Garfield

hogs the
spotlight

BY: JIM DAVIS

Ballantine Books • New York

A Ballantine Book
Published by The Random House Publishing Group

Copyright © 2000 by PAWS, Incorporated.

Published in the United States by Ballantine Books, an imprint of
The Random House Publishing Group, a division of Random House, Inc., New York, and
simultaneously in Canada by Random House of Canada Limited, Toronto.

Ballantine and colophon are registered trademarks of Random House, Inc.

"GARFIELD" and the GARFIELD characters are
registered and unregistered trademarks of Paws, Inc.

www.ballantinebooks.com

Library of Congress Catalog Card Number: 99-68499

ISBN: 978-0-345-43922-2

Printed in China

First Edition: March 2000

10   9   8

Fat Cat Classics Vol. 1

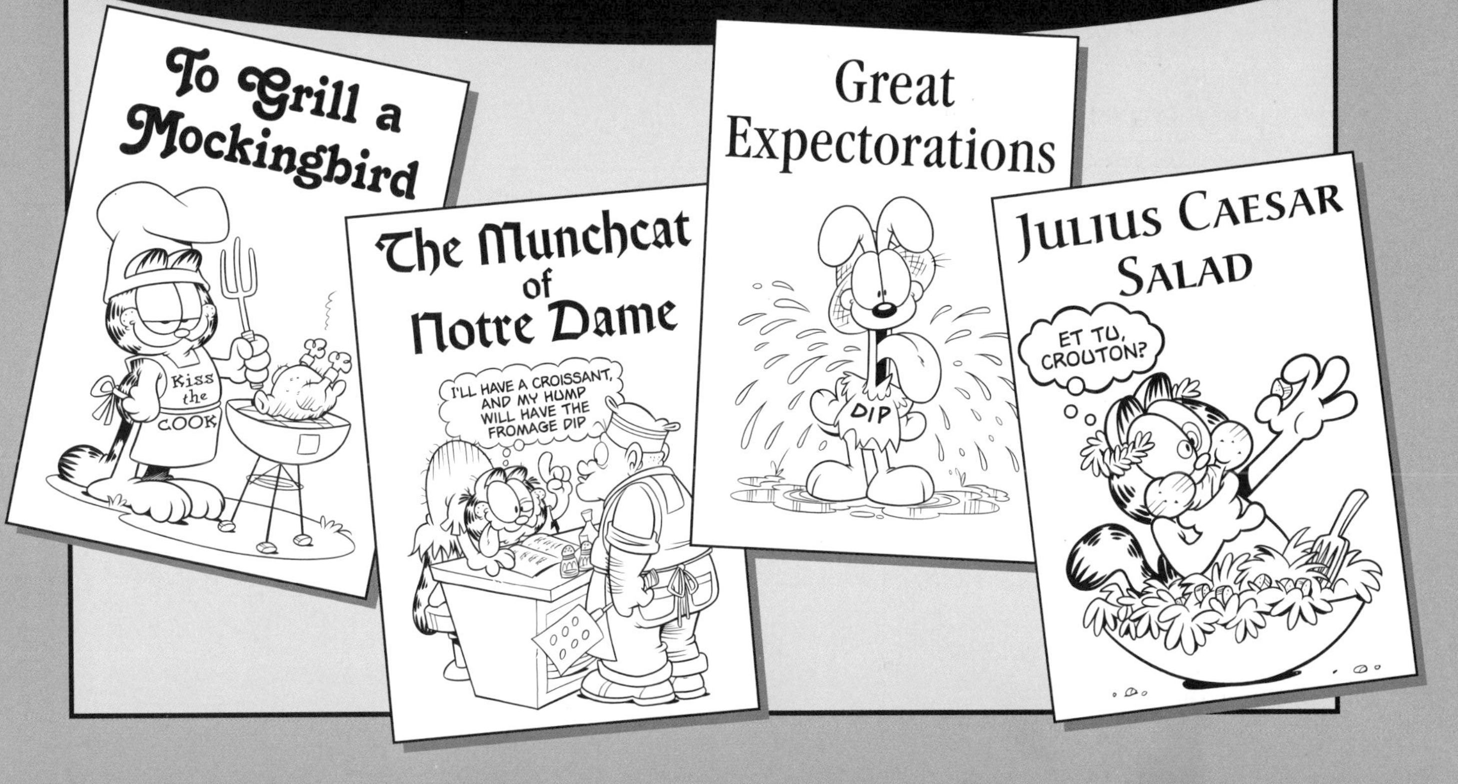

To Grill a Mockingbird
Kiss the COOK
The Munchcat of Notre Dame
I'LL HAVE A CROISSANT, AND MY HUMP WILL HAVE THE FROMAGE DIP
Great Expectorations
DIP
Julius Caesar Salad
ET TU, CROUTON?

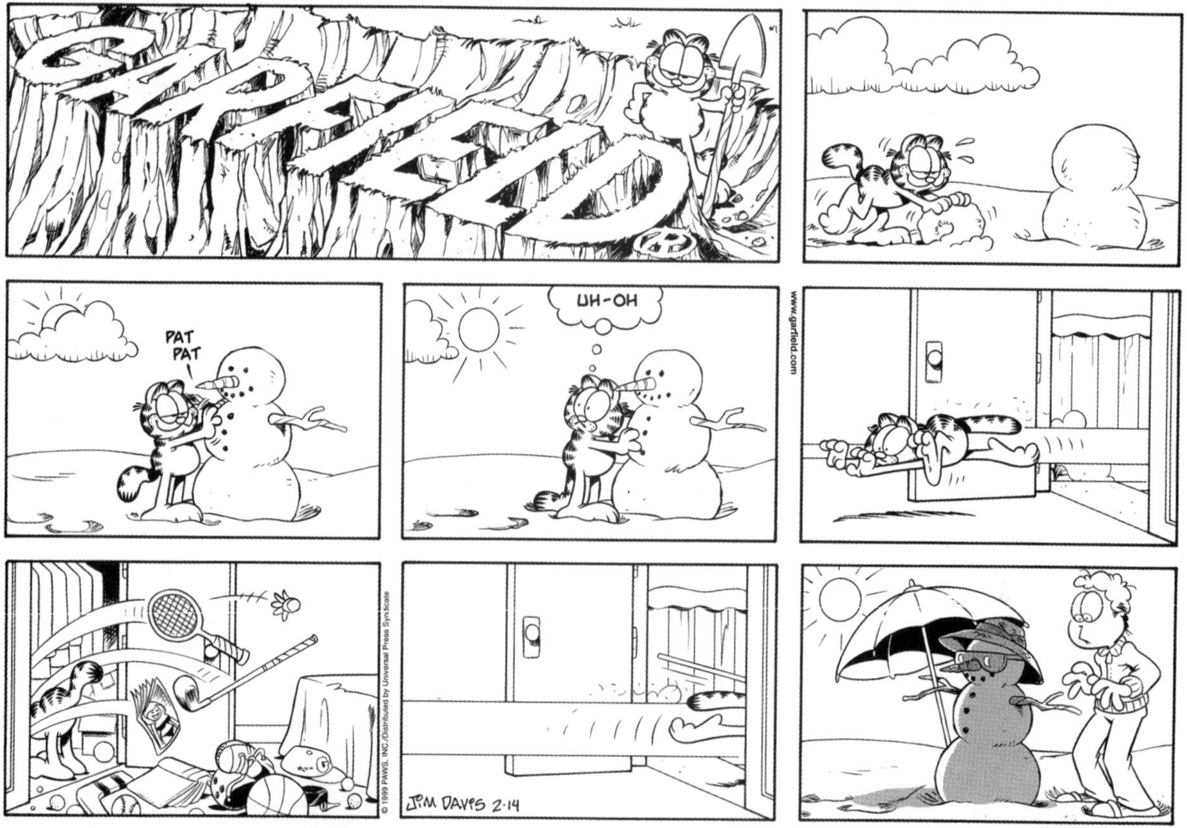
GARFIELD
PAT PAT
UH-OH
www.garfield.com
© 1999 PAWS, INC./Distributed by Universal Press Syndicate
JIM DAVIS 2-14

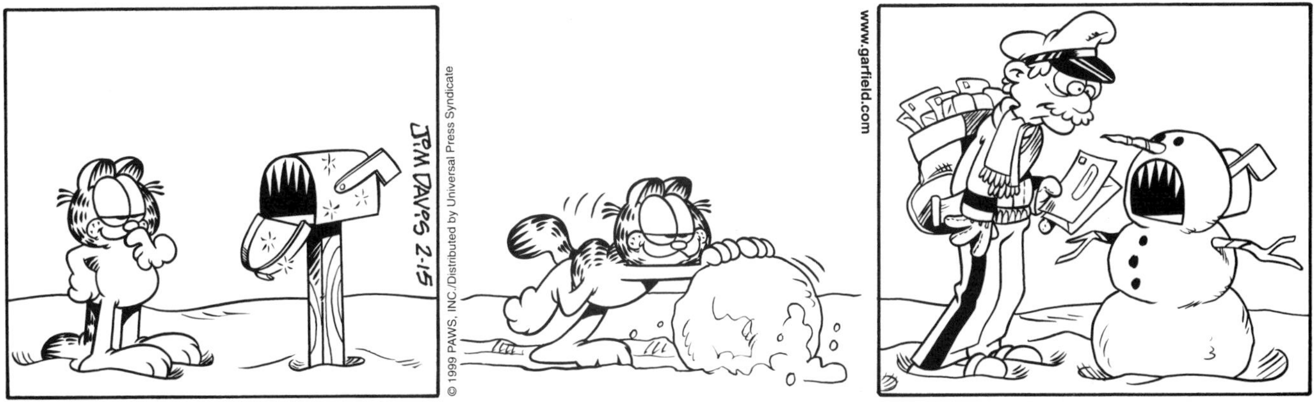
JIM DAVIS 2-15
© 1999 PAWS, INC./Distributed by Universal Press Syndicate
www.garfield.com

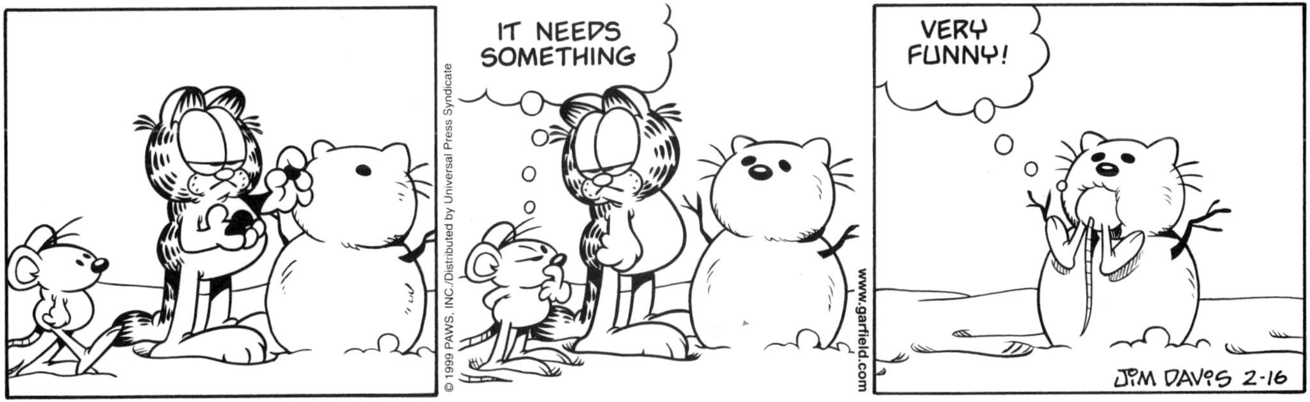
© 1999 PAWS, INC./Distributed by Universal Press Syndicate
IT NEEDS SOMETHING
www.garfield.com
VERY FUNNY!
JIM DAVIS 2-16

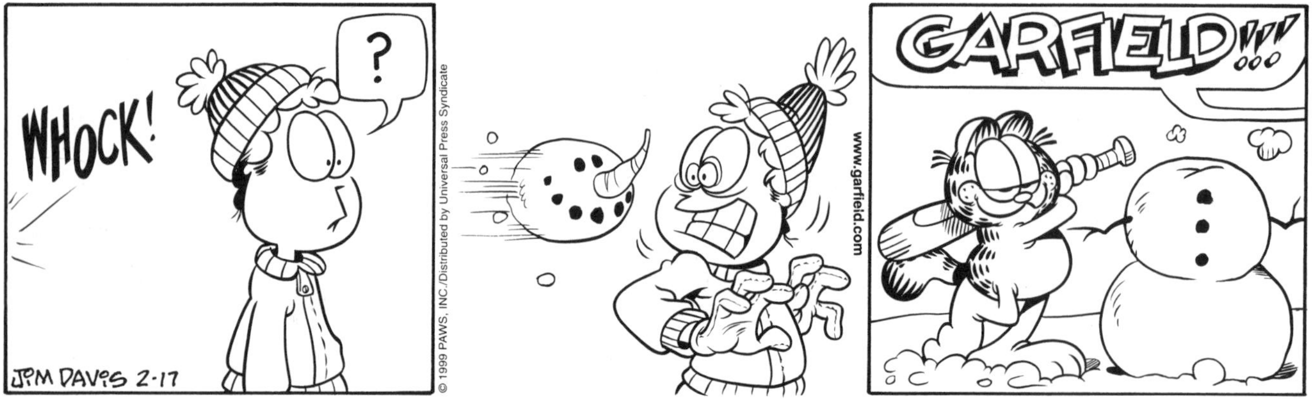
WHOCK!
?
JIM DAVIS 2-17
GARFIELD!!!
www.garfield.com

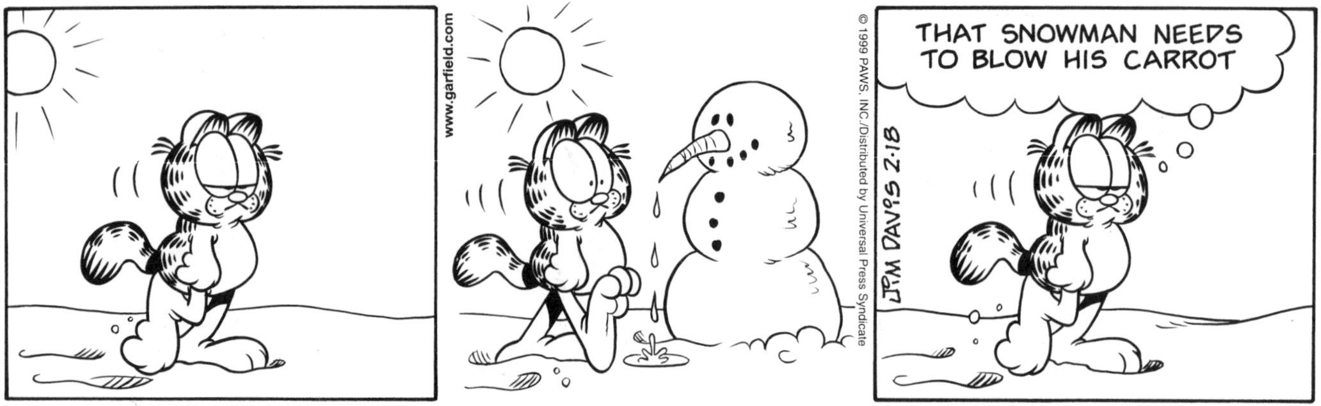
www.garfield.com
JIM DAVIS 2-18
THAT SNOWMAN NEEDS TO BLOW HIS CARROT

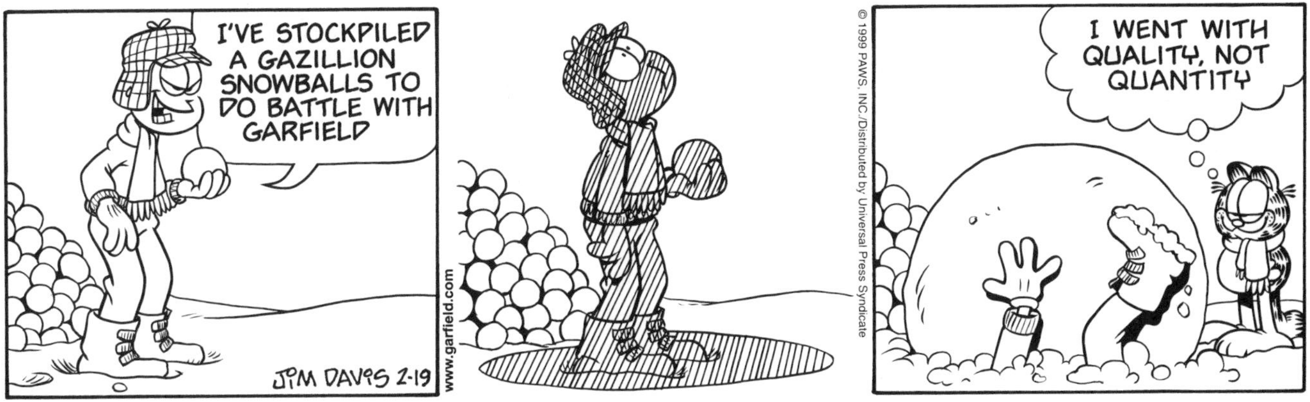
I'VE STOCKPILED A GAZILLION SNOWBALLS TO DO BATTLE WITH GARFIELD
JIM DAVIS 2-19
www.garfield.com
I WENT WITH QUALITY, NOT QUANTITY
© 1999 PAWS, INC./Distributed by Universal Press Syndicate

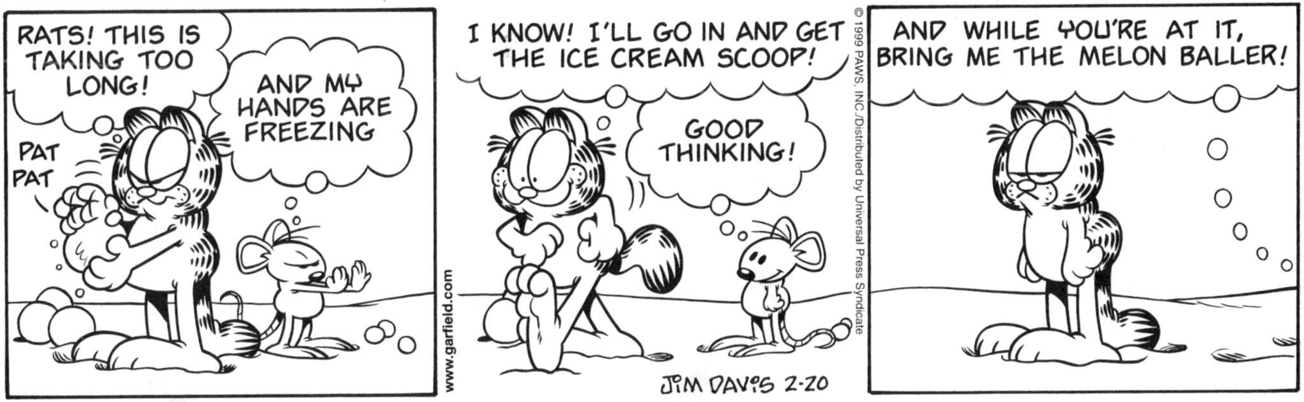
RATS! THIS IS TAKING TOO LONG!
AND MY HANDS ARE FREEZING
PAT PAT
www.garfield.com
I KNOW! I'LL GO IN AND GET THE ICE CREAM SCOOP!
GOOD THINKING!
JIM DAVIS 2-20
© 1999 PAWS, INC./Distributed by Universal Press Syndicate
AND WHILE YOU'RE AT IT, BRING ME THE MELON BALLER!

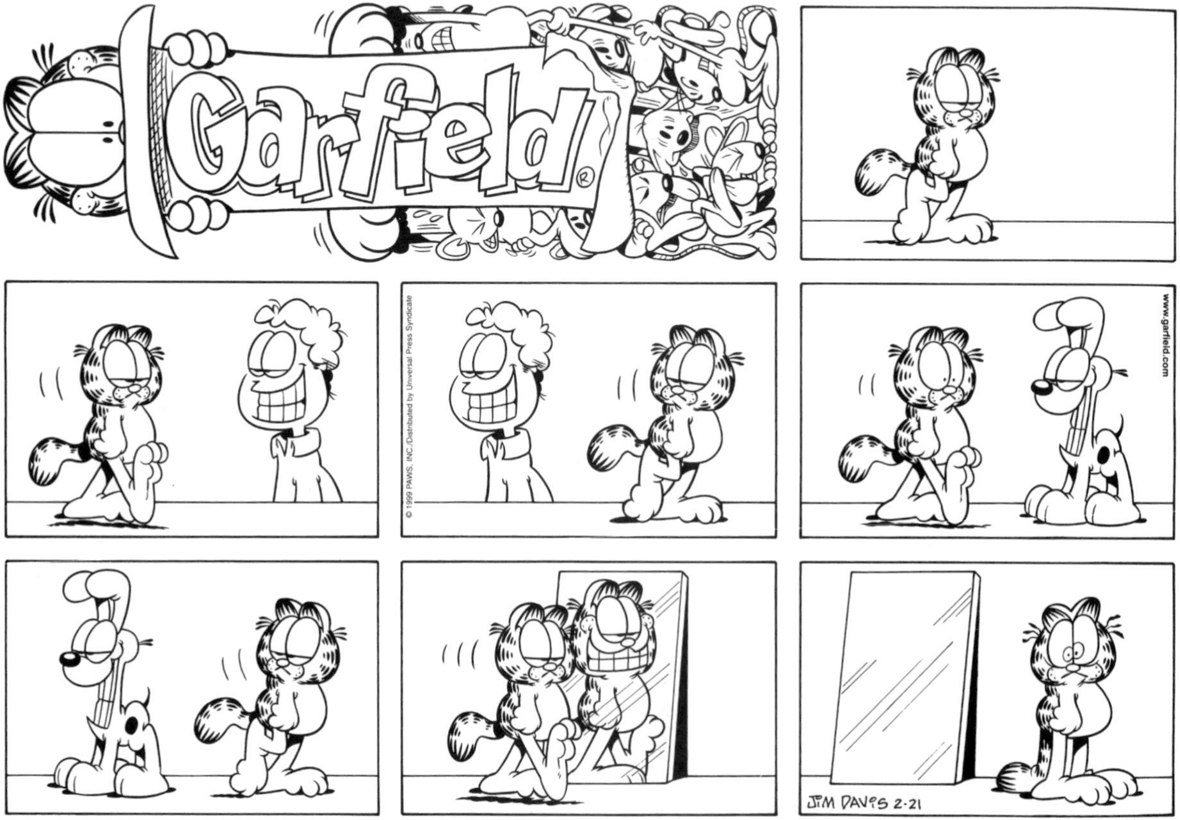
Garfield®
© 1999 PAWS, INC./Distributed by Universal Press Syndicate
www.garfield.com
JIM DAVIS 2-21

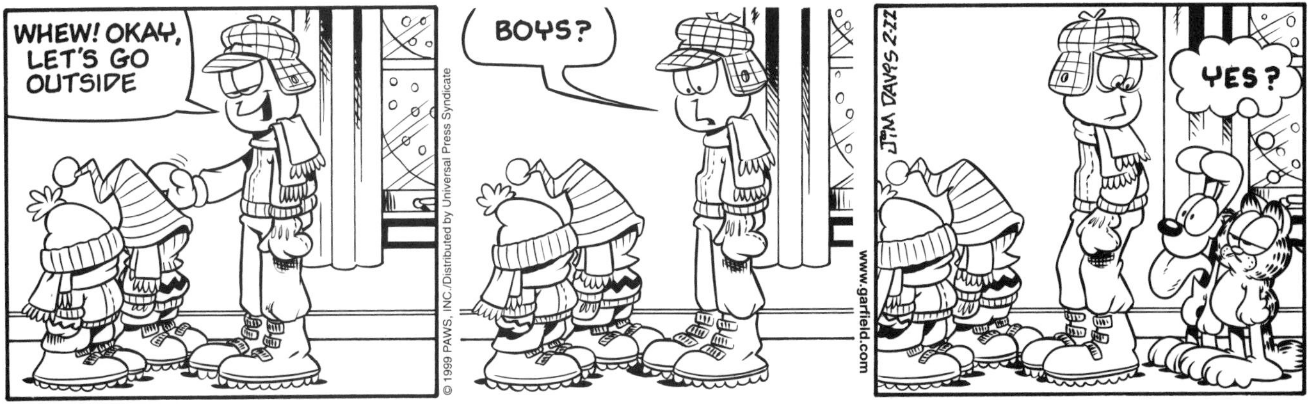
WHEW! OKAY, LET'S GO OUTSIDE
BOYS?
YES?
JIM DAVIS 2-22
© 1999 PAWS, INC./Distributed by Universal Press Syndicate
www.garfield.com

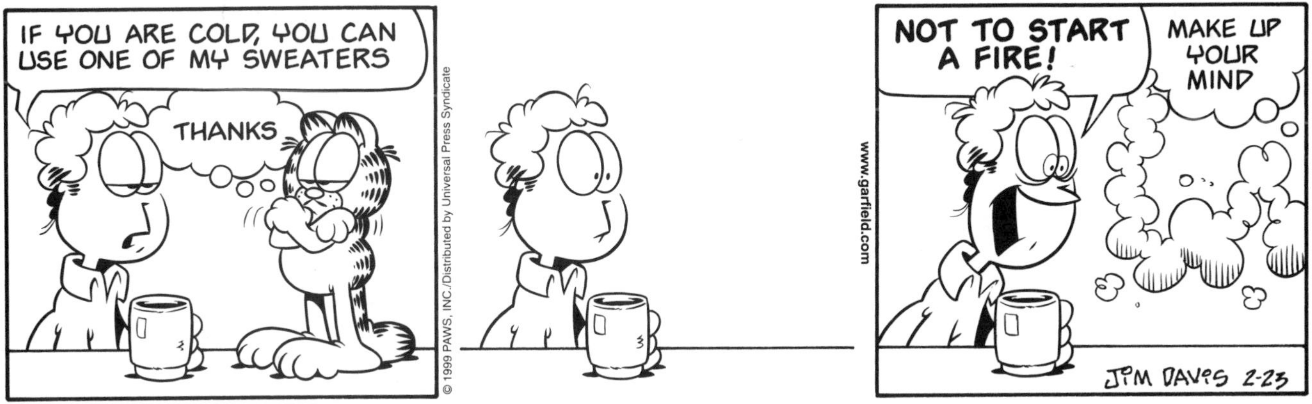
IF YOU ARE COLD, YOU CAN USE ONE OF MY SWEATERS
THANKS
NOT TO START A FIRE!
MAKE UP YOUR MIND
JIM DAVIS 2-23
© 1999 PAWS, INC./Distributed by Universal Press Syndicate
www.garfield.com

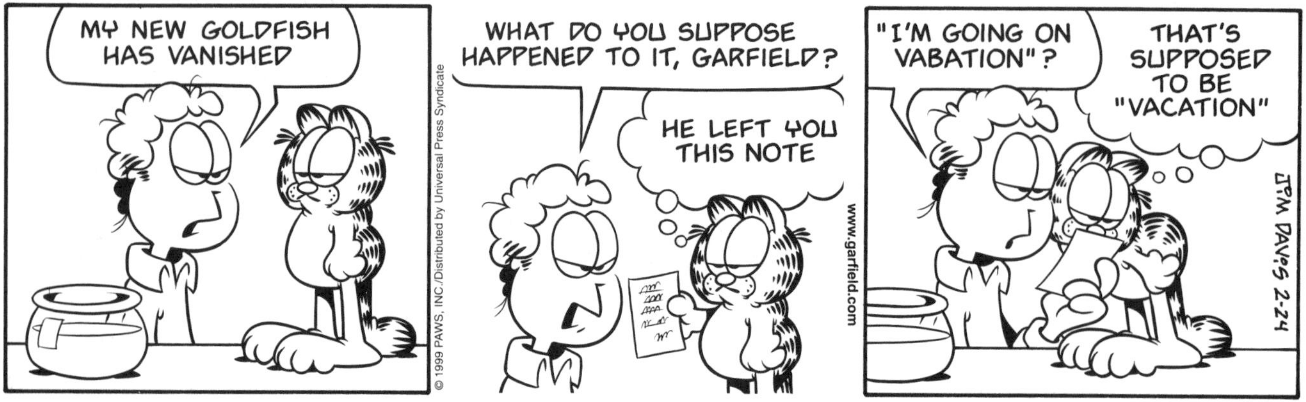
MY NEW GOLDFISH HAS VANISHED
WHAT DO YOU SUPPOSE HAPPENED TO IT, GARFIELD?
HE LEFT YOU THIS NOTE
"I'M GOING ON VABATION"?
THAT'S SUPPOSED TO BE "VACATION"
© 1999 PAWS, INC./Distributed by Universal Press Syndicate
www.garfield.com
JIM DAVIS 2-24

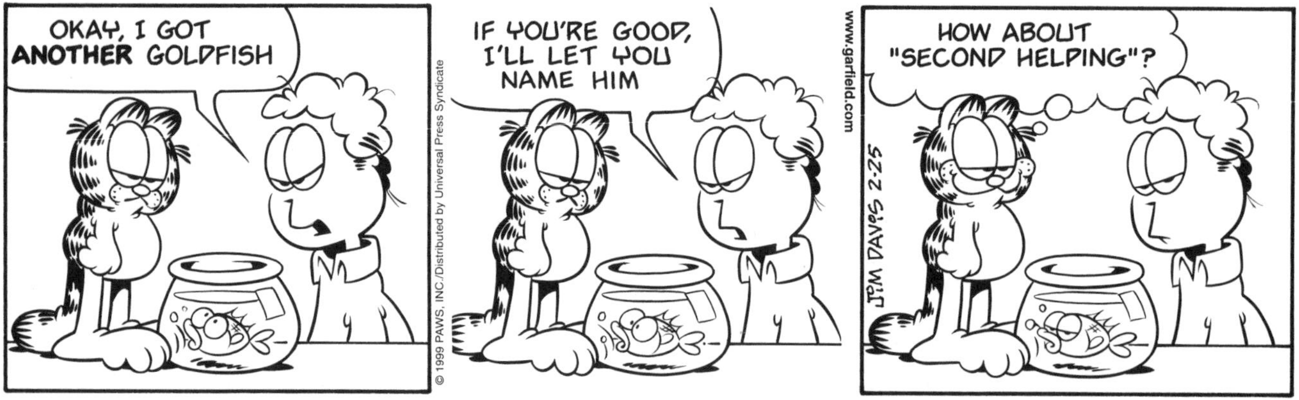
OKAY, I GOT **ANOTHER** GOLDFISH
IF YOU'RE GOOD, I'LL LET YOU NAME HIM
HOW ABOUT "SECOND HELPING"?
© 1999 PAWS, INC./Distributed by Universal Press Syndicate
www.garfield.com
JIM DAVIS 2-25

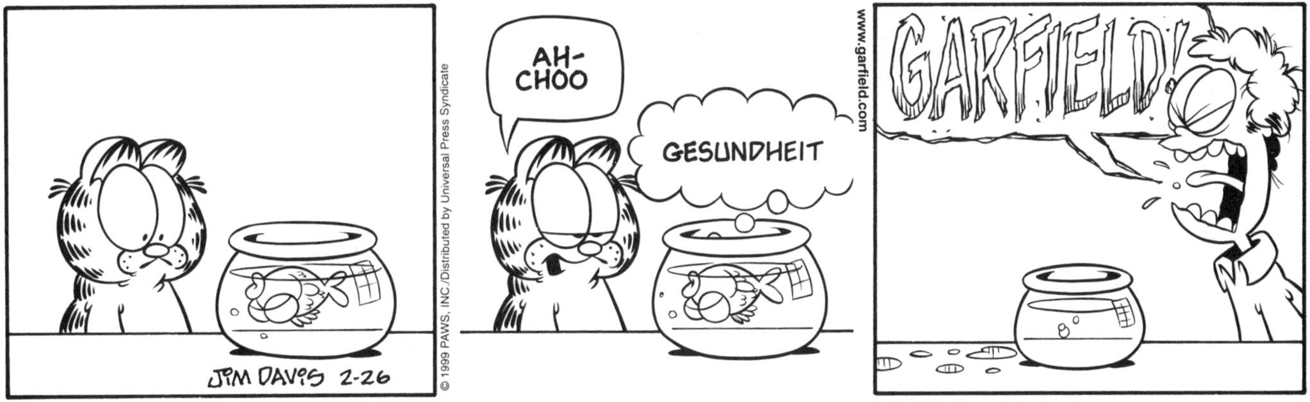
JIM DAVIS 2-26
© 1999 PAWS, INC./Distributed by Universal Press Syndicate
AH-CHOO
GESUNDHEIT
www.garfield.com
GARFIELD!

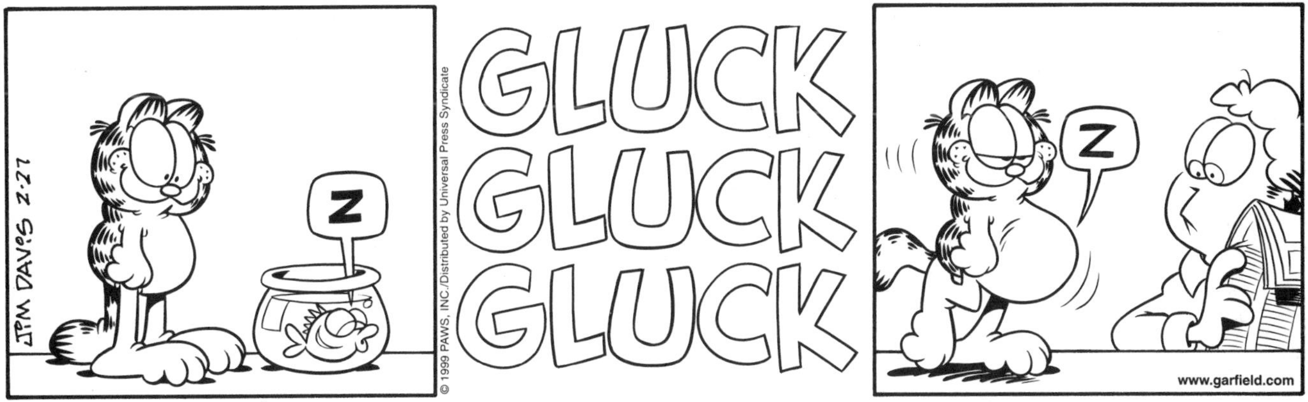
JIM DAVIS 2-27
Z
© 1999 PAWS, INC./Distributed by Universal Press Syndicate
GLUCK GLUCK GLUCK
Z
www.garfield.com

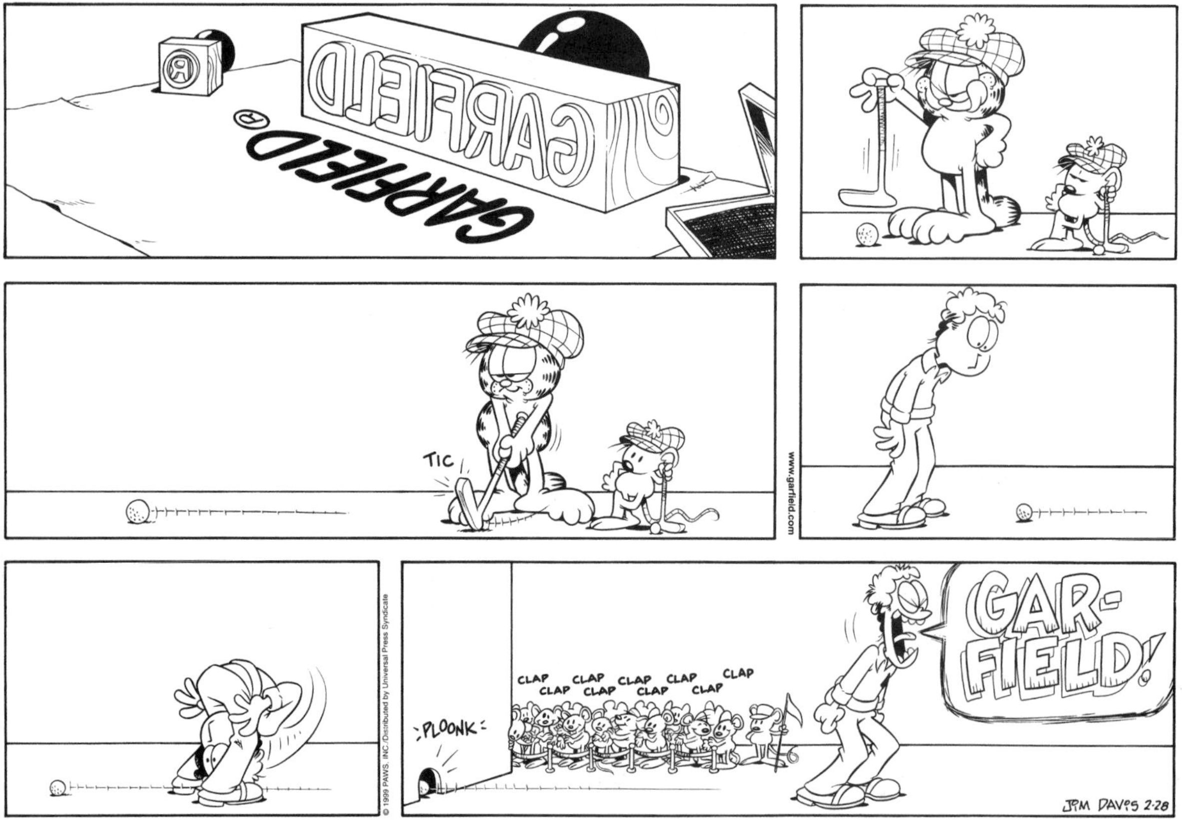
GARFIELD ®
TIC
www.garfield.com
© 1999 PAWS, INC./Distributed by Universal Press Syndicate
PLOONK
CLAP CLAP CLAP CLAP CLAP CLAP CLAP CLAP CLAP CLAP
GAR-FIELD!
JIM DAVIS 2-28

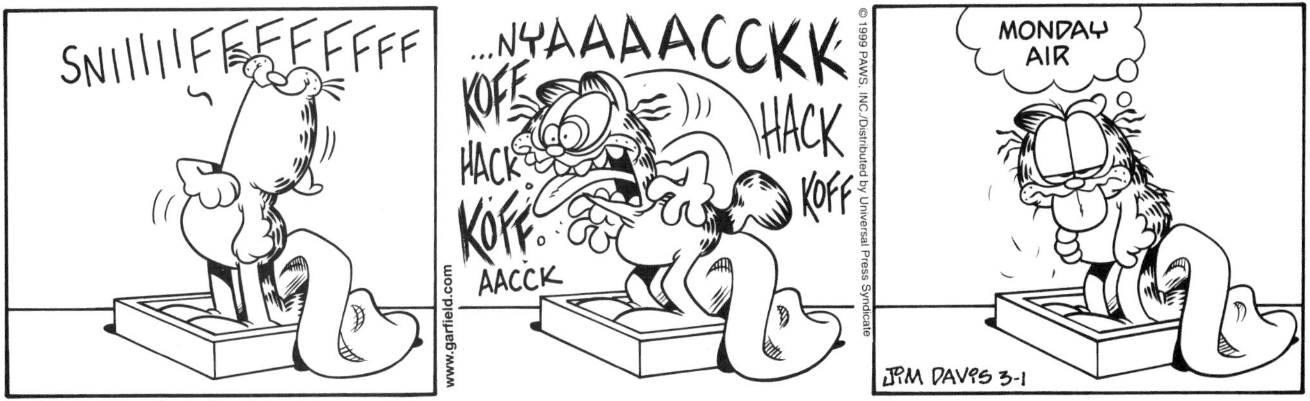
SNIIIIIFFFFFFFFF
www.garfield.com
...NYAAAAACCCKK
KOFF
HACK
KOFF
AACCK
HACK
KOFF
© 1999 PAWS, INC./Distributed by Universal Press Syndicate
MONDAY AIR
JIM DAVIS 3-1

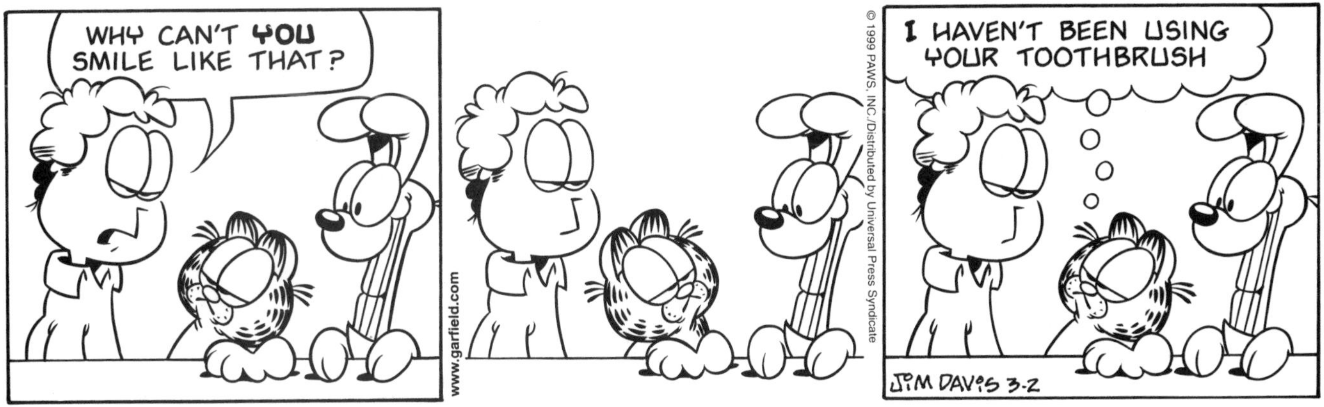
WHY CAN'T **YOU** SMILE LIKE THAT?
www.garfield.com
© 1999 PAWS, INC./Distributed by Universal Press Syndicate
I HAVEN'T BEEN USING YOUR TOOTHBRUSH
JIM DAVIS 3-2

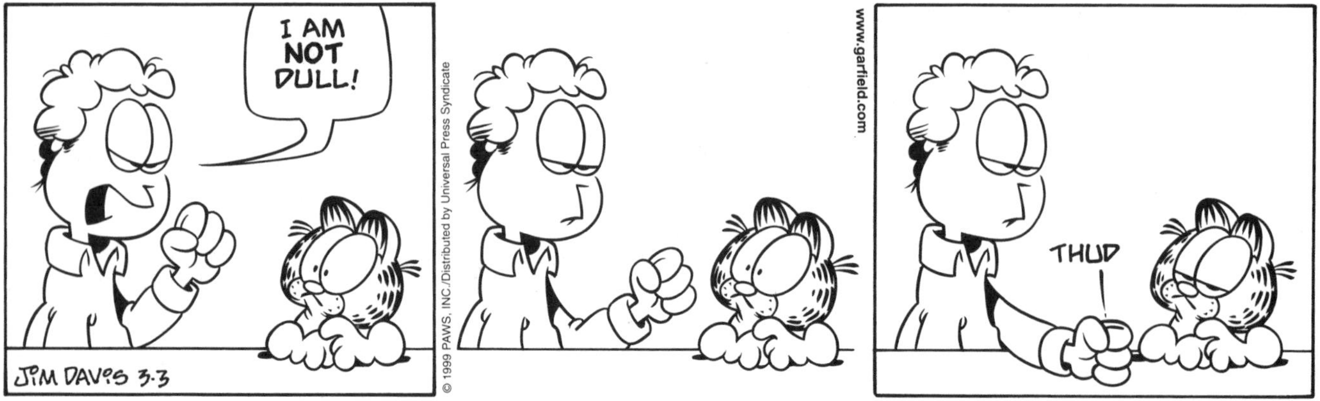
I AM NOT DULL!
JIM DAVIS 3-3
© 1999 PAWS, INC./Distributed by Universal Press Syndicate
www.garfield.com
THUD

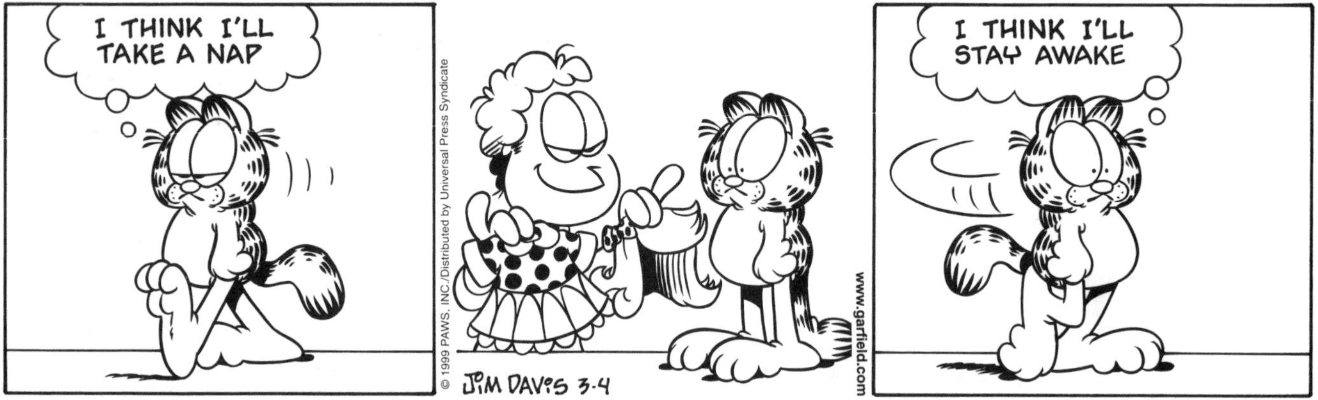
I THINK I'LL TAKE A NAP
© 1999 PAWS, INC./Distributed by Universal Press Syndicate
JIM DAVIS 3-4
www.garfield.com
I THINK I'LL STAY AWAKE

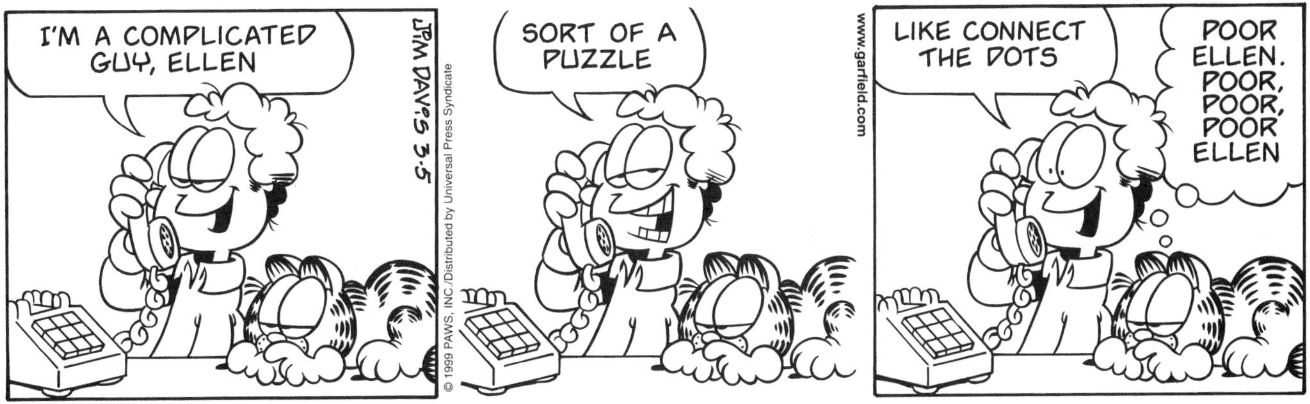
I'M A COMPLICATED GUY, ELLEN
JIM DAVIS 3-5
© 1999 PAWS, INC./Distributed by Universal Press Syndicate
SORT OF A PUZZLE
www.garfield.com
LIKE CONNECT THE DOTS
POOR ELLEN. POOR, POOR, POOR ELLEN

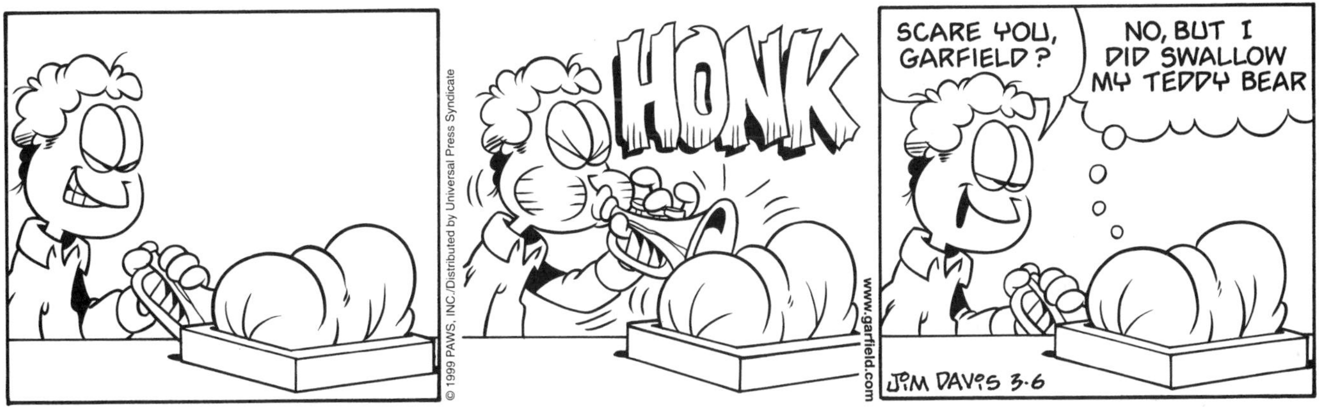
© 1999 PAWS, INC./Distributed by Universal Press Syndicate
HONK
www.garfield.com
SCARE YOU, GARFIELD?
NO, BUT I DID SWALLOW MY TEDDY BEAR
JIM DAVIS 3-6

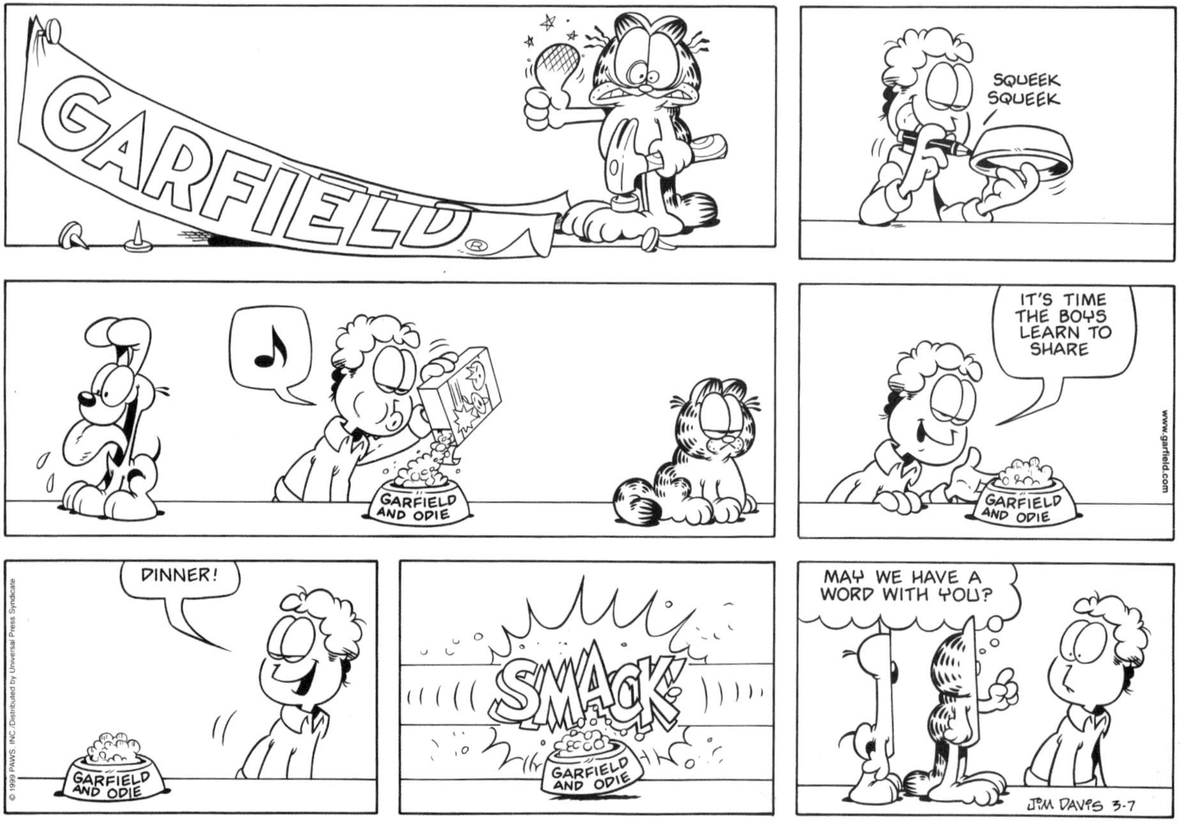
GARFIELD®
SQUEEK SQUEEK
♪
GARFIELD AND ODIE
IT'S TIME THE BOYS LEARN TO SHARE
GARFIELD AND ODIE
www.garfield.com
DINNER!
GARFIELD AND ODIE
© 1999 PAWS, INC./Distributed by Universal Press Syndicate
SMACK!
GARFIELD AND ODIE
MAY WE HAVE A WORD WITH YOU?
JIM DAVIS 3-7

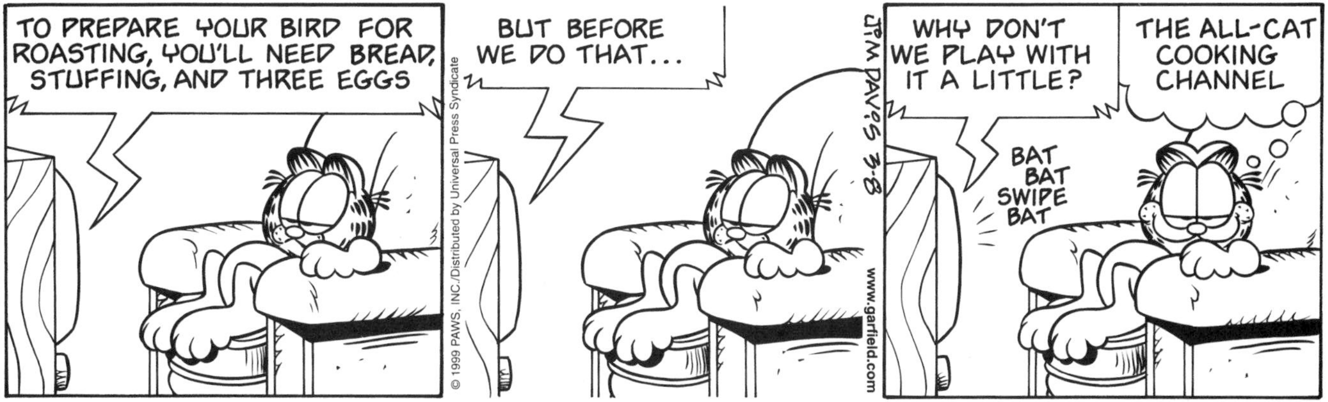
TO PREPARE YOUR BIRD FOR ROASTING, YOU'LL NEED BREAD, STUFFING, AND THREE EGGS
BUT BEFORE WE DO THAT...
WHY DON'T WE PLAY WITH IT A LITTLE?
BAT BAT SWIPE BAT
THE ALL-CAT COOKING CHANNEL
© 1999 PAWS, INC./Distributed by Universal Press Syndicate
JIM DAVIS 3-8
www.garfield.com

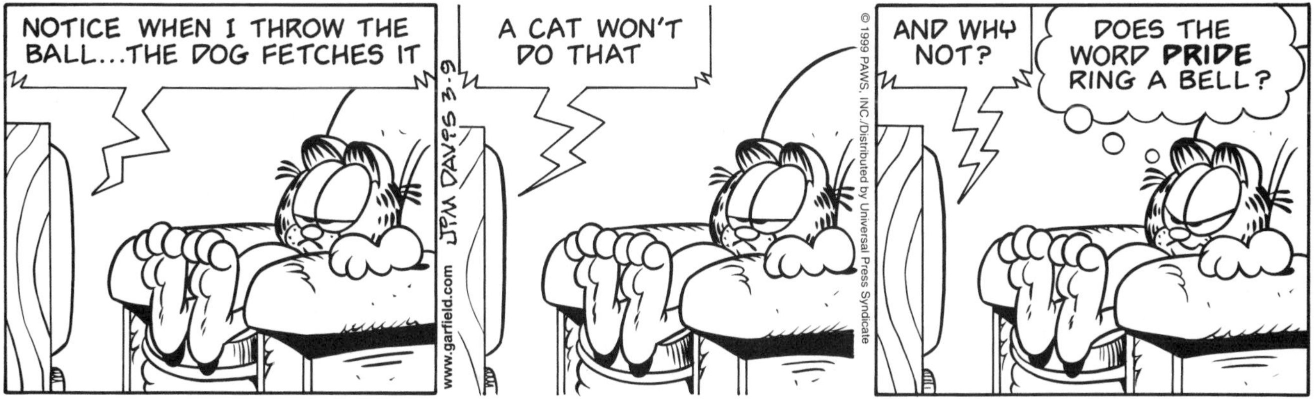
NOTICE WHEN I THROW THE BALL...THE DOG FETCHES IT
A CAT WON'T DO THAT
AND WHY NOT?
DOES THE WORD **PRIDE** RING A BELL?
JIM DAVIS 3-9
www.garfield.com
© 1999 PAWS, INC./Distributed by Universal Press Syndicate

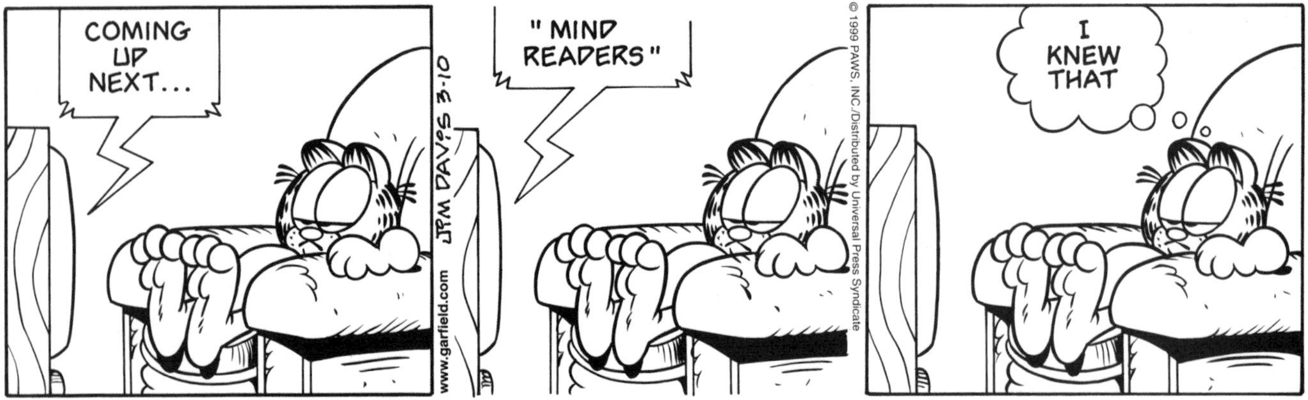
COMING UP NEXT...
JPM DAVPS 3-10
www.garfield.com
"MIND READERS"
© 1999 PAWS, INC./Distributed by Universal Press Syndicate
I KNEW THAT

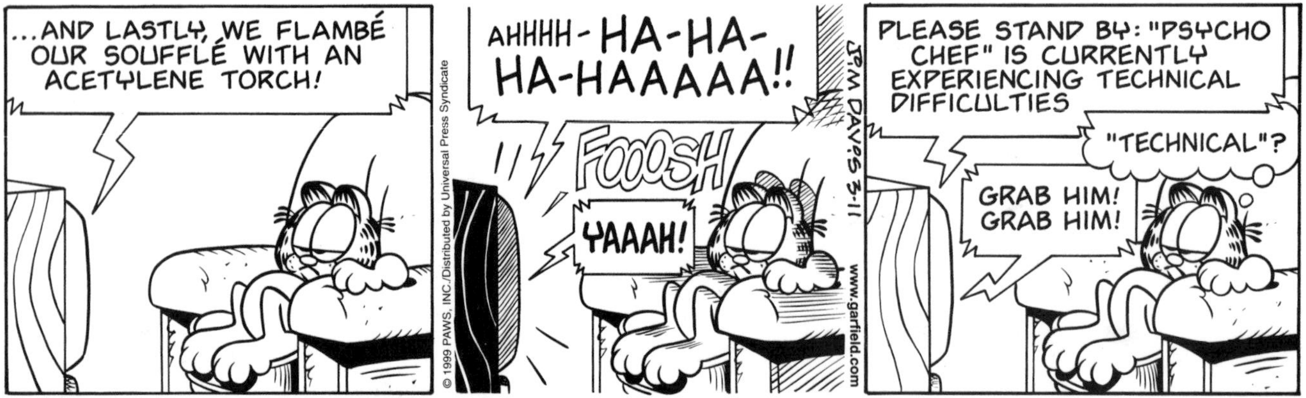
...AND LASTLY, WE FLAMBÉ OUR SOUFFLÉ WITH AN ACETYLENE TORCH!
© 1999 PAWS, INC./Distributed by Universal Press Syndicate
AHHHH-HA-HA-HA-HAAAAAA!!
FOOOSH
YAAAH!
JPM DAVPS 3-11
www.garfield.com
PLEASE STAND BY: "PSYCHO CHEF" IS CURRENTLY EXPERIENCING TECHNICAL DIFFICULTIES
GRAB HIM! GRAB HIM!
"TECHNICAL"?

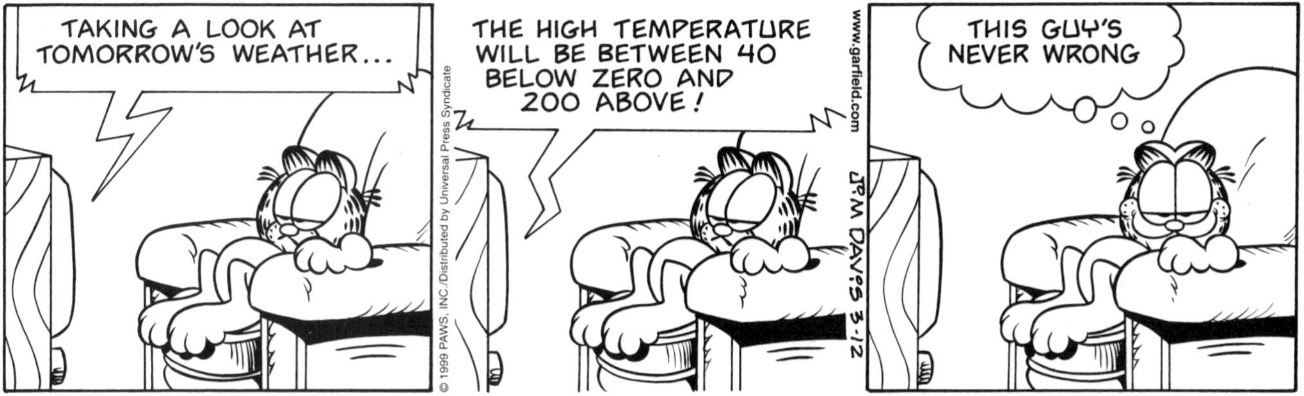
TAKING A LOOK AT TOMORROW'S WEATHER...
THE HIGH TEMPERATURE WILL BE BETWEEN 40 BELOW ZERO AND 200 ABOVE!
THIS GUY'S NEVER WRONG
JIM DAVIS 3-12
© 1999 PAWS, INC./Distributed by Universal Press Syndicate
www.garfield.com

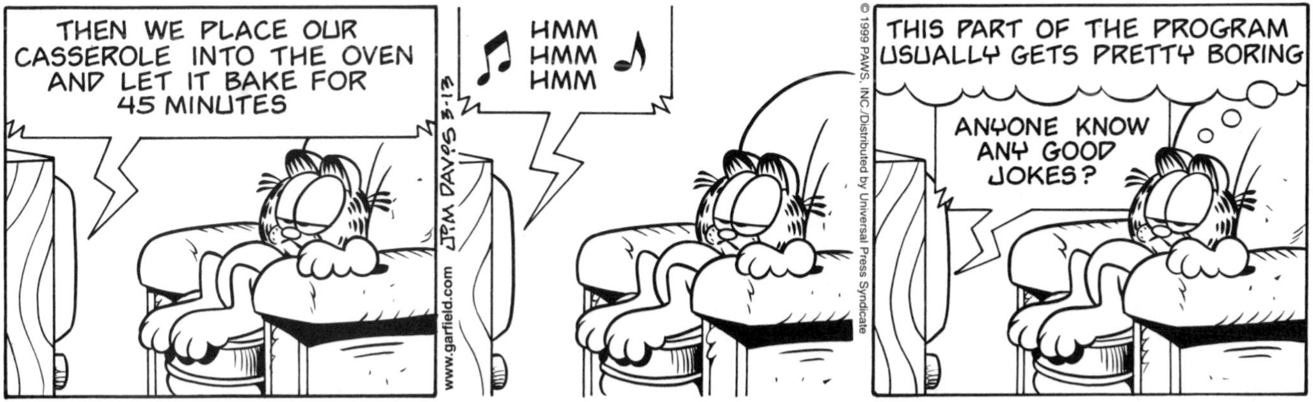
THEN WE PLACE OUR CASSEROLE INTO THE OVEN AND LET IT BAKE FOR 45 MINUTES
HMM HMM HMM
THIS PART OF THE PROGRAM USUALLY GETS PRETTY BORING
ANYONE KNOW ANY GOOD JOKES?
JIM DAVIS 3-13
www.garfield.com
© 1999 PAWS, INC./Distributed by Universal Press Syndicate

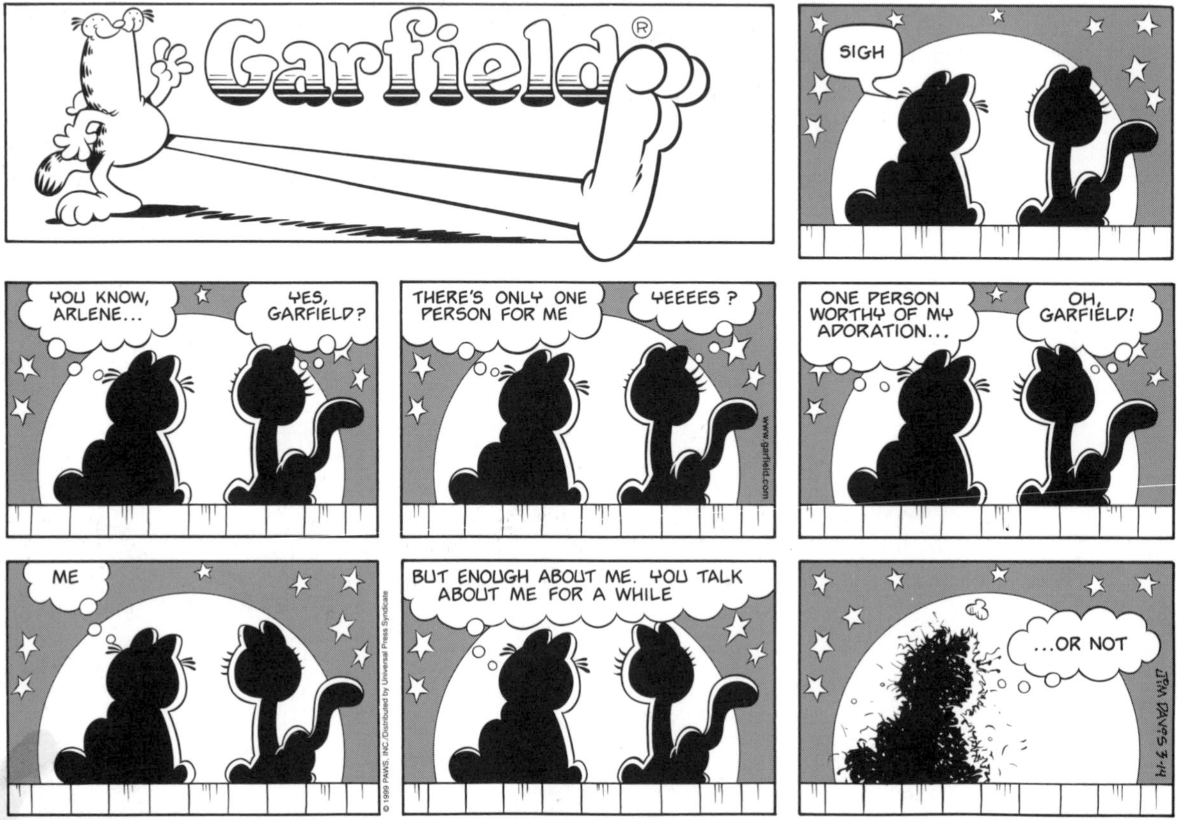
Garfield®
SIGH
YOU KNOW, ARLENE...
YES, GARFIELD?
THERE'S ONLY ONE PERSON FOR ME
YEEEES ?
www.garfield.com
ONE PERSON WORTHY OF MY ADORATION...
OH, GARFIELD!
ME
© 1999 PAWS, INC./Distributed by Universal Press Syndicate
BUT ENOUGH ABOUT ME. YOU TALK ABOUT ME FOR A WHILE
...OR NOT
JIM DAVIS 3-14

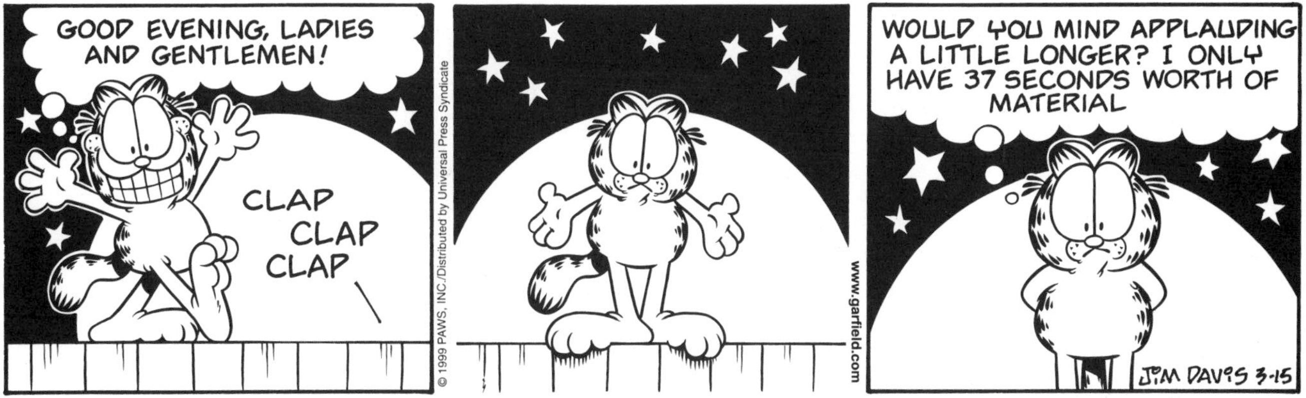
GOOD EVENING, LADIES AND GENTLEMEN!
CLAP CLAP CLAP
WOULD YOU MIND APPLAUDING A LITTLE LONGER? I ONLY HAVE 37 SECONDS WORTH OF MATERIAL
JIM DAVIS 3-15

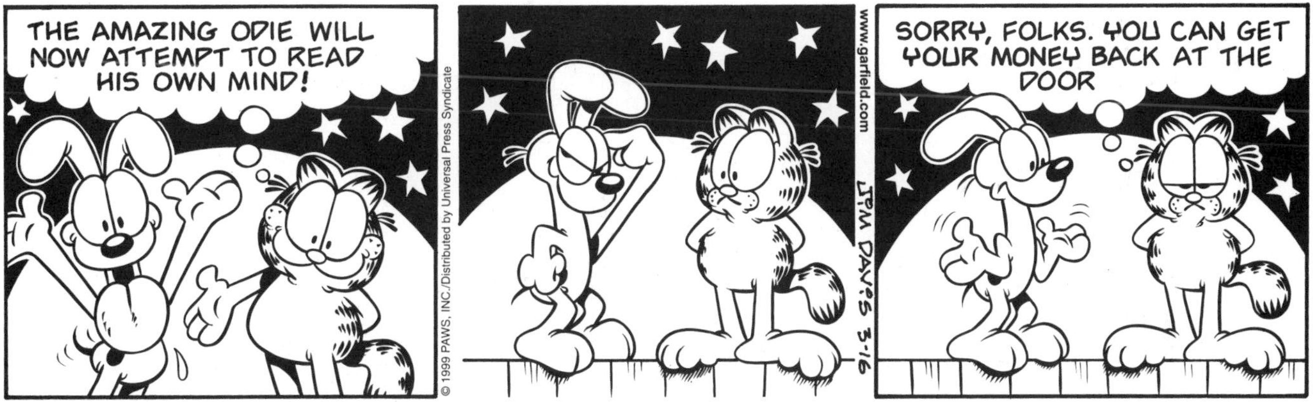
THE AMAZING ODIE WILL NOW ATTEMPT TO READ HIS OWN MIND!
SORRY, FOLKS. YOU CAN GET YOUR MONEY BACK AT THE DOOR
JIM DAVIS 3-16

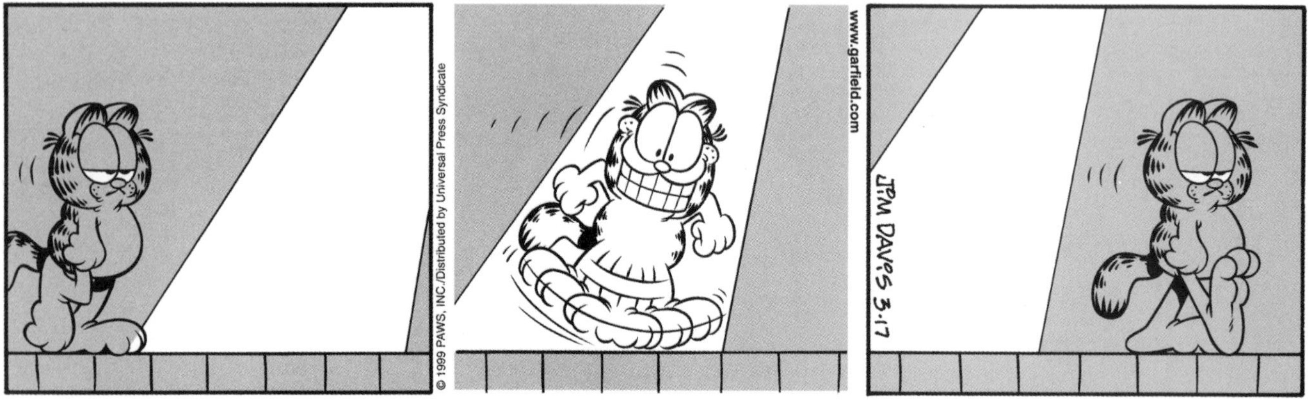
www.garfield.com
JIM DAVIS 3.17

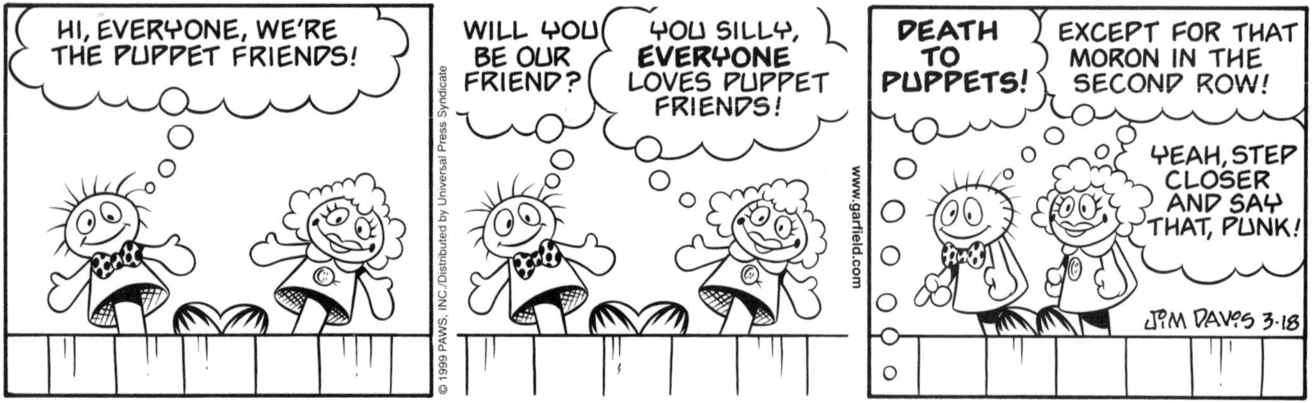
HI, EVERYONE, WE'RE THE PUPPET FRIENDS!
WILL YOU BE OUR FRIEND?
YOU SILLY, **EVERYONE** LOVES PUPPET FRIENDS!
DEATH TO PUPPETS!
EXCEPT FOR THAT MORON IN THE SECOND ROW!
YEAH, STEP CLOSER AND SAY THAT, PUNK!
JIM DAVIS 3-18
www.garfield.com
© 1999 PAWS, INC./Distributed by Universal Press Syndicate

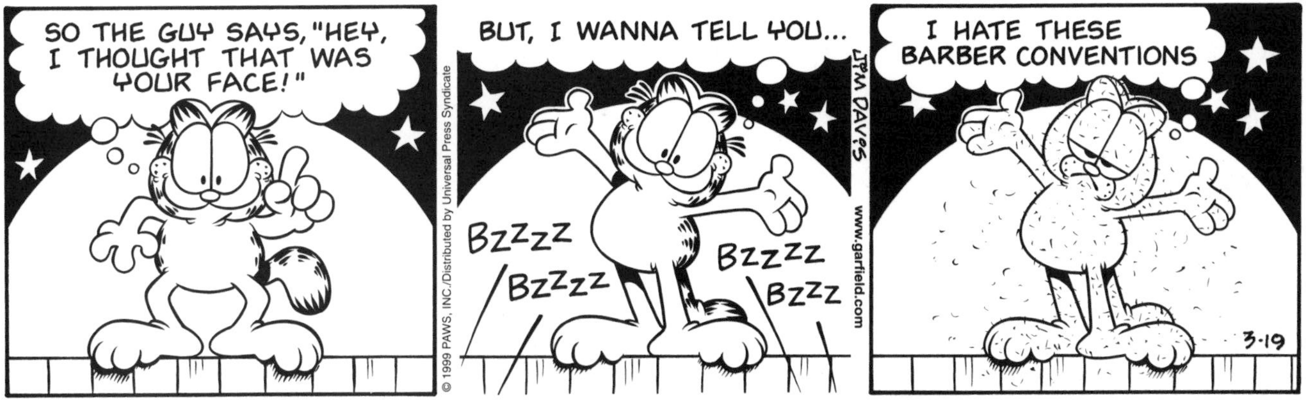
SO THE GUY SAYS, "HEY, I THOUGHT THAT WAS YOUR FACE!"
BUT, I WANNA TELL YOU...
BZZZZ
BZZZZ
BZZZZ
BZZZ
I HATE THESE BARBER CONVENTIONS
JIM DAVIS
www.garfield.com
3-19

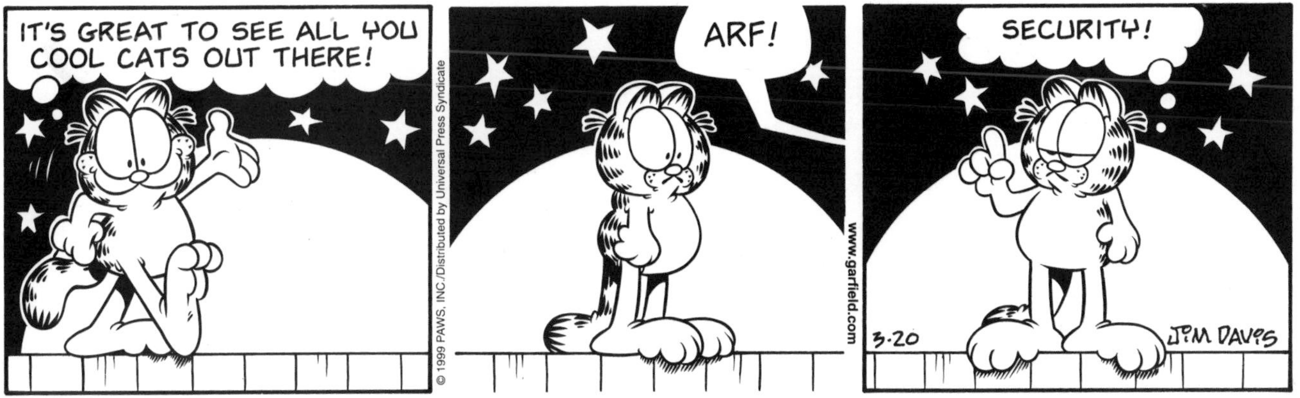
IT'S GREAT TO SEE ALL YOU COOL CATS OUT THERE!
ARF!
SECURITY!
www.garfield.com
3-20
JIM DAVIS

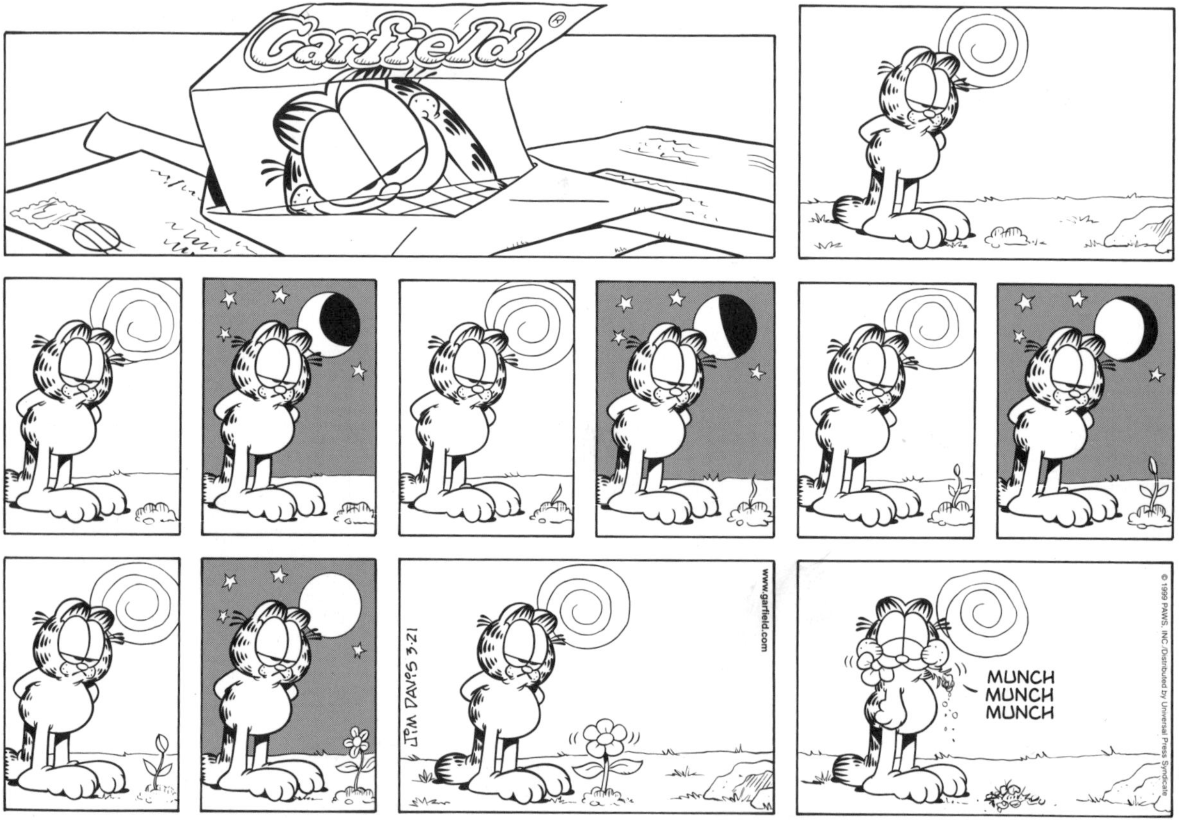
Garfield
JIM DAVIS 3-21
www.garfield.com
MUNCH
MUNCH
MUNCH
© 1999 PAWS, INC./Distributed by Universal Press Syndicate

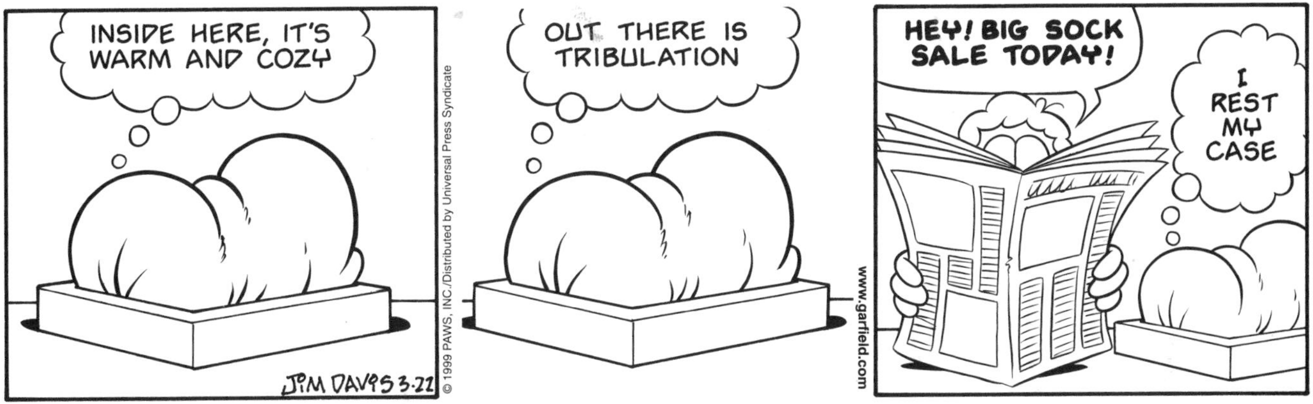
INSIDE HERE, IT'S WARM AND COZY
OUT THERE IS TRIBULATION
HEY! BIG SOCK SALE TODAY!
I REST MY CASE
JIM DAVIS 3-21
www.garfield.com

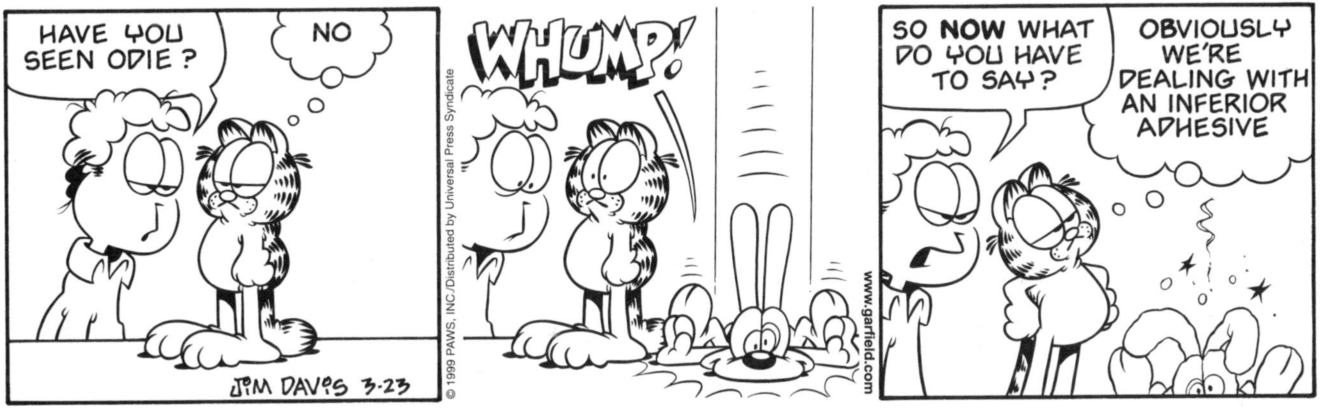
HAVE YOU SEEN ODIE ?
NO
JIM DAVIS 3-23
WHUMP!
SO NOW WHAT DO YOU HAVE TO SAY ?
OBVIOUSLY WE'RE DEALING WITH AN INFERIOR ADHESIVE
www.garfield.com

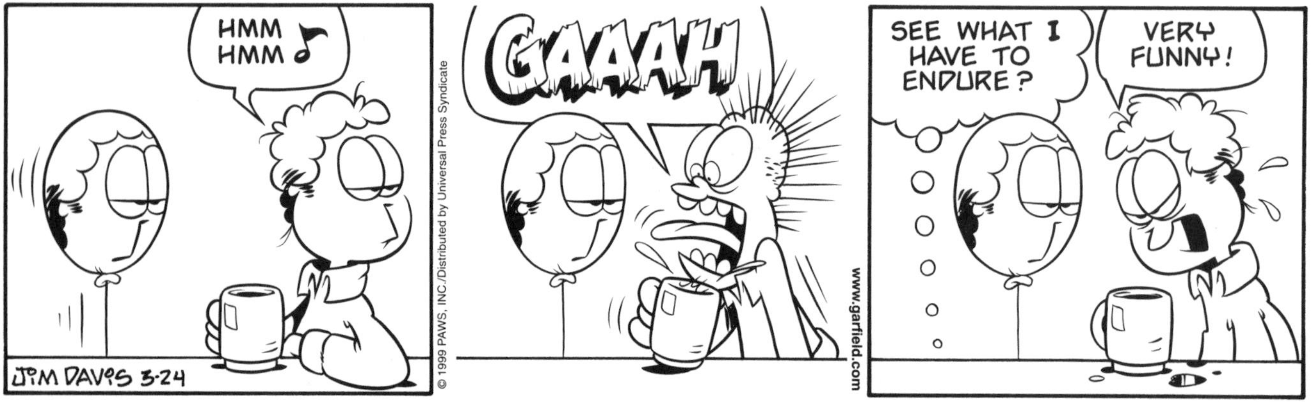
HMM HMM ♪
JIM DAVIS 3-24
© 1999 PAWS, INC./Distributed by Universal Press Syndicate
GAAAH
www.garfield.com
SEE WHAT I HAVE TO ENDURE?
VERY FUNNY!

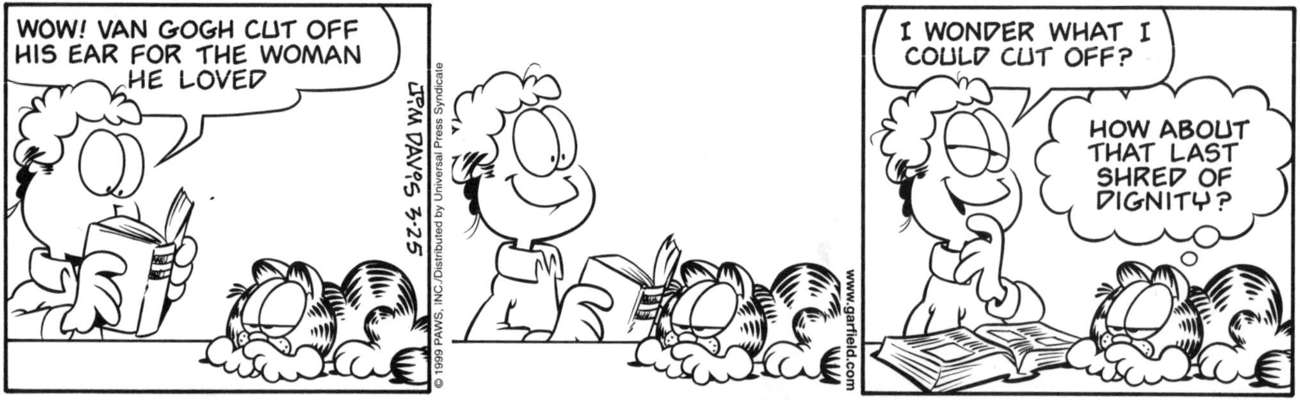
WOW! VAN GOGH CUT OFF HIS EAR FOR THE WOMAN HE LOVED
JIM DAVIS 3-25
© 1999 PAWS, INC./Distributed by Universal Press Syndicate
www.garfield.com
I WONDER WHAT I COULD CUT OFF?
HOW ABOUT THAT LAST SHRED OF DIGNITY?

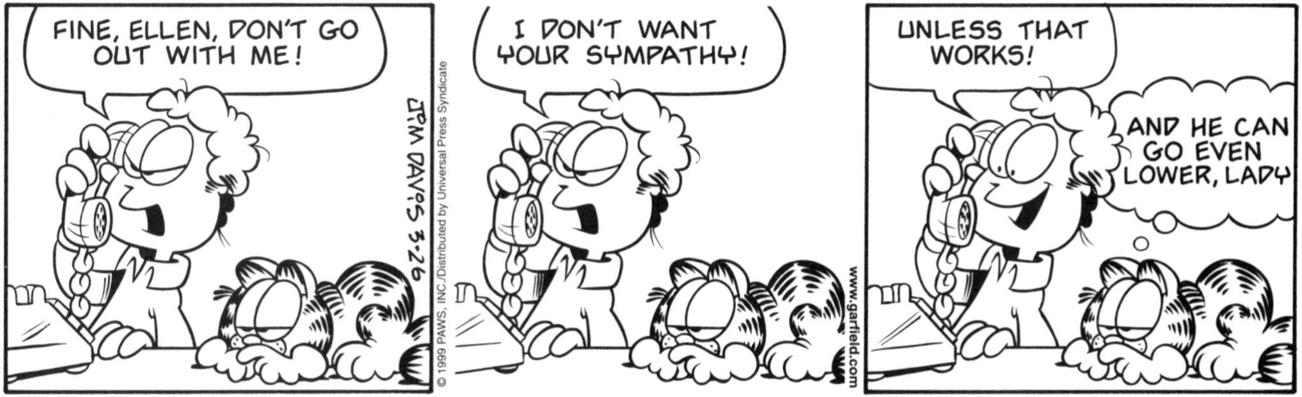
FINE, ELLEN, DON'T GO OUT WITH ME!
JIM DAVIS 3-26
© 1999 PAWS, INC./Distributed by Universal Press Syndicate
I DON'T WANT YOUR SYMPATHY!
www.garfield.com
UNLESS THAT WORKS!
AND HE CAN GO EVEN LOWER, LADY

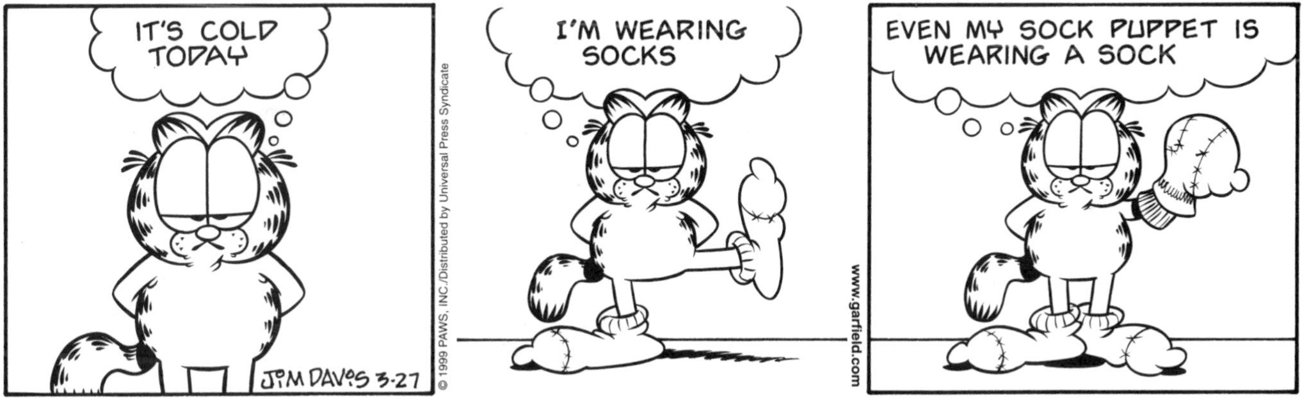
IT'S COLD TODAY
JIM DAVIS 3-27
© 1999 PAWS, INC./Distributed by Universal Press Syndicate
I'M WEARING SOCKS
www.garfield.com
EVEN MY SOCK PUPPET IS WEARING A SOCK

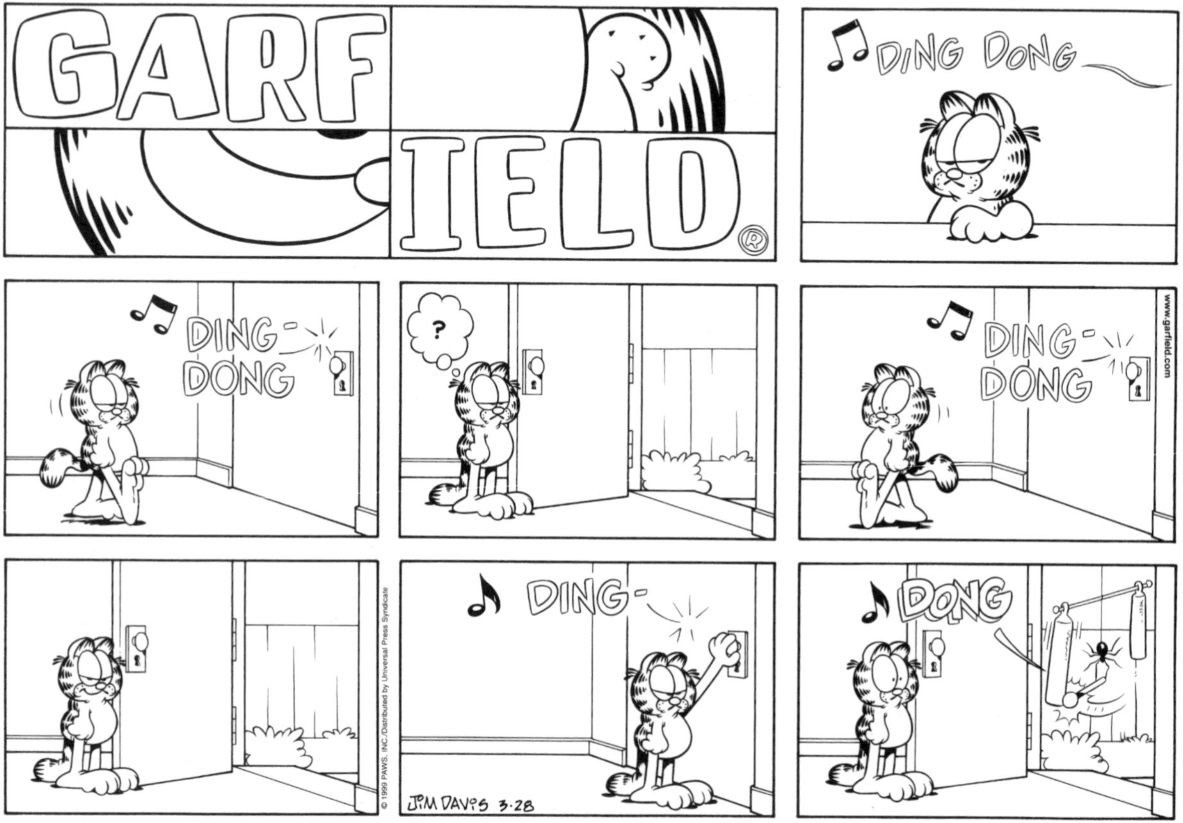
GARFIELD
DING DONG
DING-DONG
?
DING-DONG
DING-
DONG
www.garfield.com
© 1999 PAWS, INC./Distributed by Universal Press Syndicate
JIM DAVIS 3-28

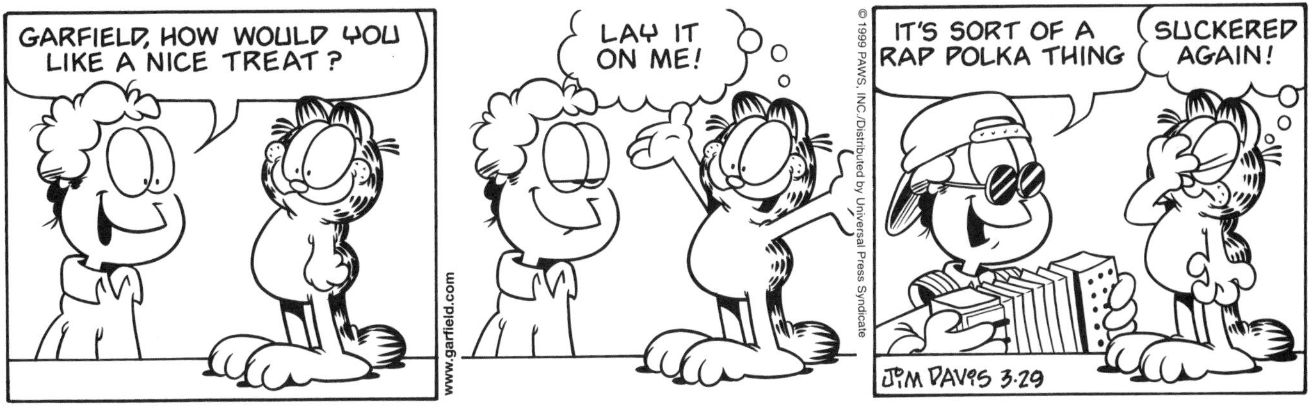
GARFIELD, HOW WOULD YOU LIKE A NICE TREAT?
LAY IT ON ME!
IT'S SORT OF A RAP POLKA THING
SUCKERED AGAIN!
www.garfield.com
© 1999 PAWS, INC./Distributed by Universal Press Syndicate
JIM DAVIS 3-29

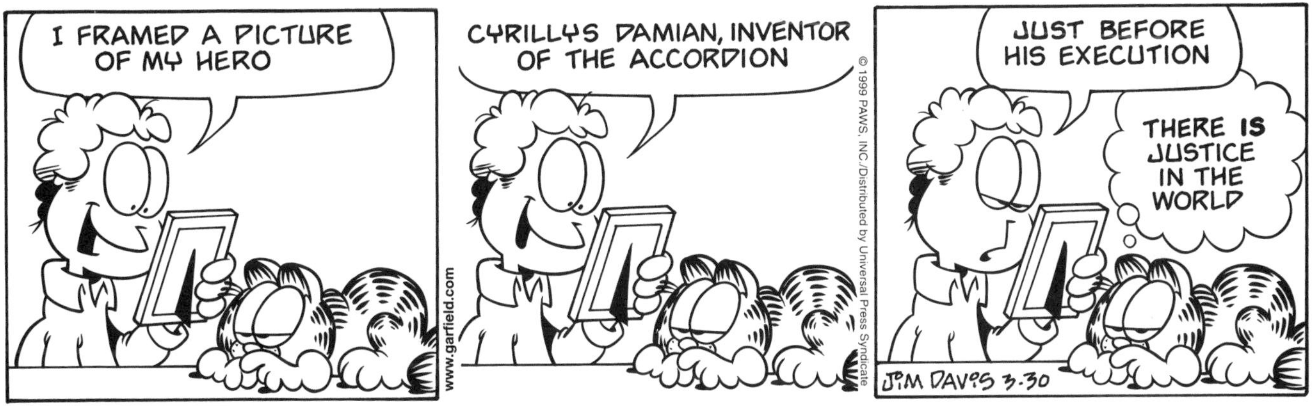
I FRAMED A PICTURE OF MY HERO
CYRILLYS DAMIAN, INVENTOR OF THE ACCORDION
JUST BEFORE HIS EXECUTION
THERE **IS** JUSTICE IN THE WORLD
www.garfield.com
© 1999 PAWS, INC./Distributed by Universal Press Syndicate
JIM DAVIS 3-30

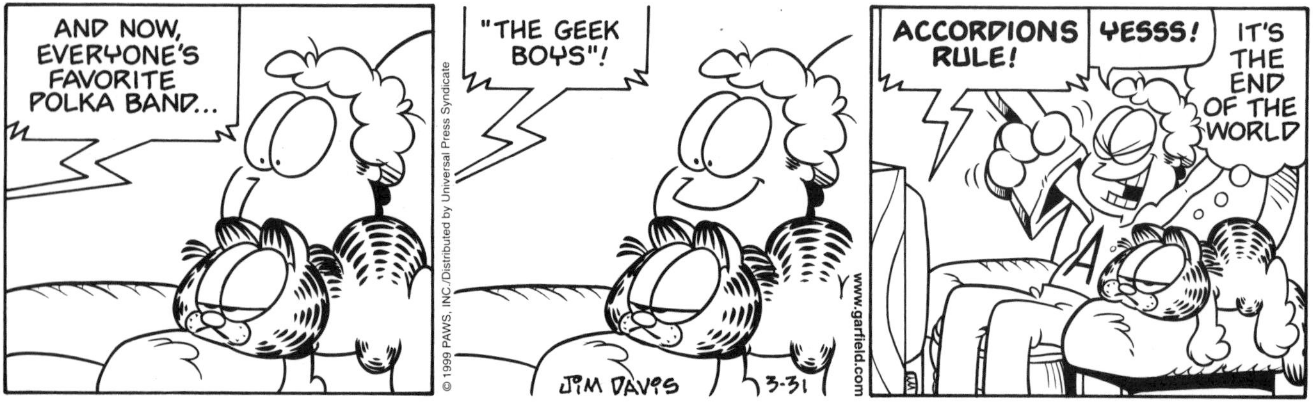
AND NOW, EVERYONE'S FAVORITE POLKA BAND...
"THE GEEK BOYS"!
ACCORDIONS RULE!
YESSS!
IT'S THE END OF THE WORLD
JIM DAVIS 3-31
© 1999 PAWS, INC./Distributed by Universal Press Syndicate
www.garfield.com

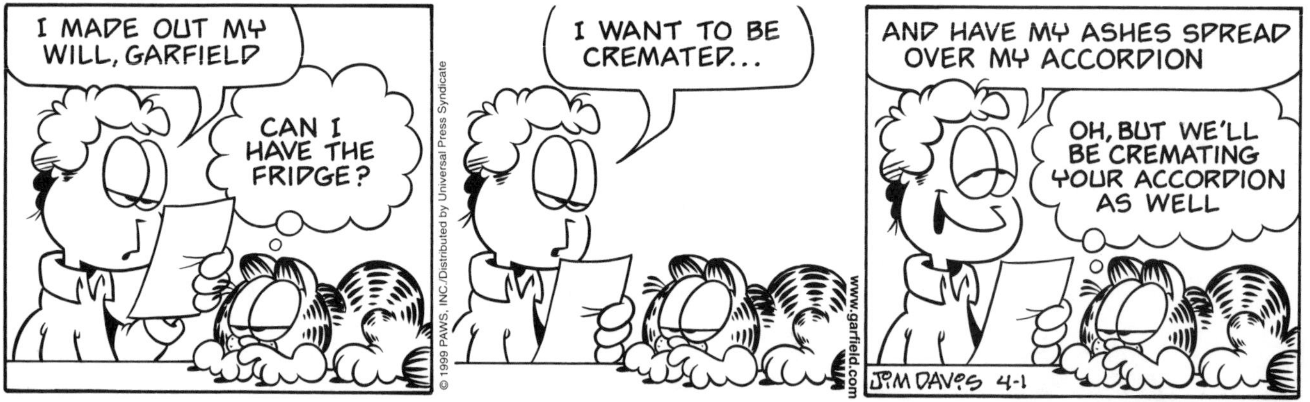
I MADE OUT MY WILL, GARFIELD
CAN I HAVE THE FRIDGE?
I WANT TO BE CREMATED...
AND HAVE MY ASHES SPREAD OVER MY ACCORDION
OH, BUT WE'LL BE CREMATING YOUR ACCORDION AS WELL
JIM DAVIS 4-1
© 1999 PAWS, INC./Distributed by Universal Press Syndicate
www.garfield.com

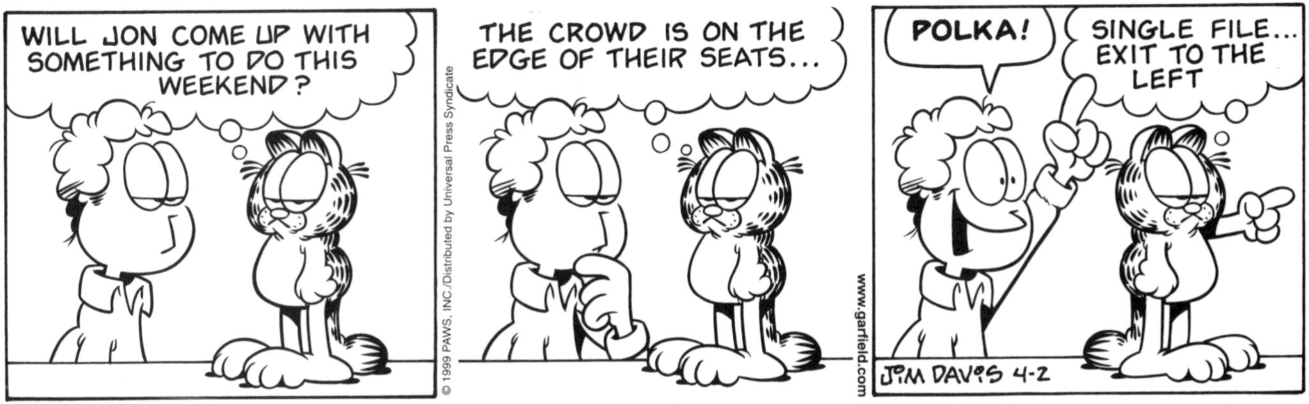
WILL JON COME UP WITH SOMETHING TO DO THIS WEEKEND?
THE CROWD IS ON THE EDGE OF THEIR SEATS...
POLKA!
SINGLE FILE... EXIT TO THE LEFT
JIM DAVIS 4-2

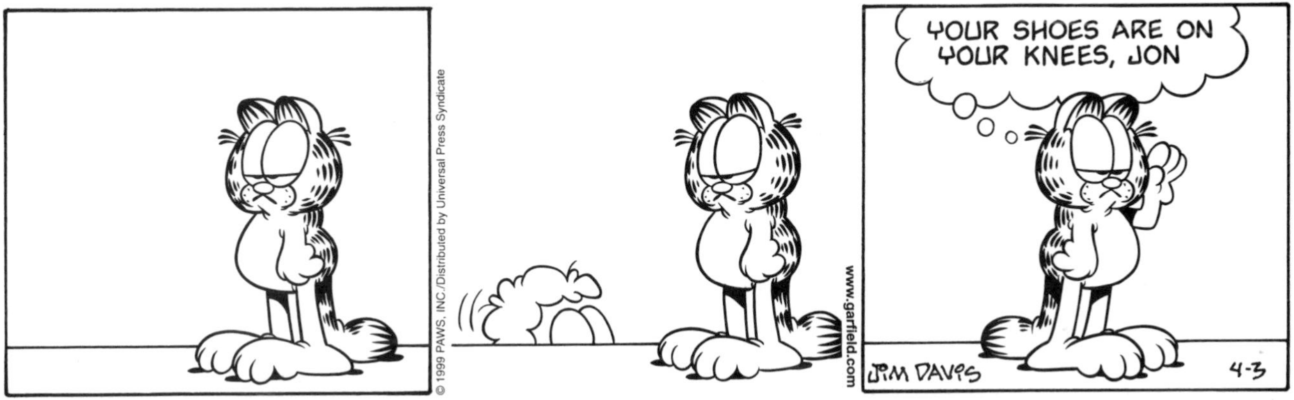
YOUR SHOES ARE ON YOUR KNEES, JON
JIM DAVIS
4-3

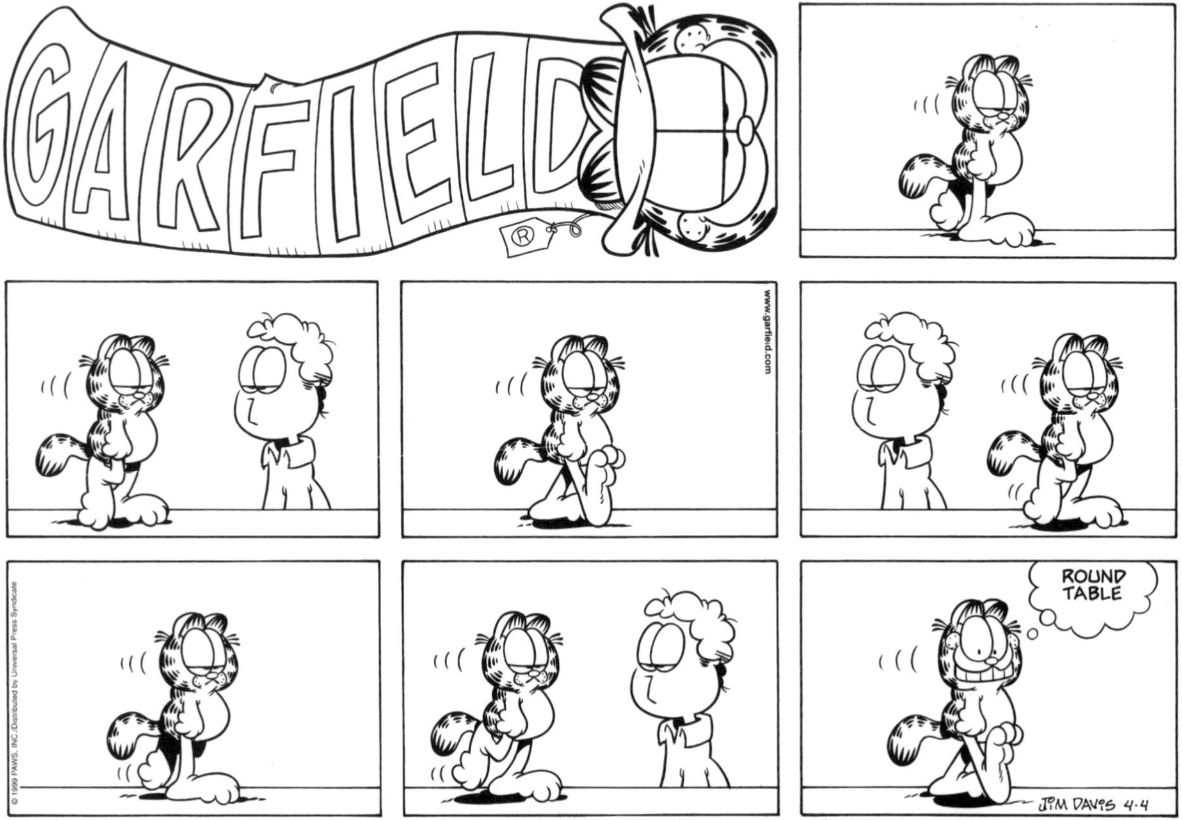
GARFIELD
www.garfield.com
© 1999 PAWS, INC./Distributed by Universal Press Syndicate
ROUND TABLE
JIM DAVIS 4-4

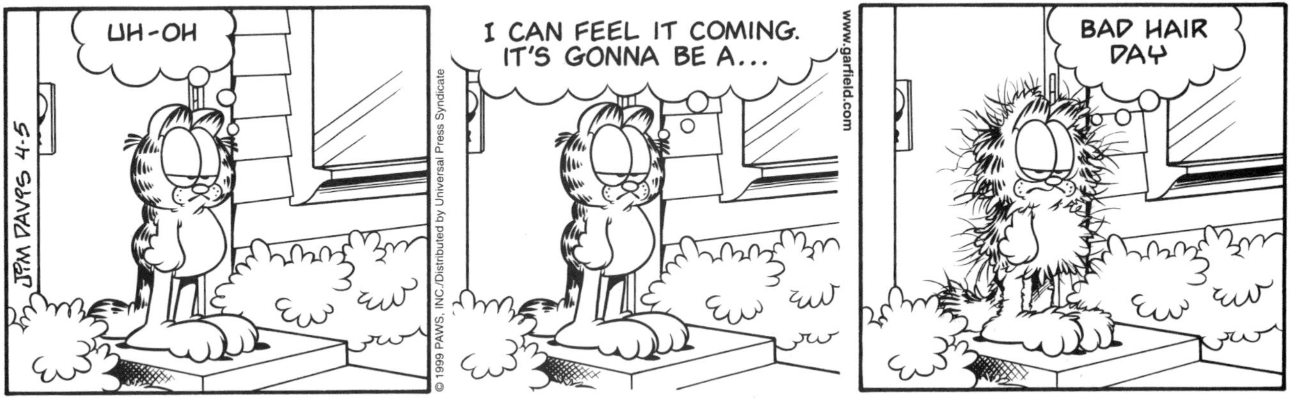
UH-OH
I CAN FEEL IT COMING. IT'S GONNA BE A...
BAD HAIR DAY
JPM DAVPS 4-5
© 1999 PAWS, INC./Distributed by Universal Press Syndicate
www.garfield.com

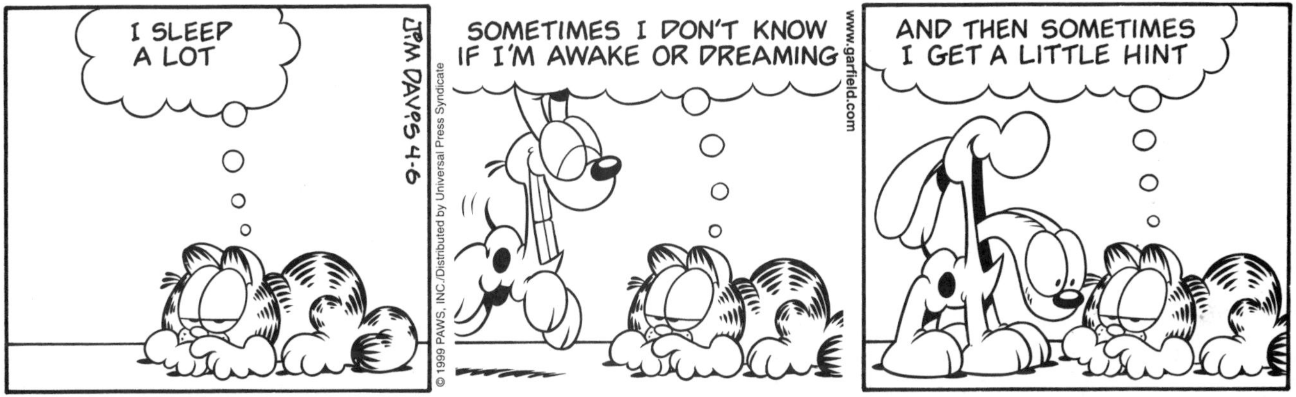
I SLEEP A LOT
SOMETIMES I DON'T KNOW IF I'M AWAKE OR DREAMING
AND THEN SOMETIMES I GET A LITTLE HINT
JPM DAVPS 4-6
© 1999 PAWS, INC./Distributed by Universal Press Syndicate
www.garfield.com

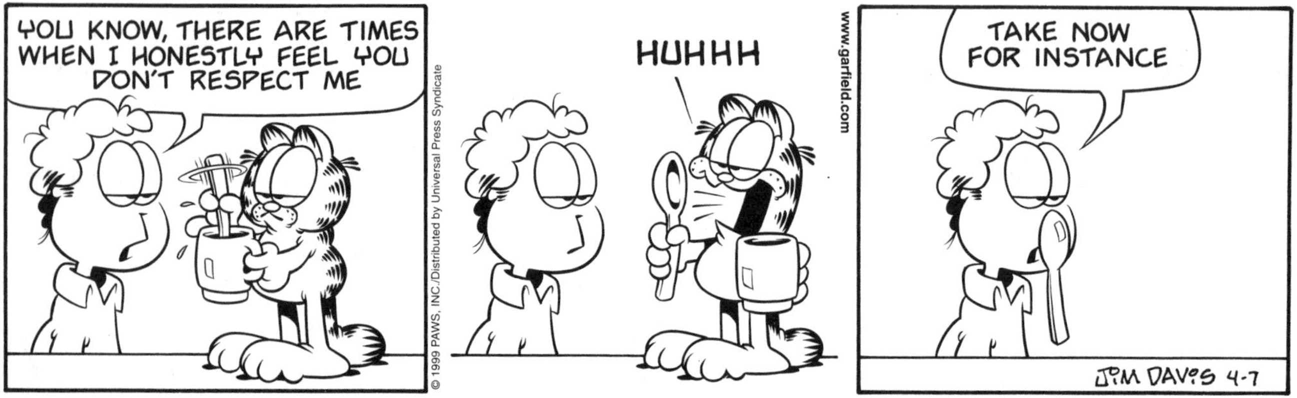
YOU KNOW, THERE ARE TIMES WHEN I HONESTLY FEEL YOU DON'T RESPECT ME
HUHHH
TAKE NOW FOR INSTANCE
JIM DAVIS 4-7
© 1999 PAWS, INC./Distributed by Universal Press Syndicate
www.garfield.com

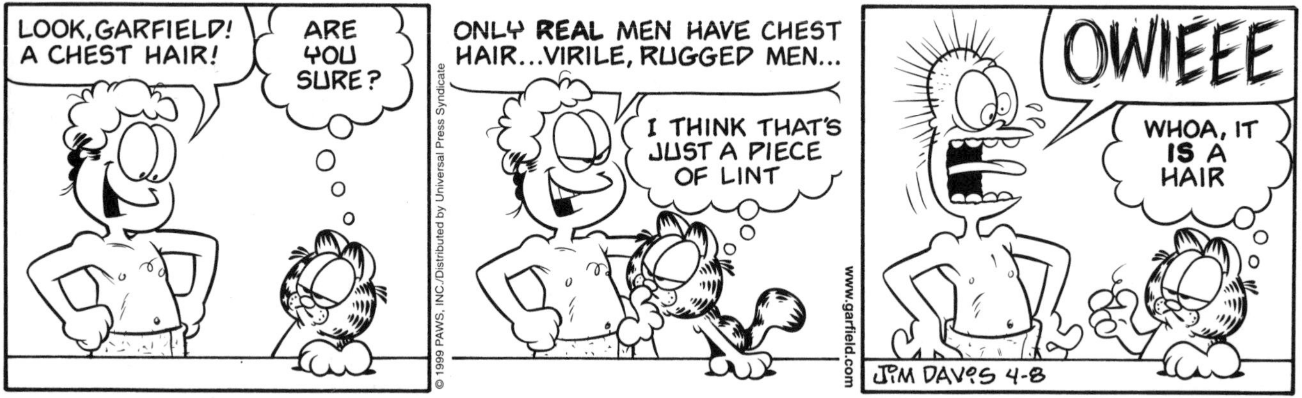
LOOK, GARFIELD! A CHEST HAIR!
ARE YOU SURE?
ONLY **REAL** MEN HAVE CHEST HAIR...VIRILE, RUGGED MEN...
I THINK THAT'S JUST A PIECE OF LINT
OWIEEE
WHOA, IT **IS** A HAIR
JIM DAVIS 4-8
© 1999 PAWS, INC./Distributed by Universal Press Syndicate
www.garfield.com

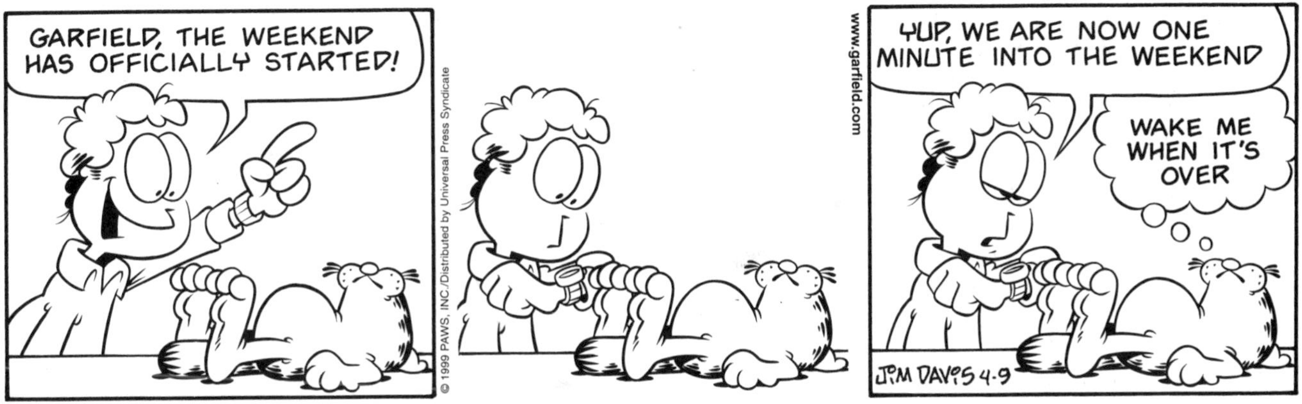
GARFIELD, THE WEEKEND HAS OFFICIALLY STARTED!
YUP, WE ARE NOW ONE MINUTE INTO THE WEEKEND
WAKE ME WHEN IT'S OVER
JIM DAVIS 4-9

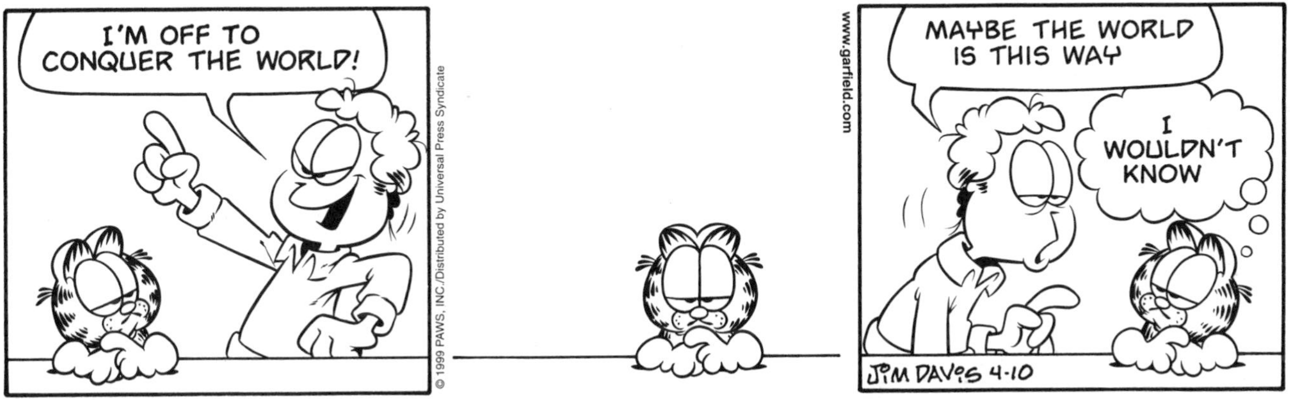
I'M OFF TO CONQUER THE WORLD!
MAYBE THE WORLD IS THIS WAY
I WOULDN'T KNOW
JIM DAVIS 4-10

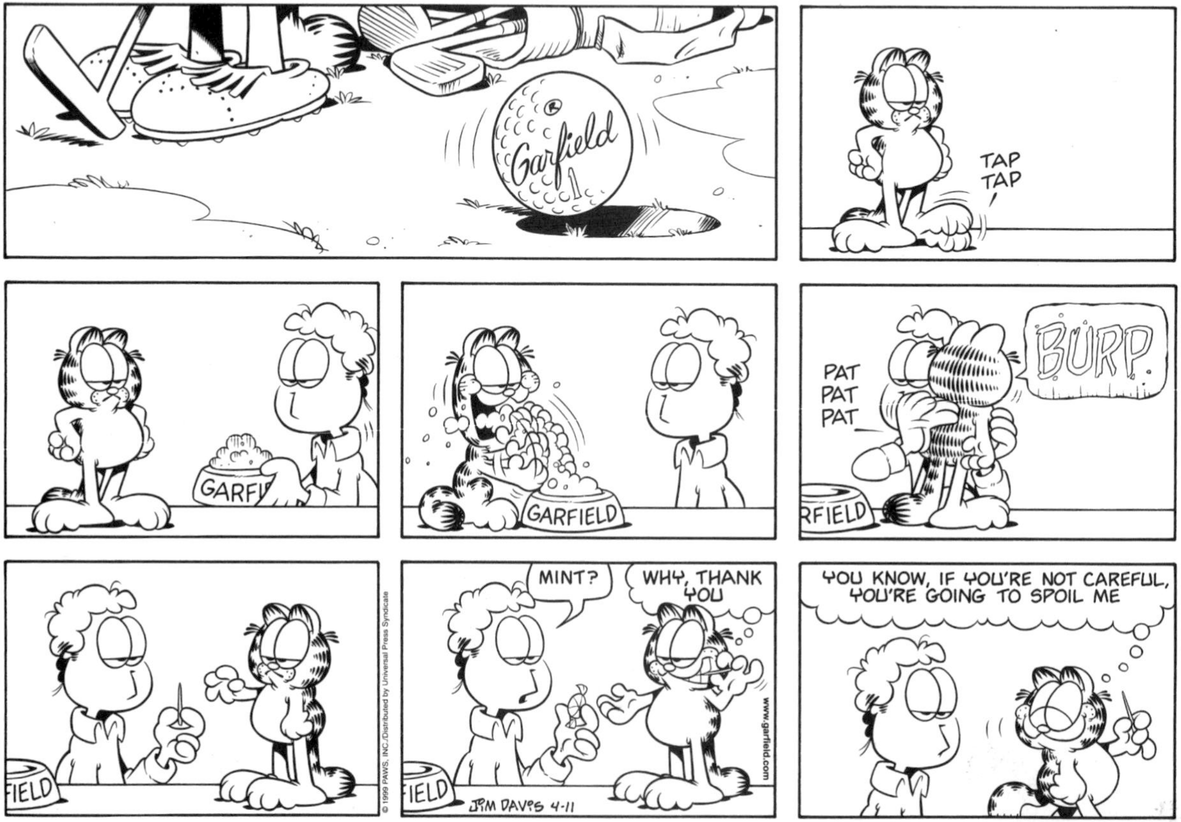
Garfield
TAP
TAP
GARFI
GARFIELD
PAT
PAT
PAT
BURP
RFIELD
FIELD
MINT?
WHY, THANK YOU
FIELD
JIM DAVIS 4-11
YOU KNOW, IF YOU'RE NOT CAREFUL, YOU'RE GOING TO SPOIL ME
© 1999 PAWS, INC./Distributed by Universal Press Syndicate
www.garfield.com

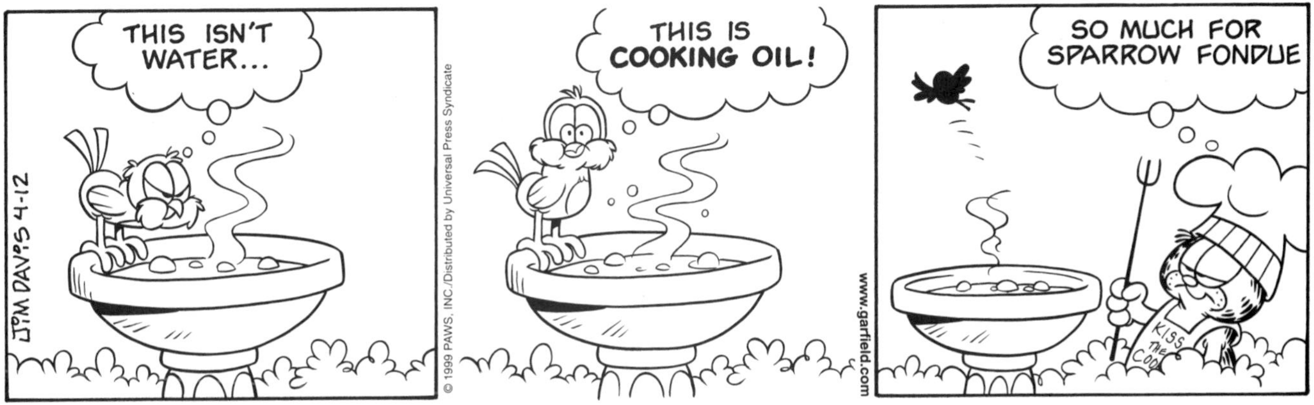

THIS ISN'T WATER...
THIS IS COOKING OIL!
SO MUCH FOR SPARROW FONDUE
KISS THE COO
JIM DAVIS 4-12
© 1999 PAWS, INC./Distributed by Universal Press Syndicate
www.garfield.com

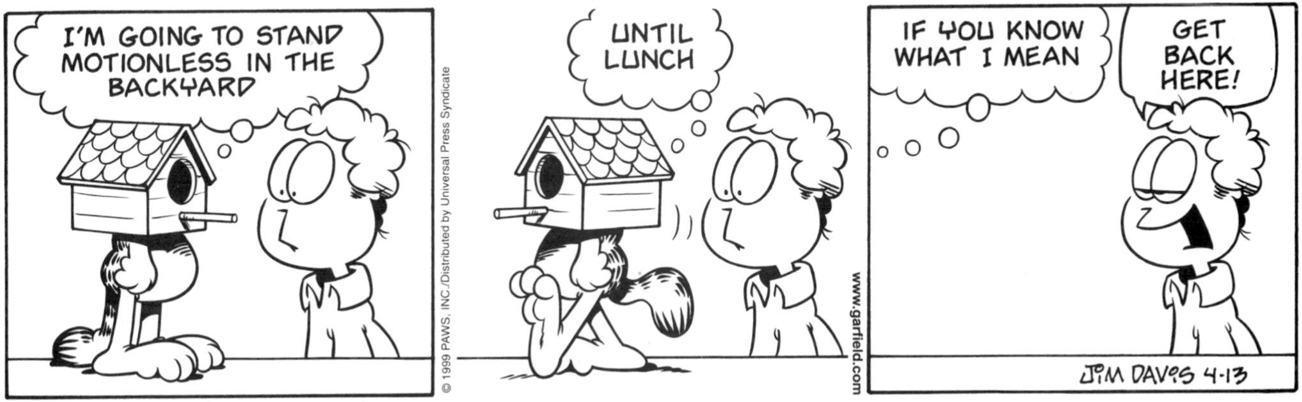

I'M GOING TO STAND MOTIONLESS IN THE BACKYARD
UNTIL LUNCH
IF YOU KNOW WHAT I MEAN
GET BACK HERE!
JIM DAVIS 4-13
© 1999 PAWS, INC./Distributed by Universal Press Syndicate
www.garfield.com

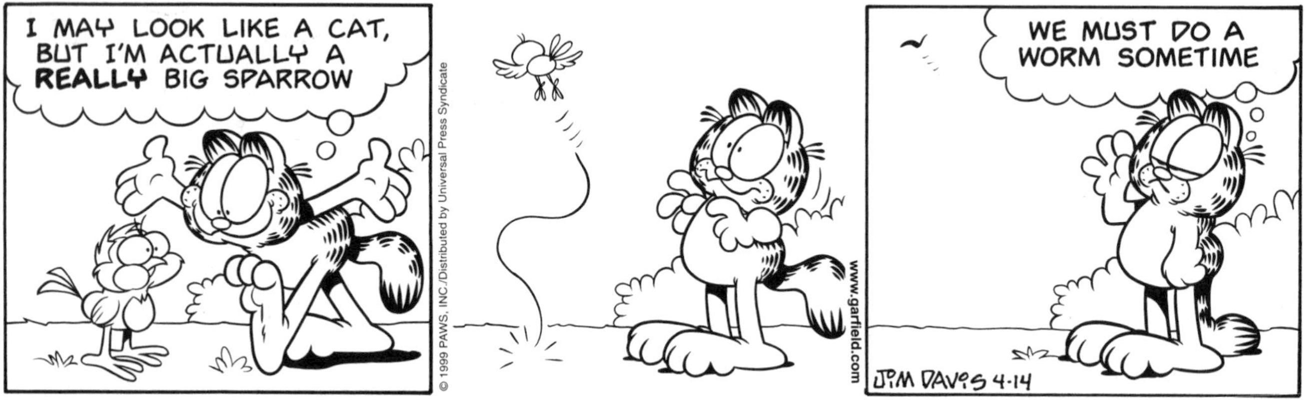
I MAY LOOK LIKE A CAT, BUT I'M ACTUALLY A **REALLY** BIG SPARROW
WE MUST DO A WORM SOMETIME
© 1999 PAWS, INC./Distributed by Universal Press Syndicate
www.garfield.com
JIM DAVIS 4-14

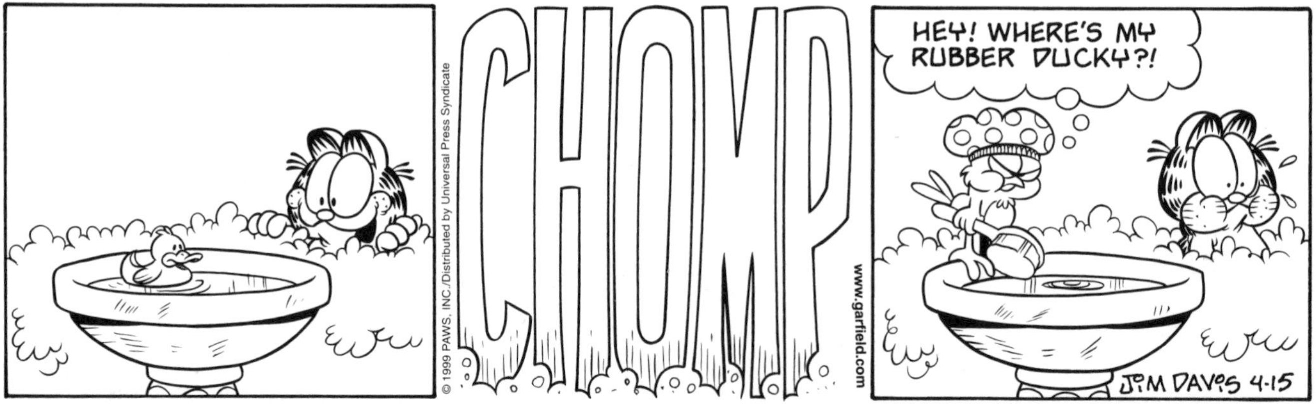
CHOMP
HEY! WHERE'S MY RUBBER DUCKY?!
© 1999 PAWS, INC./Distributed by Universal Press Syndicate
www.garfield.com
JIM DAVIS 4-15

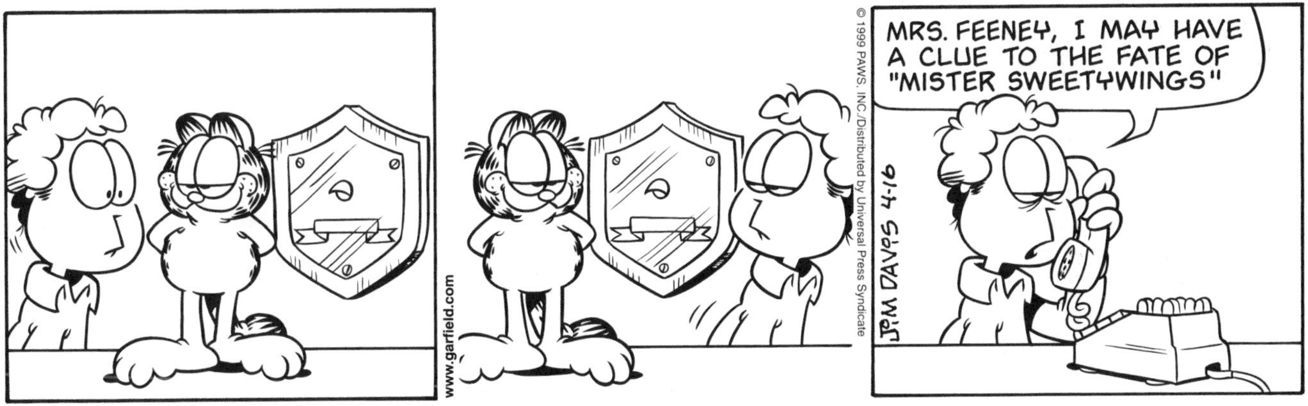
MRS. FEENEY, I MAY HAVE A CLUE TO THE FATE OF "MISTER SWEETYWINGS"
JIM DAVIS 4-16
www.garfield.com
© 1999 PAWS, INC./Distributed by Universal Press Syndicate

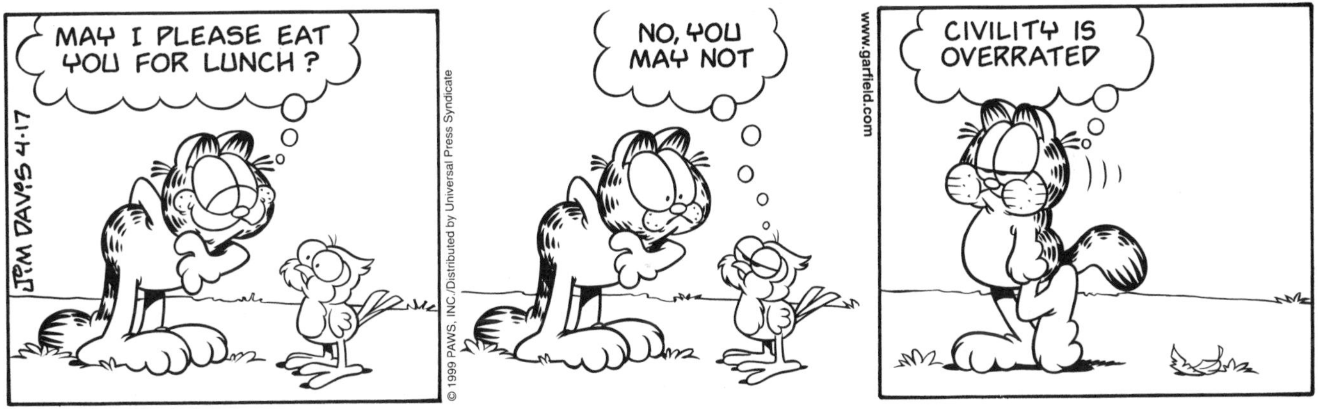
MAY I PLEASE EAT YOU FOR LUNCH?
NO, YOU MAY NOT
CIVILITY IS OVERRATED
JIM DAVIS 4-17
© 1999 PAWS, INC./Distributed by Universal Press Syndicate
www.garfield.com

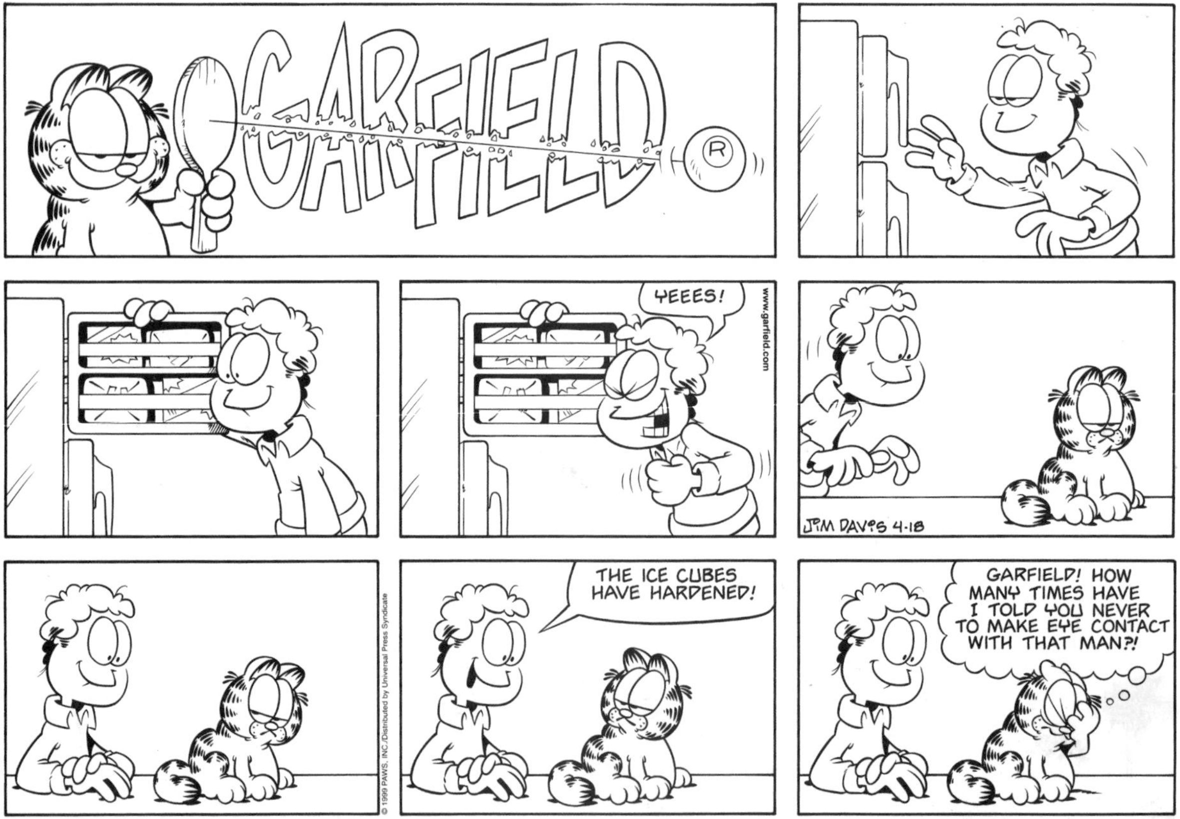

GARFIELD
YEEES!
www.garfield.com
JIM DAVIS 4-18
© 1999 PAWS, INC./Distributed by Universal Press Syndicate
THE ICE CUBES HAVE HARDENED!
GARFIELD! HOW MANY TIMES HAVE I TOLD YOU NEVER TO MAKE EYE CONTACT WITH THAT MAN?!

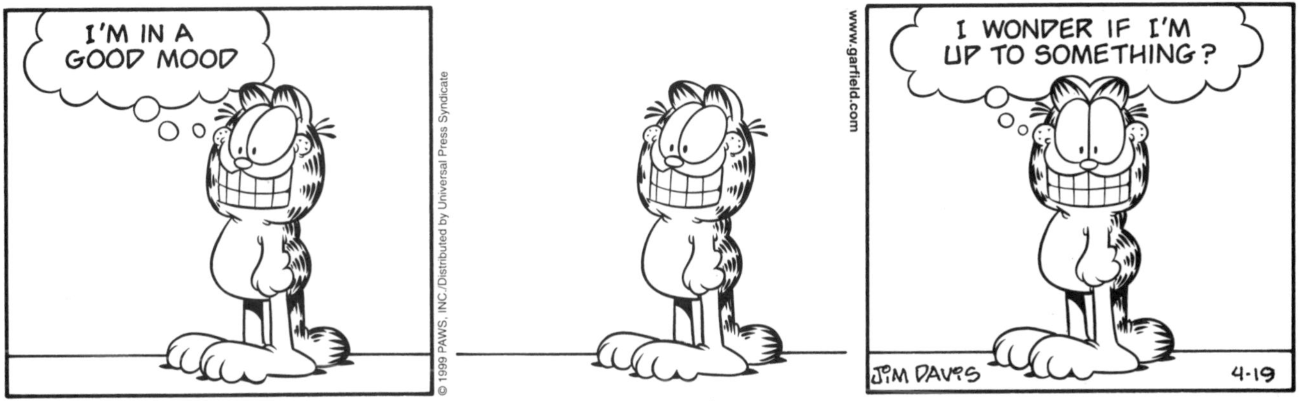
I'M IN A GOOD MOOD
I WONDER IF I'M UP TO SOMETHING?
JIM DAVIS
4-19
© 1999 PAWS, INC./Distributed by Universal Press Syndicate
www.garfield.com

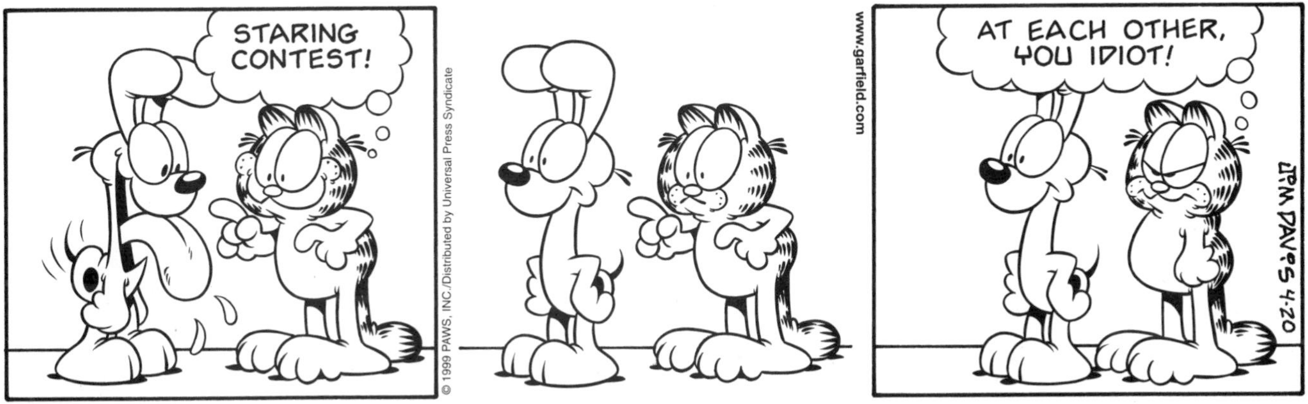
STARING CONTEST!
AT EACH OTHER, YOU IDIOT!
JIM DAVIS 4-20
© 1999 PAWS, INC./Distributed by Universal Press Syndicate
www.garfield.com

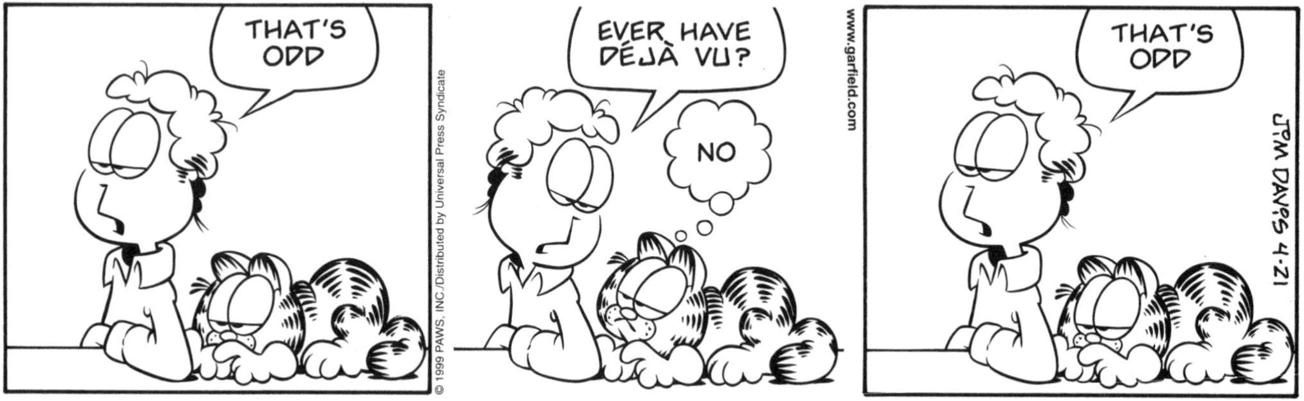
THAT'S ODD
EVER HAVE DÉJÀ VU?
NO
THAT'S ODD
JIM DAVIS 4-21

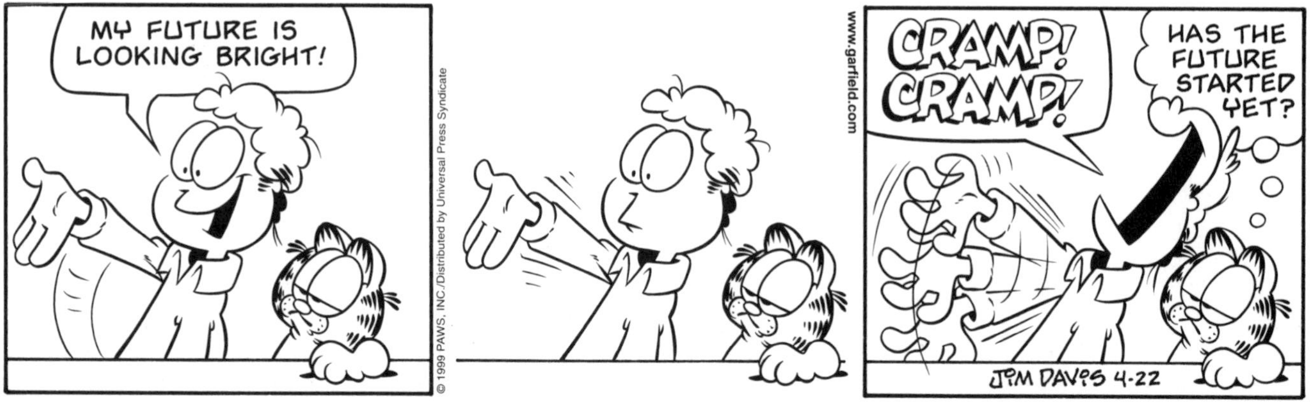
MY FUTURE IS LOOKING BRIGHT!
CRAMP! CRAMP!
HAS THE FUTURE STARTED YET?
JIM DAVIS 4-22

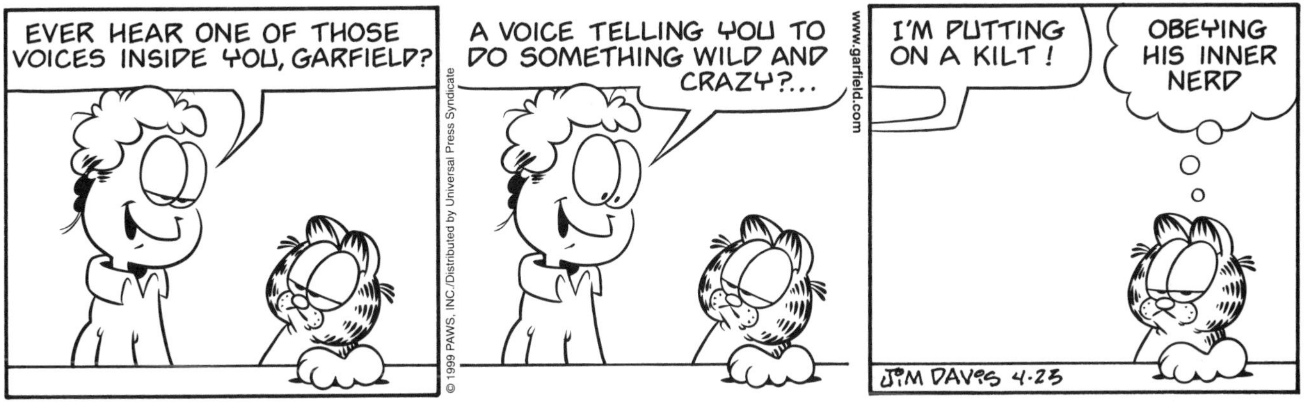
EVER HEAR ONE OF THOSE VOICES INSIDE YOU, GARFIELD?
© 1999 PAWS, INC./Distributed by Universal Press Syndicate
A VOICE TELLING YOU TO DO SOMETHING WILD AND CRAZY?...
www.garfield.com
I'M PUTTING ON A KILT!
OBEYING HIS INNER NERD
JIM DAVIS 4-23

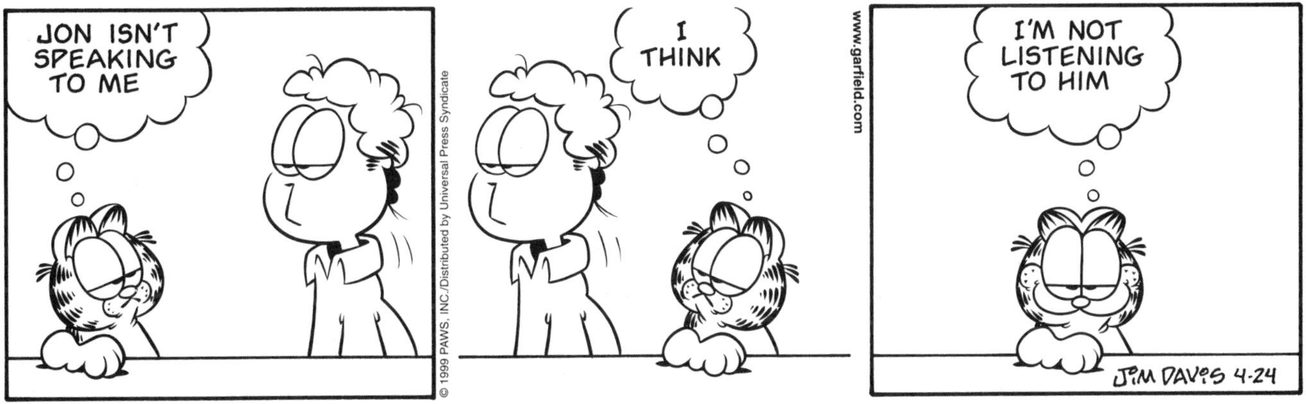
JON ISN'T SPEAKING TO ME
© 1999 PAWS, INC./Distributed by Universal Press Syndicate
I THINK
www.garfield.com
I'M NOT LISTENING TO HIM
JIM DAVIS 4-24

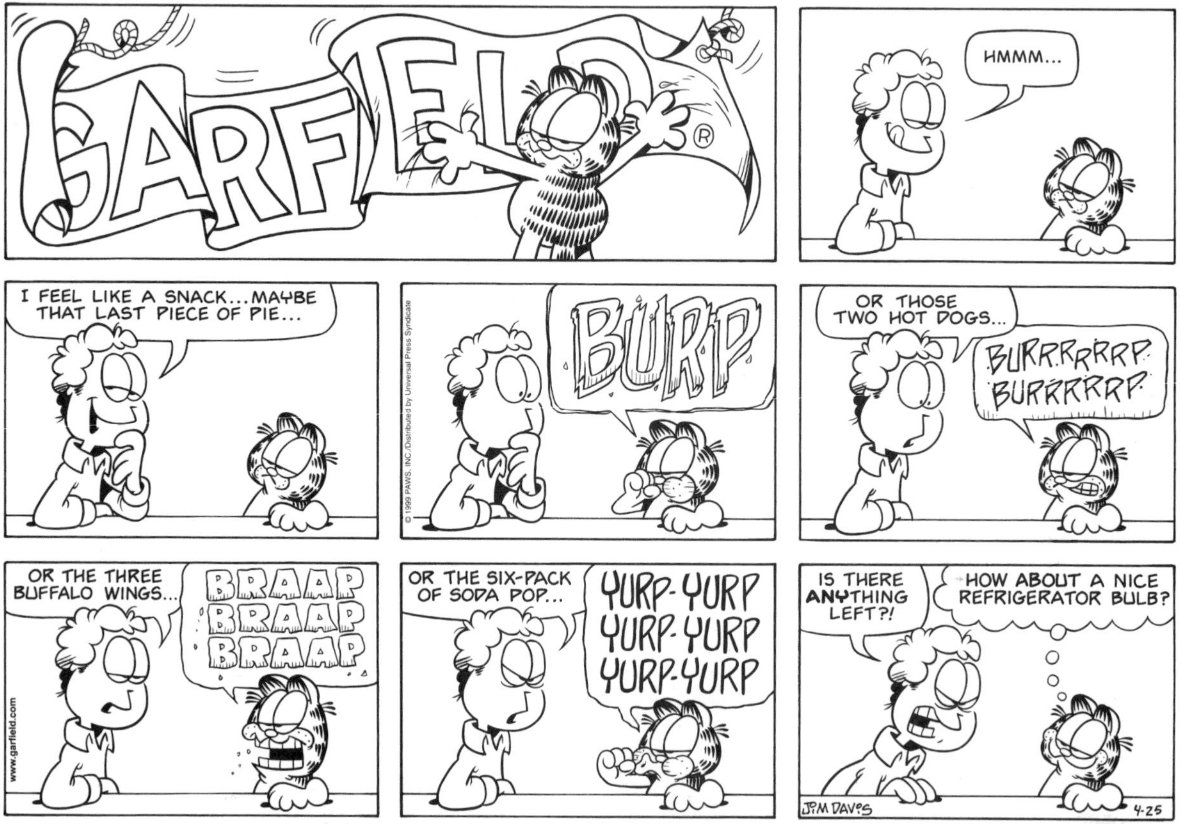
GARFIELD®
HMMM...
I FEEL LIKE A SNACK... MAYBE THAT LAST PIECE OF PIE...
BURP
OR THOSE TWO HOT DOGS...
BURRRRRRP BURRRRRRP
OR THE THREE BUFFALO WINGS...
BRAAAP BRAAAP BRAAAP
OR THE SIX-PACK OF SODA POP...
YURP-YURP YURP-YURP YURP-YURP
IS THERE ANYTHING LEFT?!
HOW ABOUT A NICE REFRIGERATOR BULB?
JIM DAVIS
4-25
© 1999 PAWS, INC./Distributed by Universal Press Syndicate
www.garfield.com

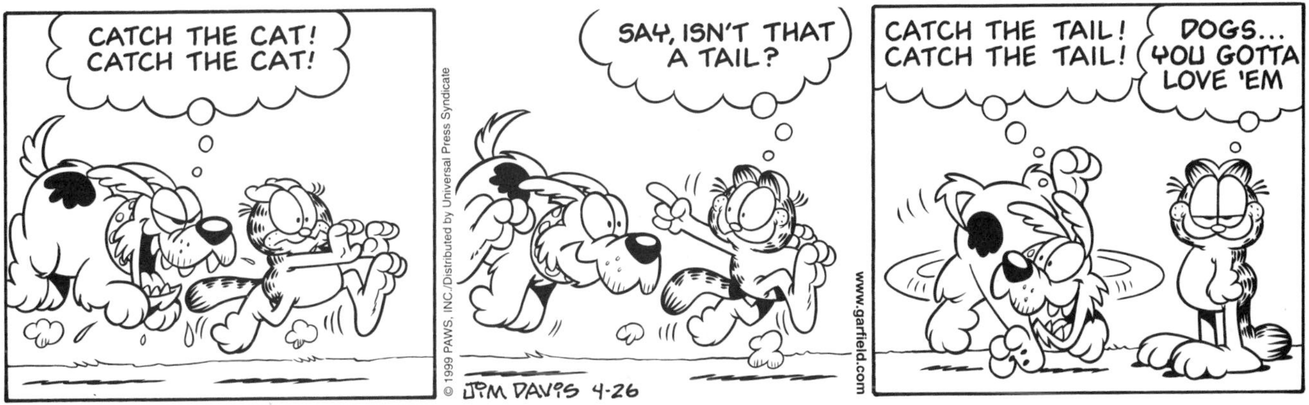
CATCH THE CAT! CATCH THE CAT!
SAY, ISN'T THAT A TAIL?
CATCH THE TAIL! CATCH THE TAIL!
DOGS... YOU GOTTA LOVE 'EM
JIM DAVIS 4-26
© 1999 PAWS, INC./Distributed by Universal Press Syndicate
www.garfield.com

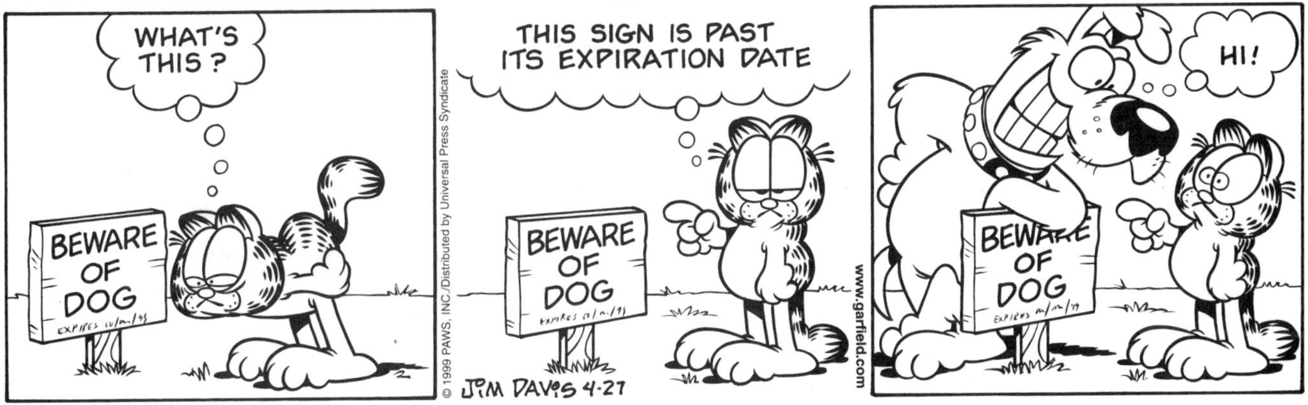
WHAT'S THIS?
BEWARE OF DOG
THIS SIGN IS PAST ITS EXPIRATION DATE
BEWARE OF DOG
HI!
BEWARE OF DOG
JIM DAVIS 4-27
© 1999 PAWS, INC./Distributed by Universal Press Syndicate
www.garfield.com

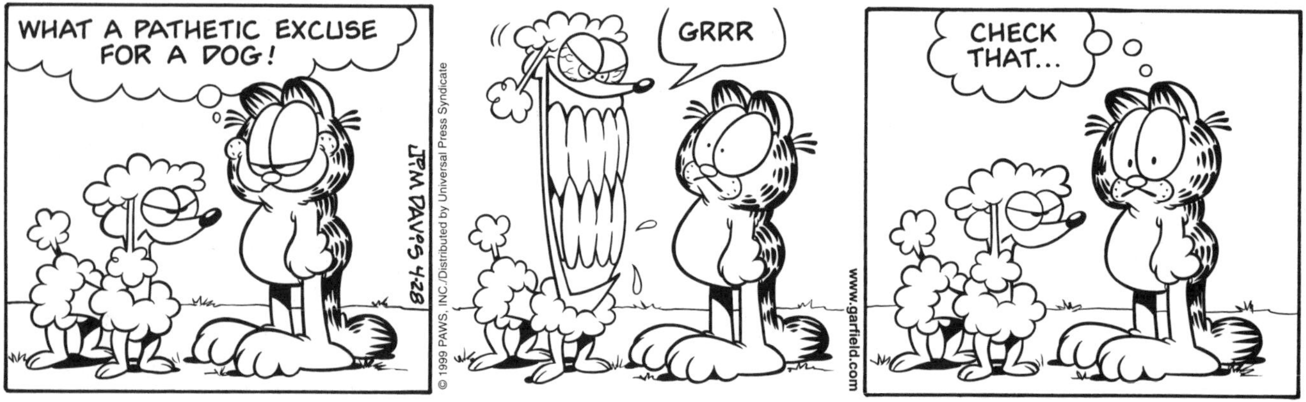
WHAT A PATHETIC EXCUSE FOR A DOG!
JIM DAVIS 4-28
© 1999 PAWS, INC./Distributed by Universal Press Syndicate
GRRR
www.garfield.com
CHECK THAT...

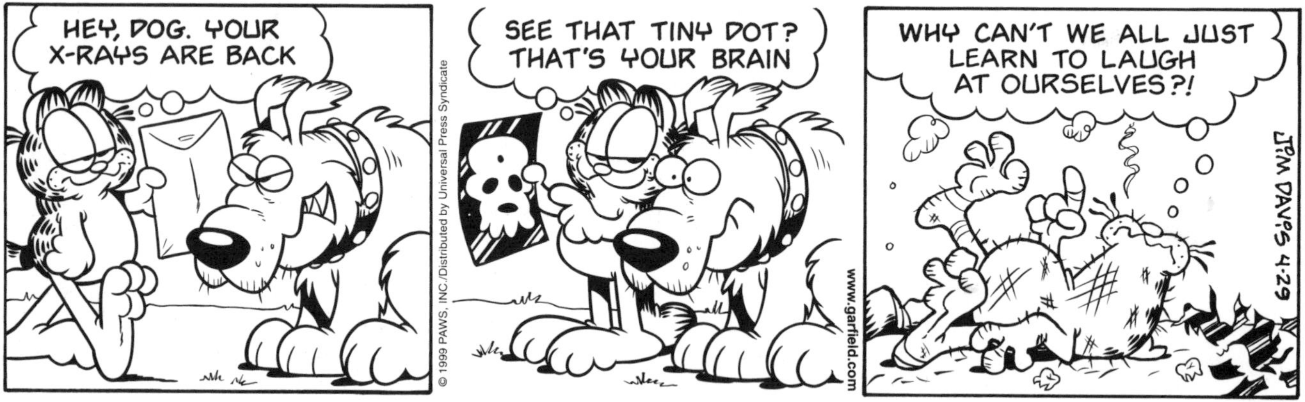
HEY, DOG. YOUR X-RAYS ARE BACK
© 1999 PAWS, INC./Distributed by Universal Press Syndicate
SEE THAT TINY DOT? THAT'S YOUR BRAIN
www.garfield.com
WHY CAN'T WE ALL JUST LEARN TO LAUGH AT OURSELVES?!
JIM DAVIS 4-29

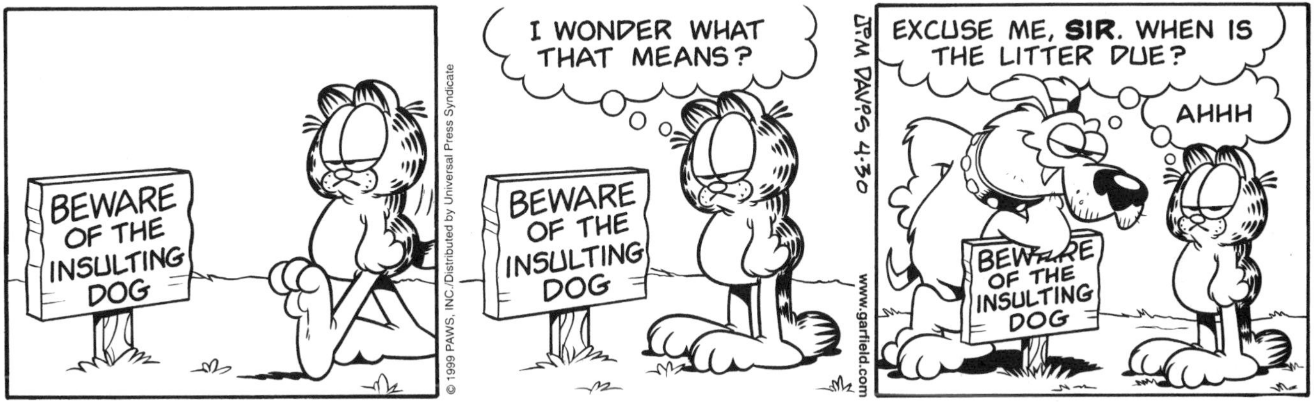
BEWARE OF THE INSULTING DOG
© 1999 PAWS, INC./Distributed by Universal Press Syndicate
I WONDER WHAT THAT MEANS?
BEWARE OF THE INSULTING DOG
JIM DAVIS 4-30
www.garfield.com
EXCUSE ME, **SIR**. WHEN IS THE LITTER DUE?
AHHH
BEWARE OF THE INSULTING DOG

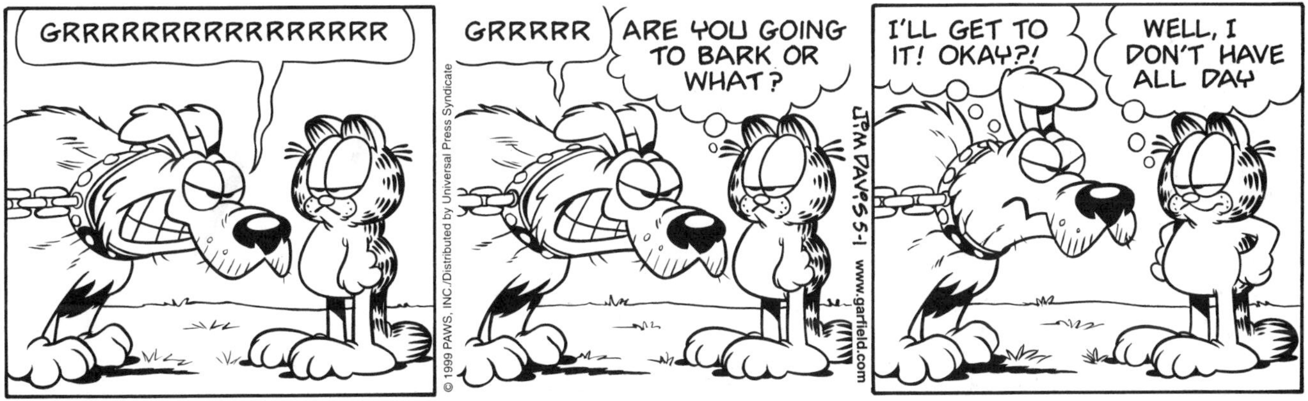
GRRRRRRRRRRRRRRRR
© 1999 PAWS, INC./Distributed by Universal Press Syndicate
GRRRRR
ARE YOU GOING TO BARK OR WHAT?
JIM DAVIS 5-1
www.garfield.com
I'LL GET TO IT! OKAY?!
WELL, I DON'T HAVE ALL DAY

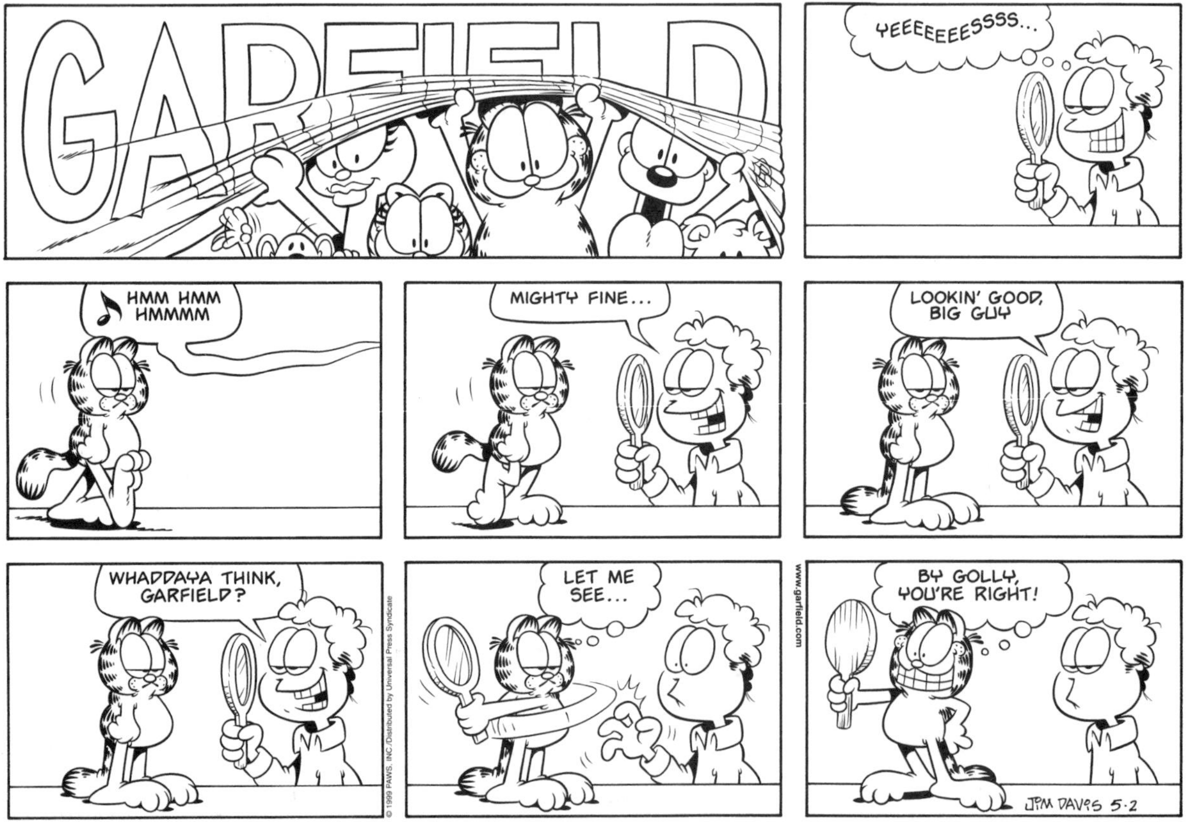
GARFIELD
YEEEEEEEESSSS...
HMM HMM HMMMM
MIGHTY FINE...
LOOKIN' GOOD, BIG GUY
WHADDAYA THINK, GARFIELD?
LET ME SEE...
BY GOLLY, YOU'RE RIGHT!
JIM DAVIS 5·2
www.garfield.com

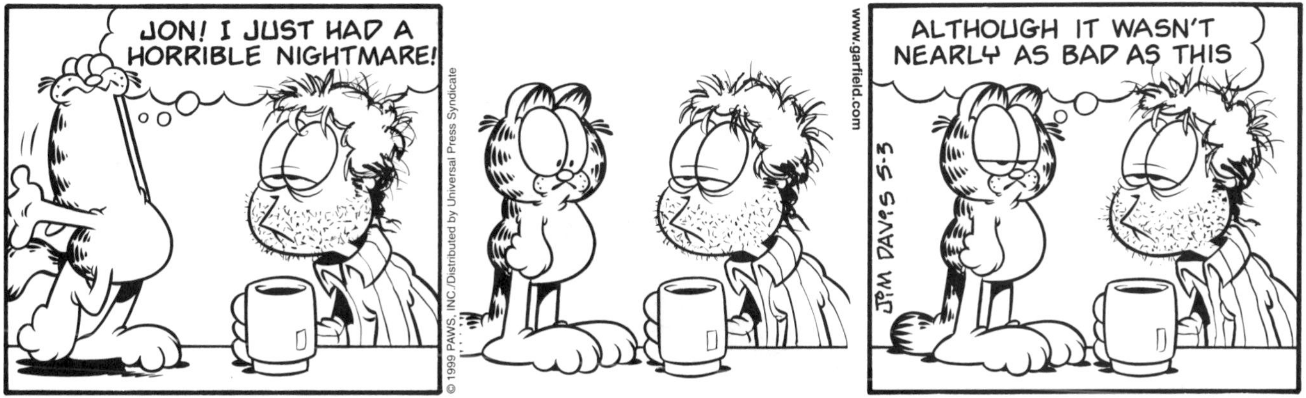
JON! I JUST HAD A HORRIBLE NIGHTMARE!
ALTHOUGH IT WASN'T NEARLY AS BAD AS THIS
JIM DAVIS 5-3
© 1999 PAWS, INC./Distributed by Universal Press Syndicate
www.garfield.com

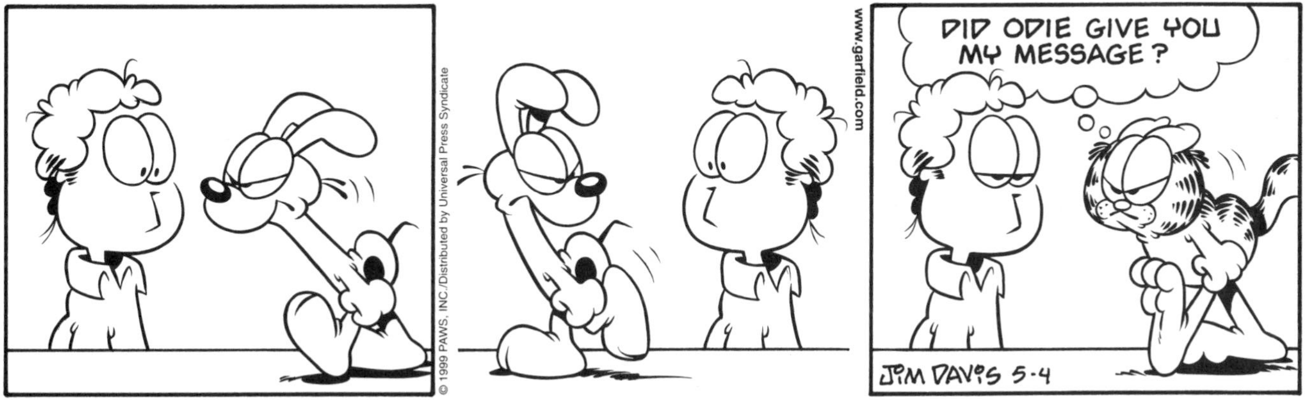
DID ODIE GIVE YOU MY MESSAGE?
JIM DAVIS 5-4
© 1999 PAWS, INC./Distributed by Universal Press Syndicate
www.garfield.com

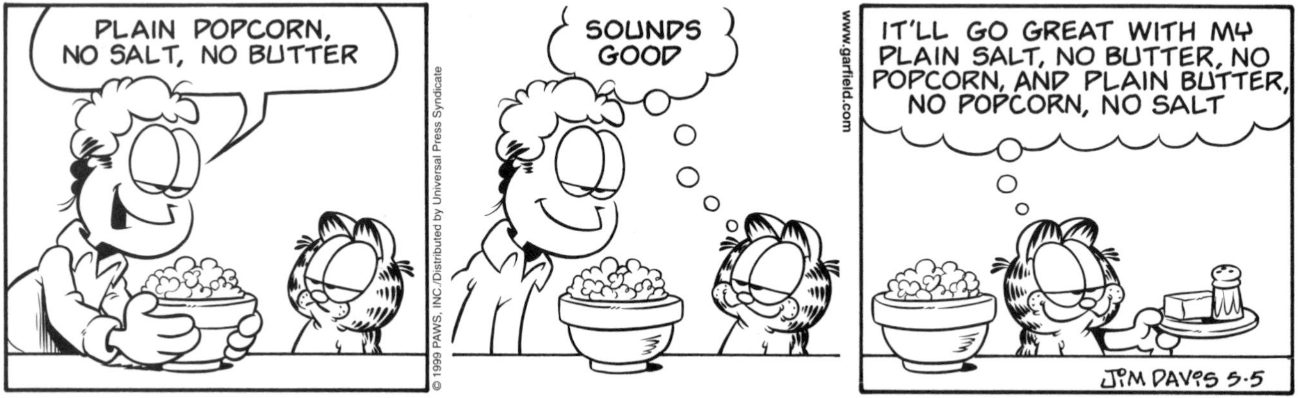
PLAIN POPCORN, NO SALT, NO BUTTER
SOUNDS GOOD
IT'LL GO GREAT WITH MY PLAIN SALT, NO BUTTER, NO POPCORN, AND PLAIN BUTTER, NO POPCORN, NO SALT
JIM DAVIS 5-5

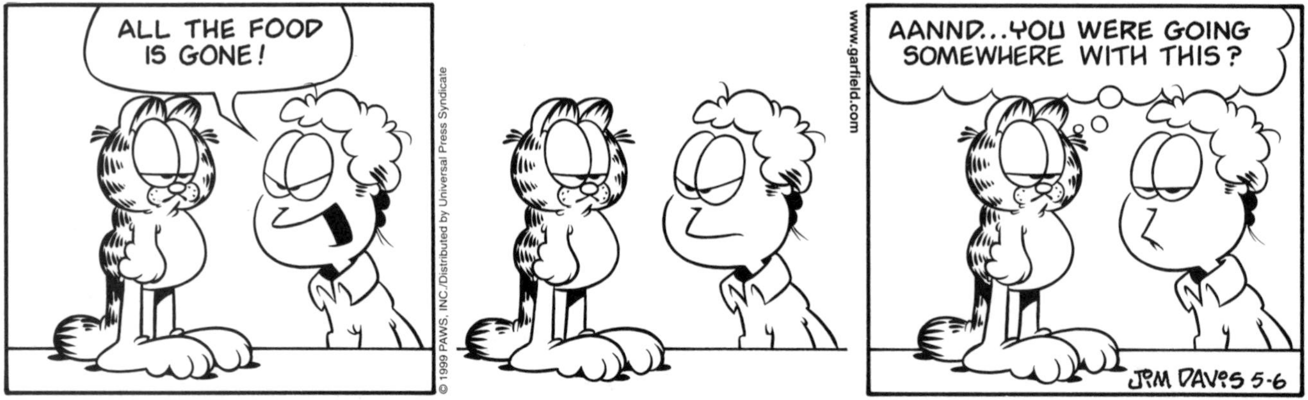
ALL THE FOOD IS GONE!
AANND...YOU WERE GOING SOMEWHERE WITH THIS?
JIM DAVIS 5-6

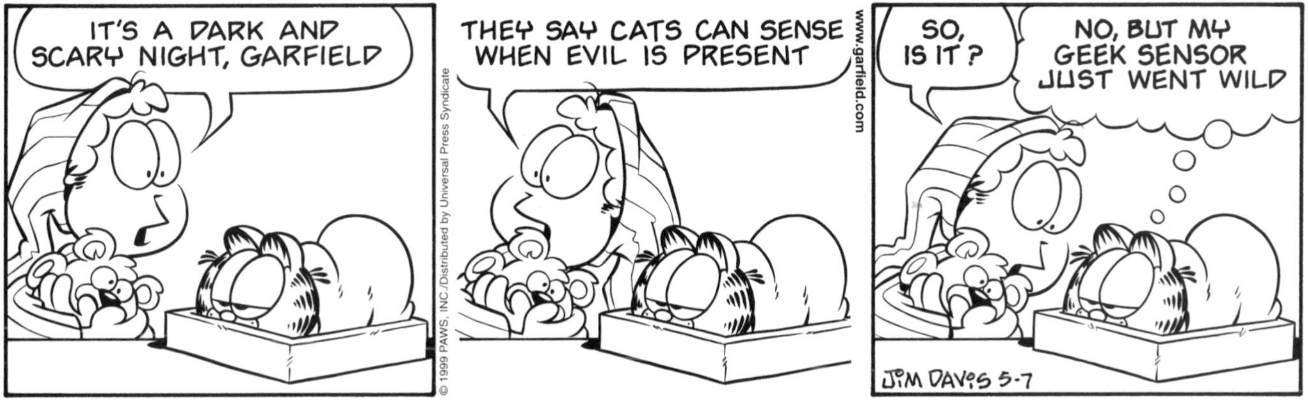
IT'S A DARK AND SCARY NIGHT, GARFIELD
THEY SAY CATS CAN SENSE WHEN EVIL IS PRESENT
SO, IS IT ?
NO, BUT MY GEEK SENSOR JUST WENT WILD
JIM DAVIS 5-7
www.garfield.com

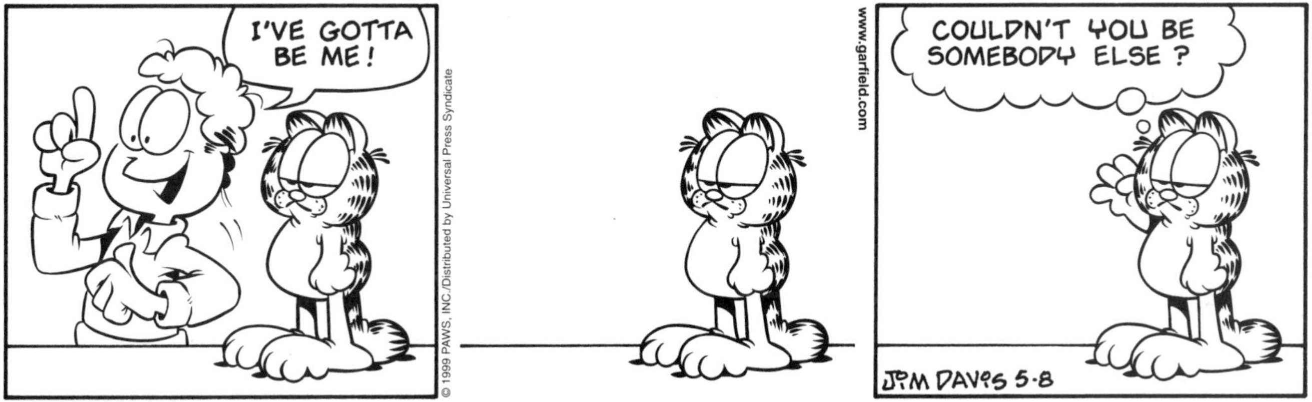
I'VE GOTTA BE ME !
COULDN'T YOU BE SOMEBODY ELSE ?
JIM DAVIS 5-8
www.garfield.com

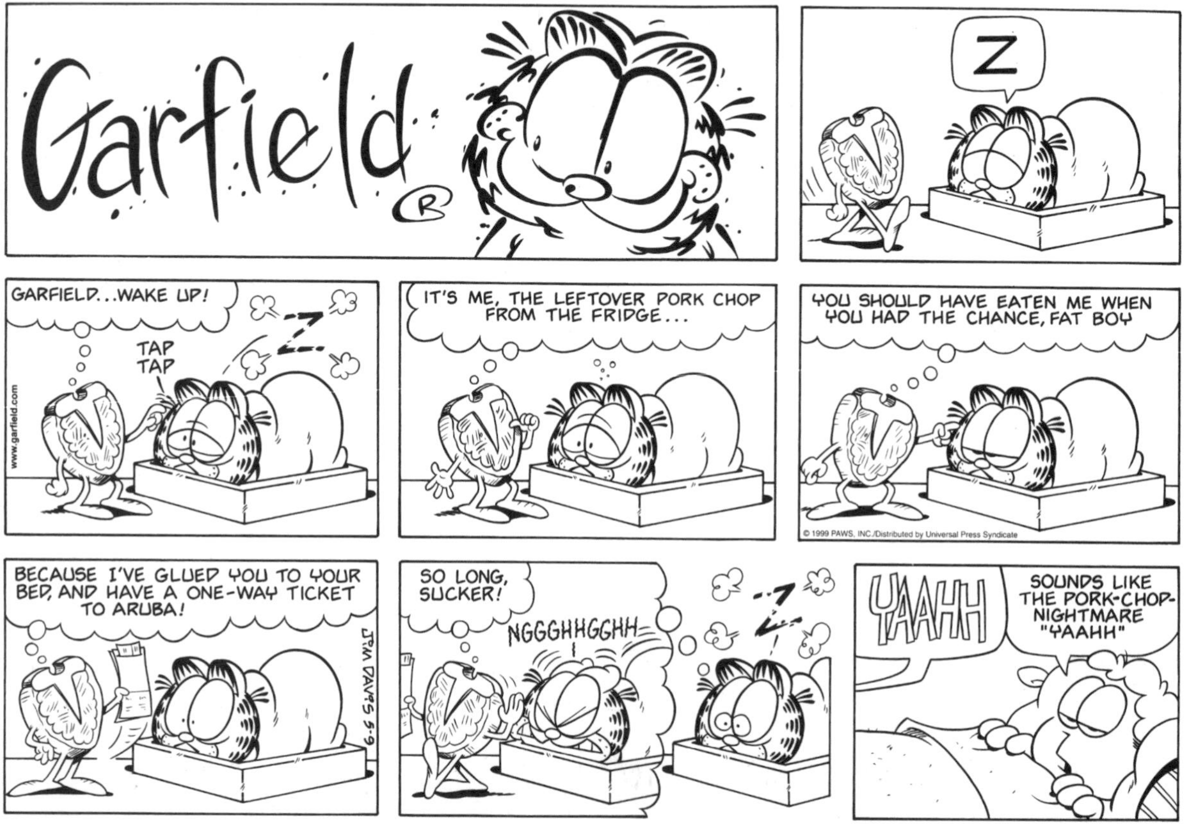
Garfield®
Z
GARFIELD...WAKE UP!
TAP TAP
www.garfield.com
IT'S ME, THE LEFTOVER PORK CHOP FROM THE FRIDGE...
YOU SHOULD HAVE EATEN ME WHEN YOU HAD THE CHANCE, FAT BOY
© 1999 PAWS, INC./Distributed by Universal Press Syndicate
BECAUSE I'VE GLUED YOU TO YOUR BED, AND HAVE A ONE-WAY TICKET TO ARUBA!
JIM DAVIS 5-9
SO LONG, SUCKER!
NGGGHHGGHH
YAAHH
SOUNDS LIKE THE PORK-CHOP-NIGHTMARE "YAAHH"

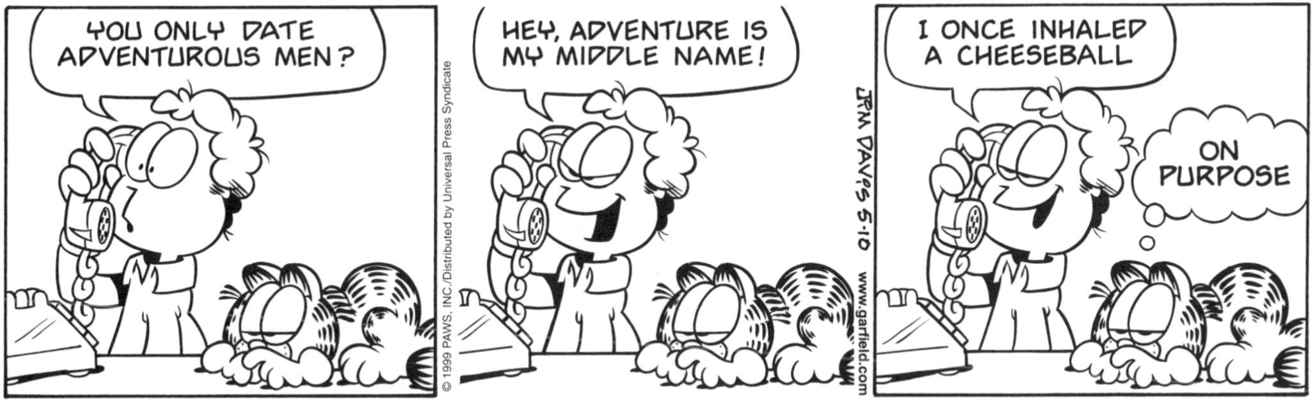
YOU ONLY DATE ADVENTUROUS MEN?
© 1999 PAWS, INC./Distributed by Universal Press Syndicate
HEY, ADVENTURE IS MY MIDDLE NAME!
JIM DAVIS 5-10
www.garfield.com
I ONCE INHALED A CHEESEBALL
ON PURPOSE

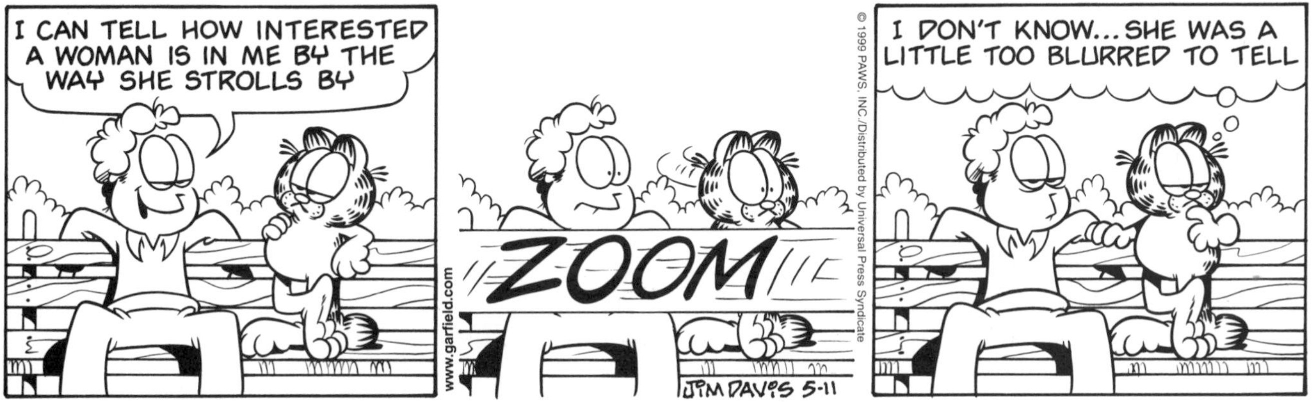
I CAN TELL HOW INTERESTED A WOMAN IS IN ME BY THE WAY SHE STROLLS BY
www.garfield.com
ZOOM
JIM DAVIS 5-11
© 1999 PAWS, INC./Distributed by Universal Press Syndicate
I DON'T KNOW... SHE WAS A LITTLE TOO BLURRED TO TELL

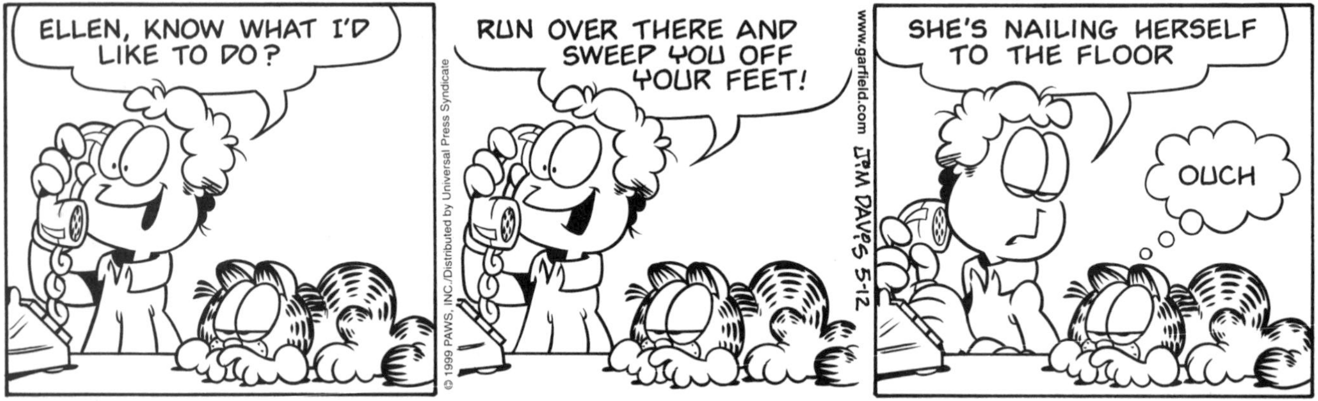
ELLEN, KNOW WHAT I'D LIKE TO DO?
RUN OVER THERE AND SWEEP YOU OFF YOUR FEET!
SHE'S NAILING HERSELF TO THE FLOOR
OUCH
© 1999 PAWS, INC./Distributed by Universal Press Syndicate
www.garfield.com
JIM DAVIS 5-12

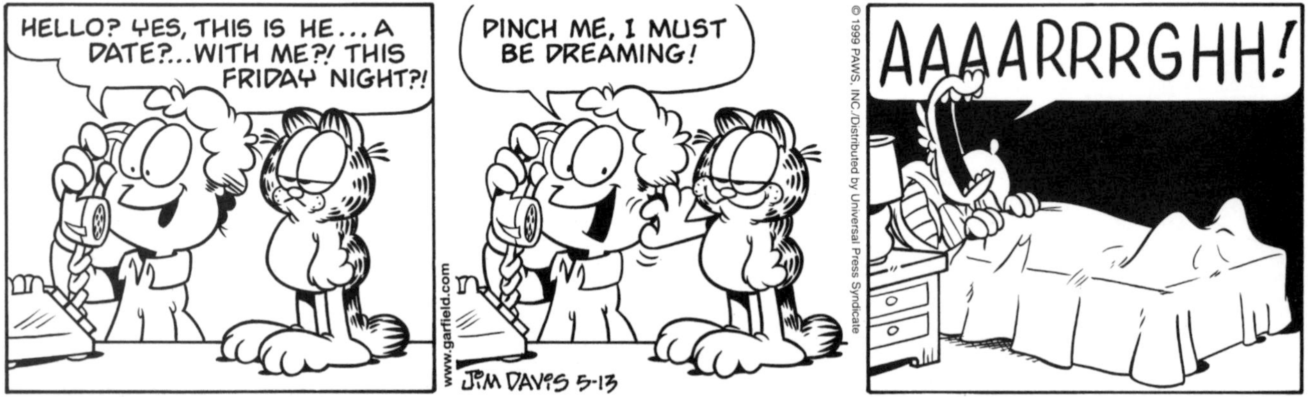
HELLO? YES, THIS IS HE... A DATE?...WITH ME?! THIS FRIDAY NIGHT?!
PINCH ME, I MUST BE DREAMING!
AAAARRRGHH!
www.garfield.com
JIM DAVIS 5-13
© 1999 PAWS, INC./Distributed by Universal Press Syndicate

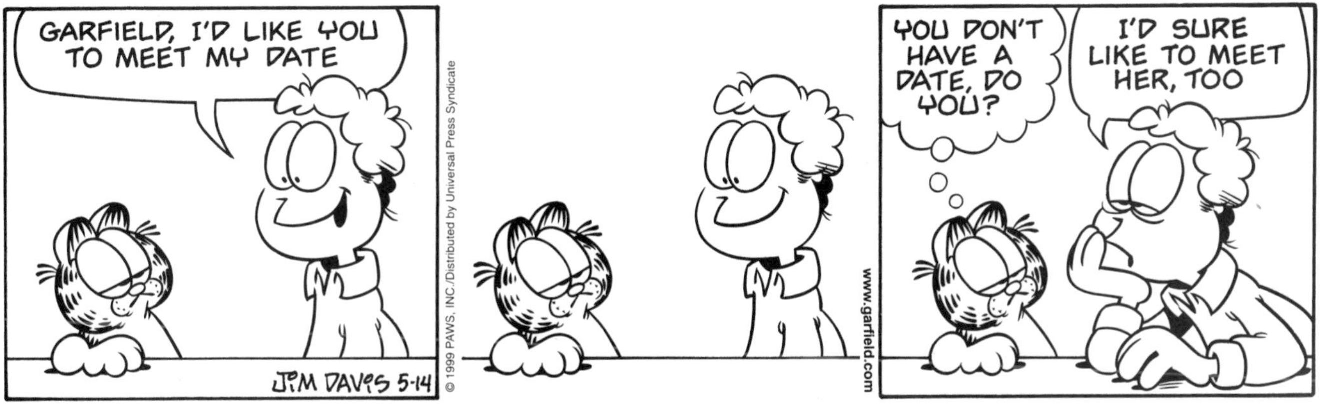
GARFIELD, I'D LIKE YOU TO MEET MY DATE
JIM DAVIS 5-14
© 1999 PAWS, INC./Distributed by Universal Press Syndicate
www.garfield.com
YOU DON'T HAVE A DATE, DO YOU?
I'D SURE LIKE TO MEET HER, TOO

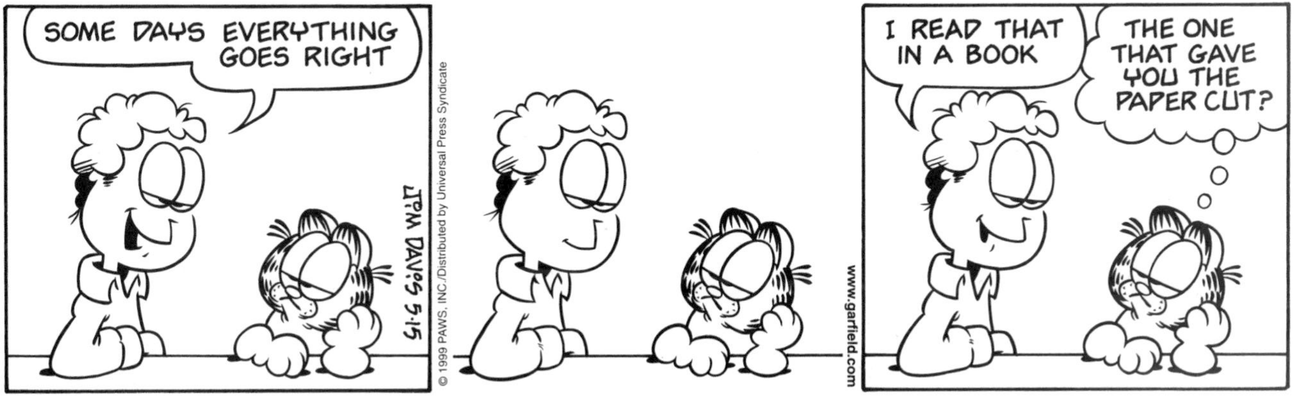
SOME DAYS EVERYTHING GOES RIGHT
JIM DAVIS 5-15
© 1999 PAWS, INC./Distributed by Universal Press Syndicate
www.garfield.com
I READ THAT IN A BOOK
THE ONE THAT GAVE YOU THE PAPER CUT?

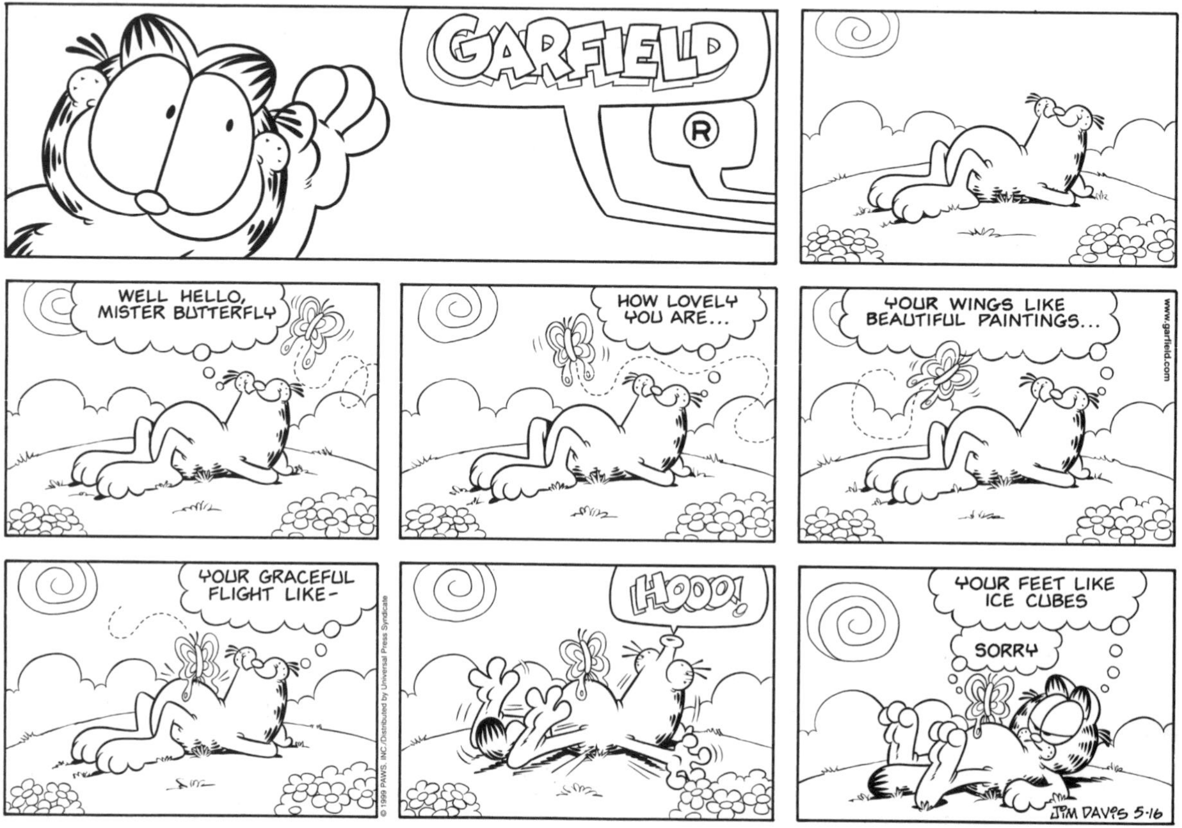
GARFIELD ®
WELL HELLO, MISTER BUTTERFLY
HOW LOVELY YOU ARE...
YOUR WINGS LIKE BEAUTIFUL PAINTINGS...
www.garfield.com
YOUR GRACEFUL FLIGHT LIKE-
© 1999 PAWS, INC./Distributed by Universal Press Syndicate
HOOO!
YOUR FEET LIKE ICE CUBES
SORRY
JIM DAVIS 5-16

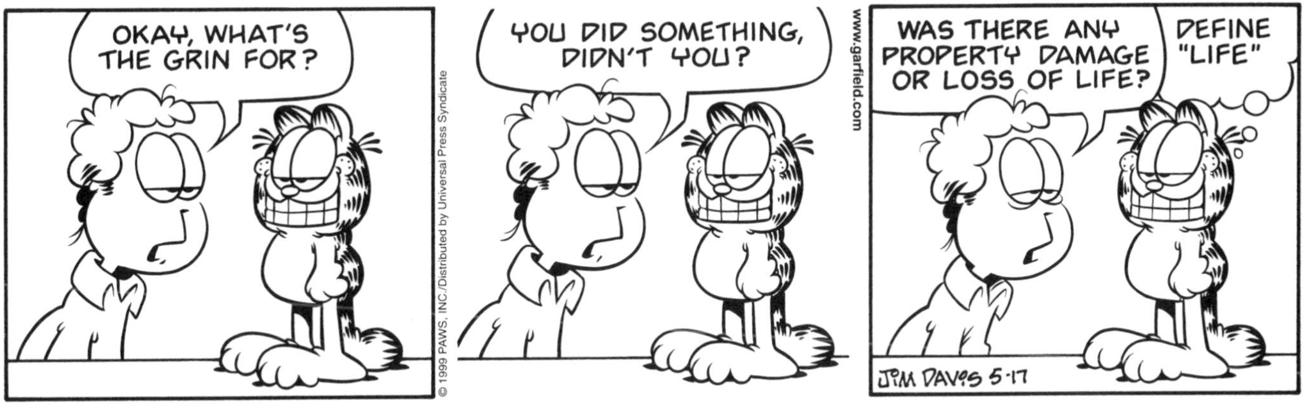
OKAY, WHAT'S THE GRIN FOR?
YOU DID SOMETHING, DIDN'T YOU?
WAS THERE ANY PROPERTY DAMAGE OR LOSS OF LIFE?
DEFINE "LIFE"
JIM DAVIS 5-17
www.garfield.com

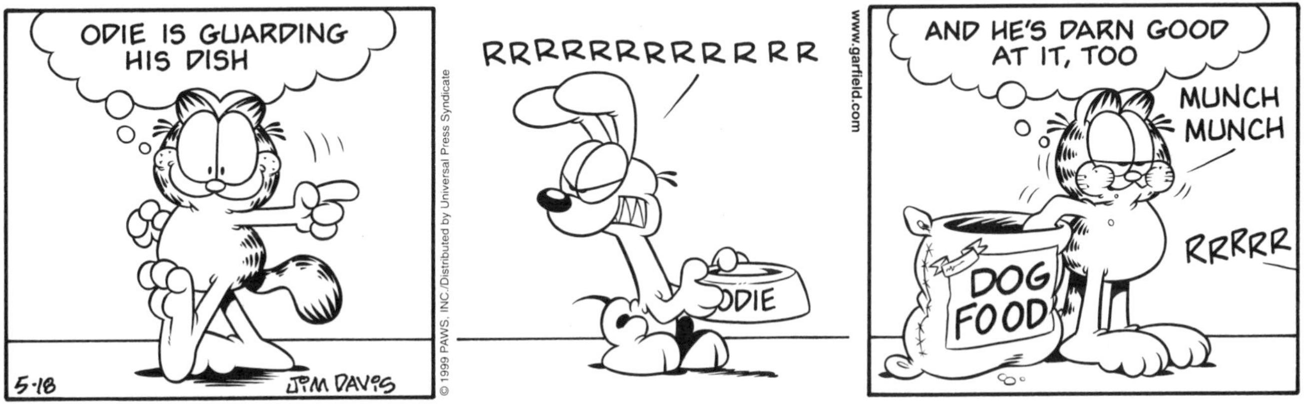
ODIE IS GUARDING HIS DISH
5-18
JIM DAVIS
RRRRRRRRRRRRR
ODIE
AND HE'S DARN GOOD AT IT, TOO
MUNCH MUNCH
RRRRR
DOG FOOD
www.garfield.com

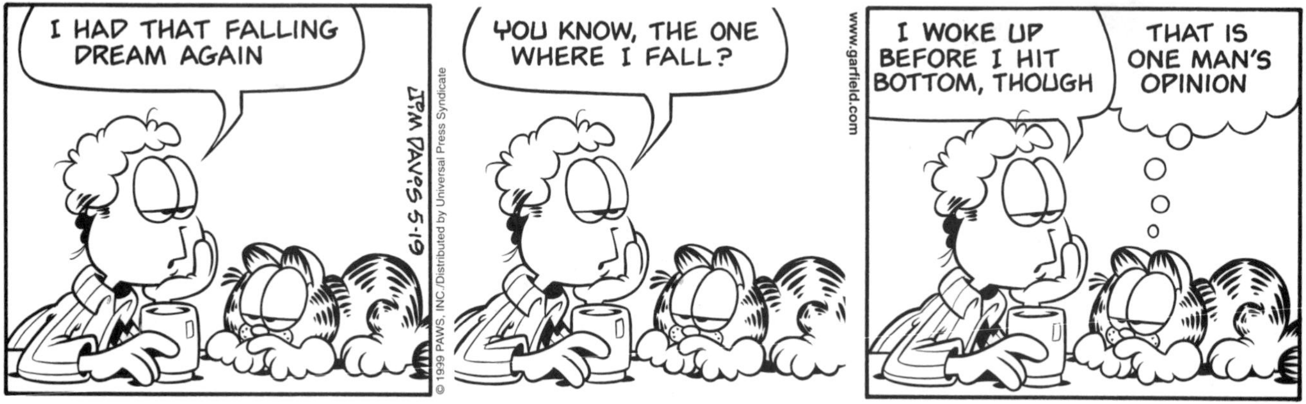
I HAD THAT FALLING DREAM AGAIN
JIM DAVIS 5-19
© 1999 PAWS, INC./Distributed by Universal Press Syndicate
YOU KNOW, THE ONE WHERE I FALL?
www.garfield.com
I WOKE UP BEFORE I HIT BOTTOM, THOUGH
THAT IS ONE MAN'S OPINION

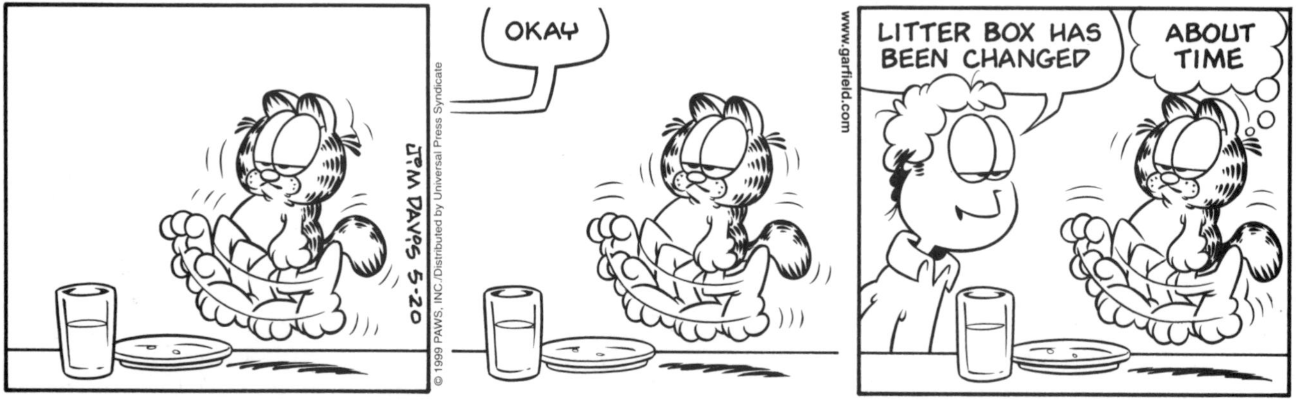
JIM DAVIS 5-20
© 1999 PAWS, INC./Distributed by Universal Press Syndicate
OKAY
www.garfield.com
LITTER BOX HAS BEEN CHANGED
ABOUT TIME

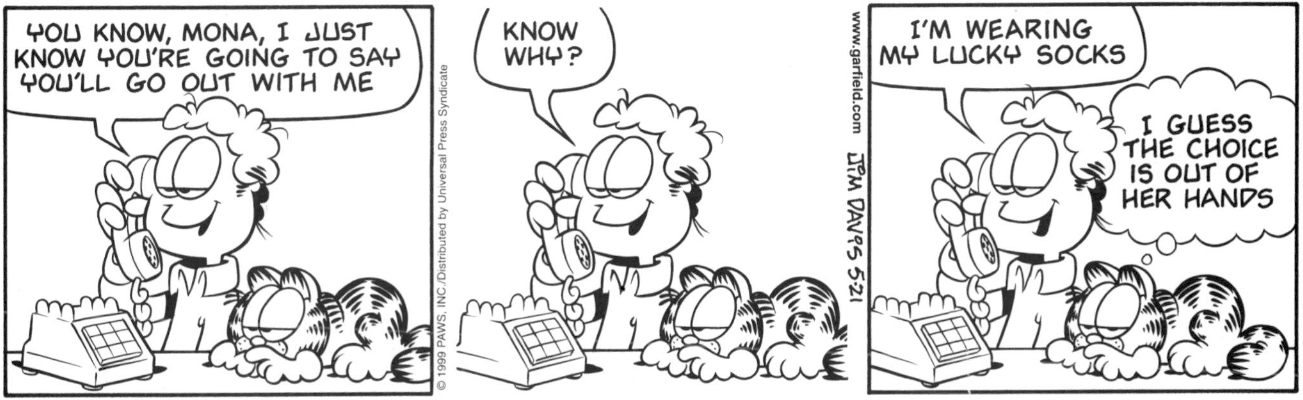
YOU KNOW, MONA, I JUST KNOW YOU'RE GOING TO SAY YOU'LL GO OUT WITH ME
KNOW WHY?
I'M WEARING MY LUCKY SOCKS
I GUESS THE CHOICE IS OUT OF HER HANDS
JIM DAVIS 5-21

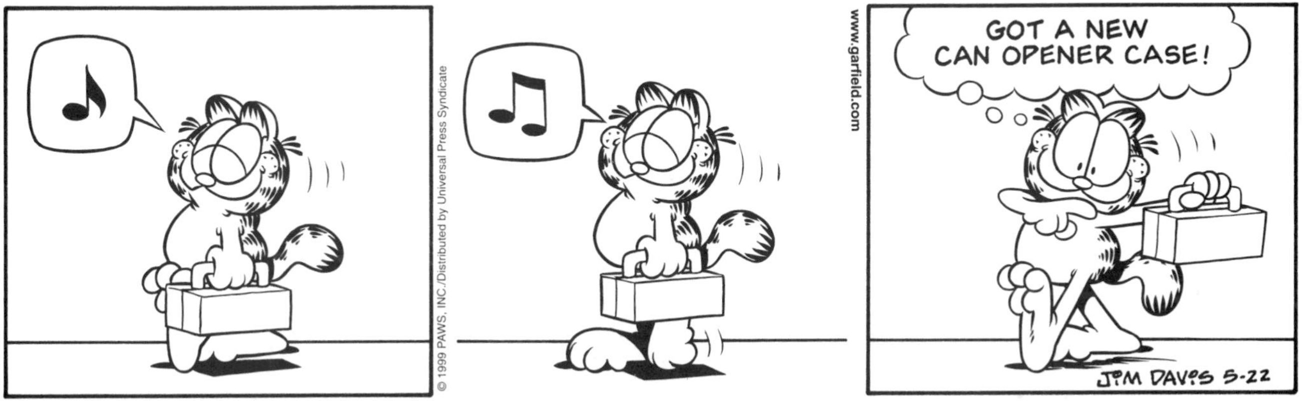
GOT A NEW CAN OPENER CASE!
JIM DAVIS 5-22

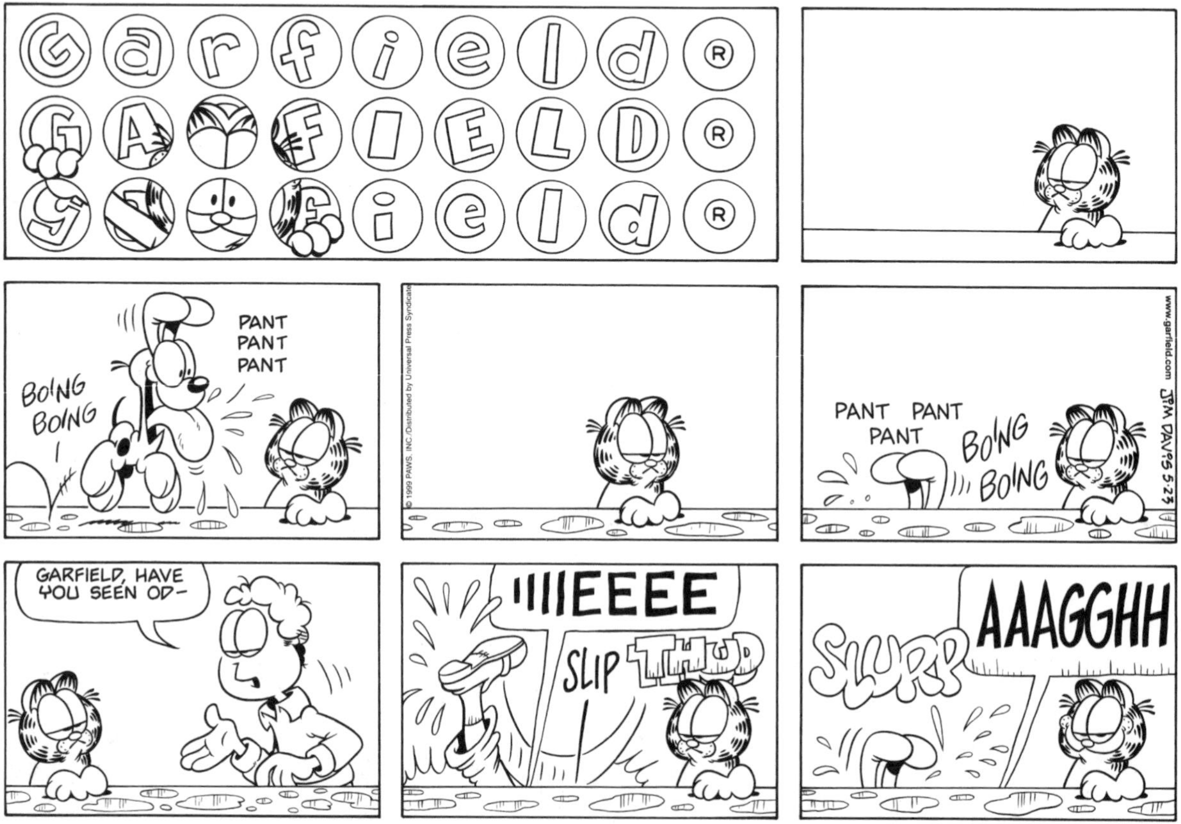
Garfield®
GARFIELD®
PANT
PANT
PANT
BOING
BOING
© 1999 PAWS. INC./Distributed by Universal Press Syndicate
PANT PANT
PANT
BOING
BOING
www.garfield.com
JPM DAVIS 5-23
GARFIELD, HAVE YOU SEEN OD-
IIIIEEEE
SLIP
THUD
SLURP
AAAGGHH

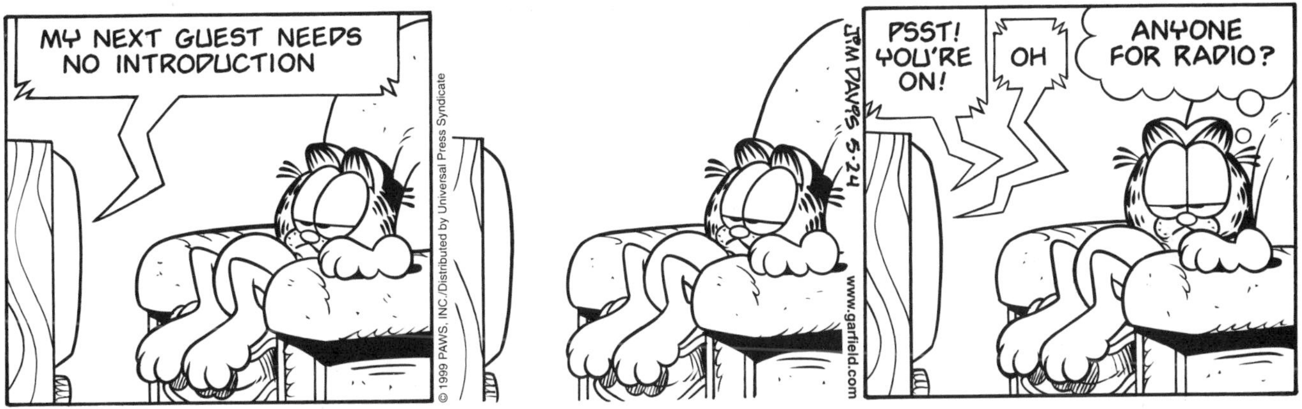
MY NEXT GUEST NEEDS NO INTRODUCTION
PSST! YOU'RE ON!
OH
ANYONE FOR RADIO?
JPM DAVPS 5·24

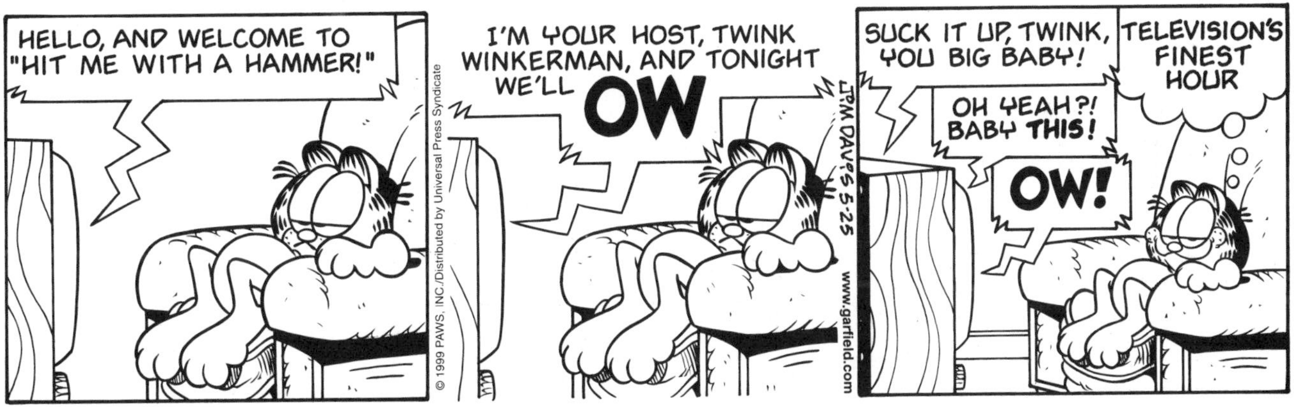
HELLO, AND WELCOME TO "HIT ME WITH A HAMMER!"
I'M YOUR HOST, TWINK WINKERMAN, AND TONIGHT WE'LL
OW
SUCK IT UP, TWINK, YOU BIG BABY!
OH YEAH?! BABY THIS!
OW!
TELEVISION'S FINEST HOUR
JPM DAVPS 5·25

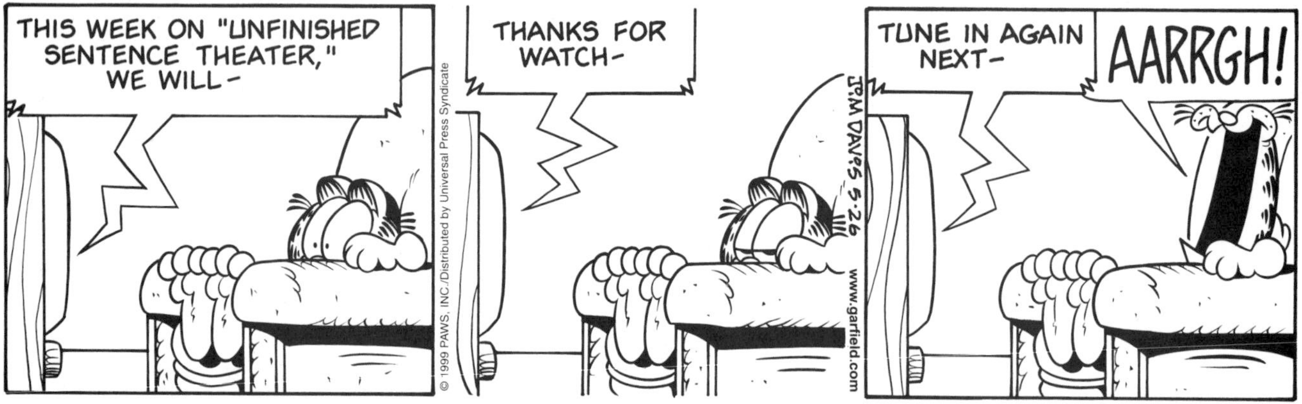
THIS WEEK ON "UNFINISHED SENTENCE THEATER," WE WILL-
THANKS FOR WATCH-
TUNE IN AGAIN NEXT-
AARRGH!
JIM DAVIS 5-26
© 1999 PAWS, INC./Distributed by Universal Press Syndicate
www.garfield.com

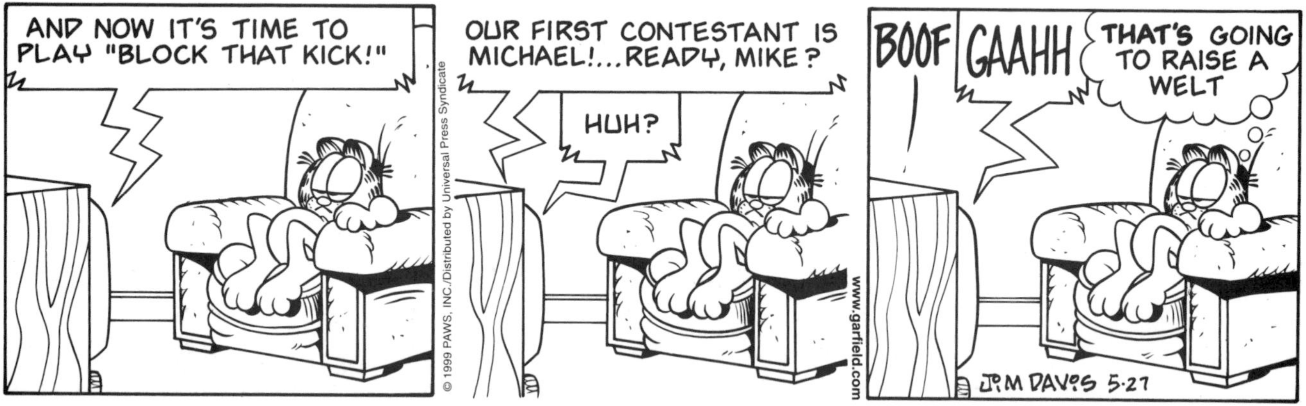
AND NOW IT'S TIME TO PLAY "BLOCK THAT KICK!"
OUR FIRST CONTESTANT IS MICHAEL!...READY, MIKE?
HUH?
BOOF
GAAHH
THAT'S GOING TO RAISE A WELT
JIM DAVIS 5-27
© 1999 PAWS, INC./Distributed by Universal Press Syndicate
www.garfield.com

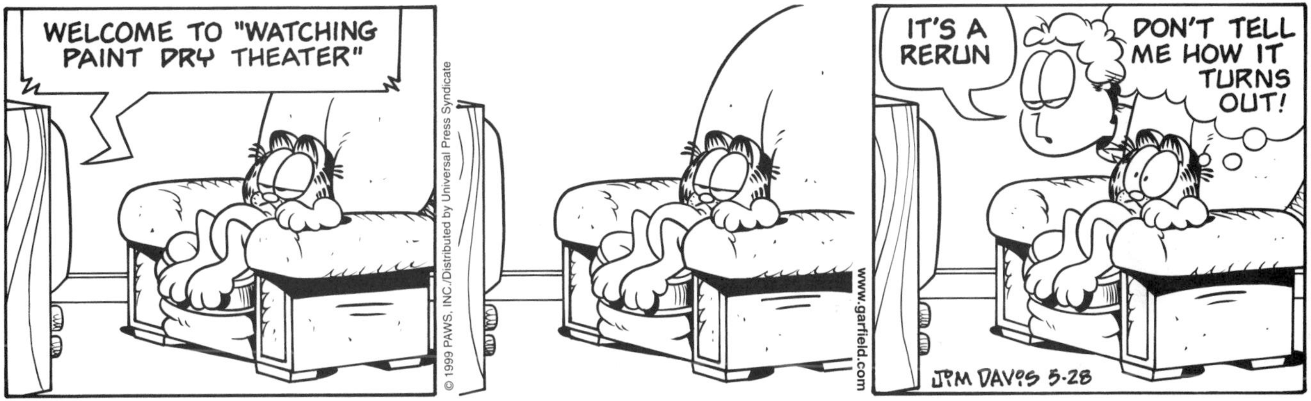
WELCOME TO "WATCHING PAINT DRY THEATER"
© 1999 PAWS, INC./Distributed by Universal Press Syndicate
www.garfield.com
IT'S A RERUN
DON'T TELL ME HOW IT TURNS OUT!
JIM DAVIS 5-28

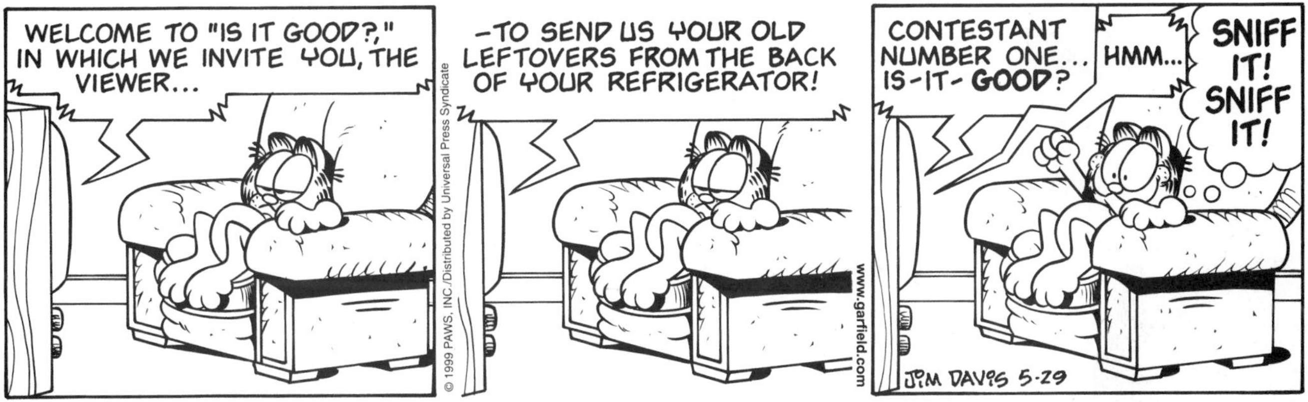
WELCOME TO "IS IT GOOD?," IN WHICH WE INVITE YOU, THE VIEWER...
© 1999 PAWS, INC./Distributed by Universal Press Syndicate
–TO SEND US YOUR OLD LEFTOVERS FROM THE BACK OF YOUR REFRIGERATOR!
www.garfield.com
CONTESTANT NUMBER ONE... IS-IT-**GOOD**?
HMM...
SNIFF IT! SNIFF IT!
JIM DAVIS 5-29

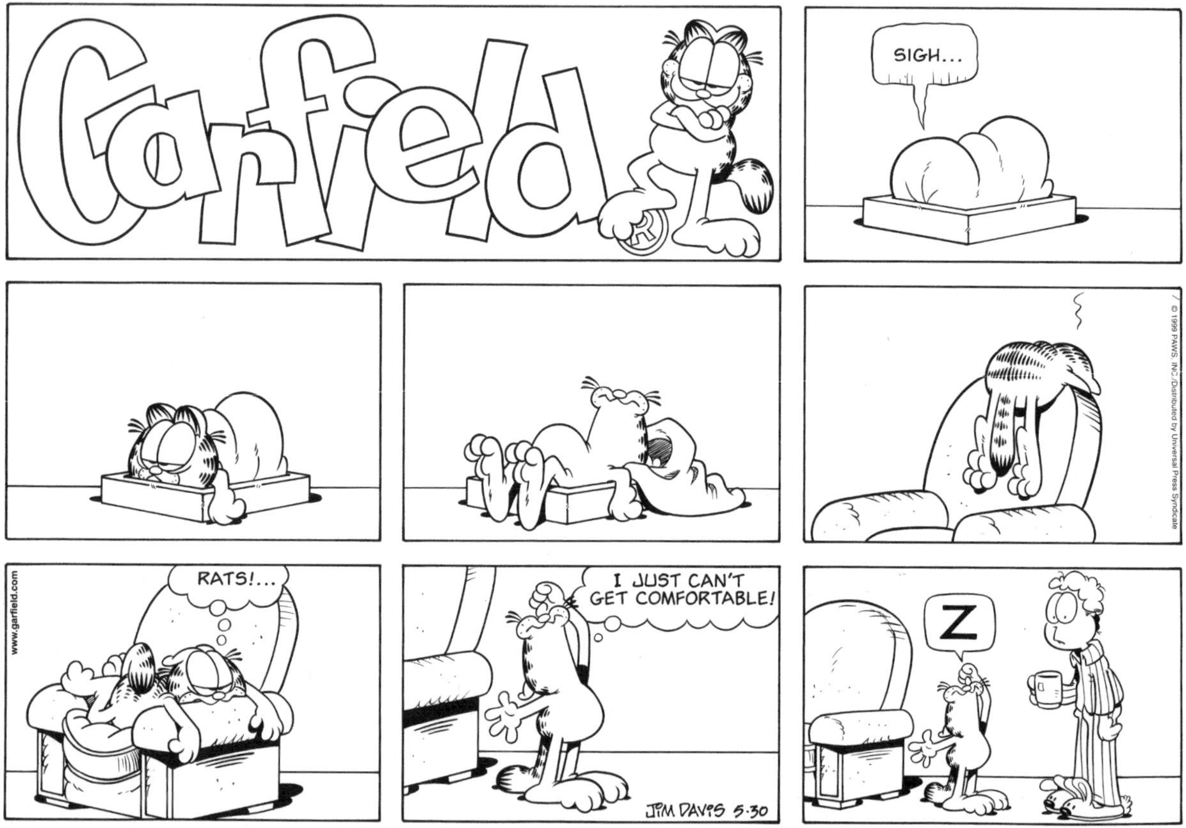
Garfield
SIGH...
© 1999 PAWS, INC./Distributed by Universal Press Syndicate
www.garfield.com
RATS!...
I JUST CAN'T GET COMFORTABLE!
JIM DAVIS 5·30
Z

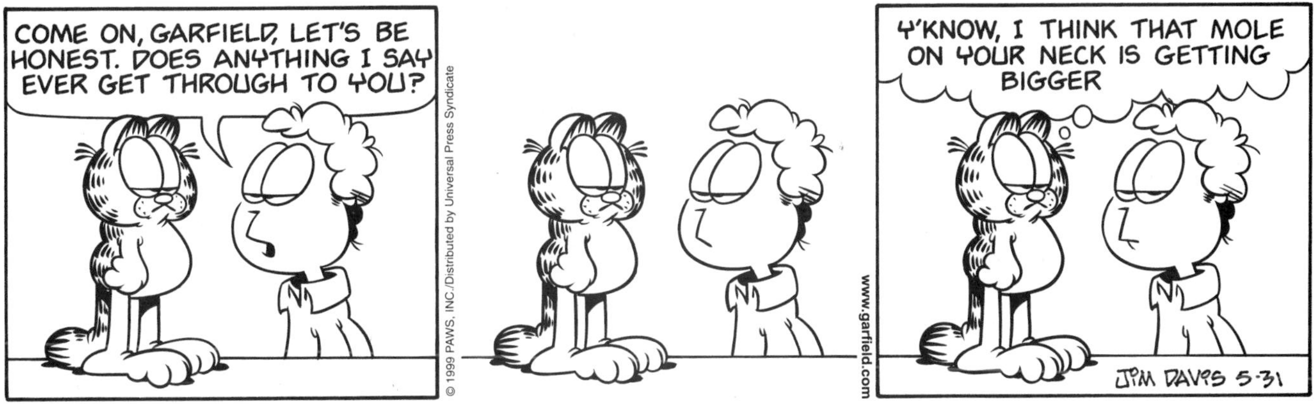
COME ON, GARFIELD, LET'S BE HONEST. DOES ANYTHING I SAY EVER GET THROUGH TO YOU?
Y'KNOW, I THINK THAT MOLE ON YOUR NECK IS GETTING BIGGER
JIM DAVIS 5-31
© 1999 PAWS, INC./Distributed by Universal Press Syndicate
www.garfield.com

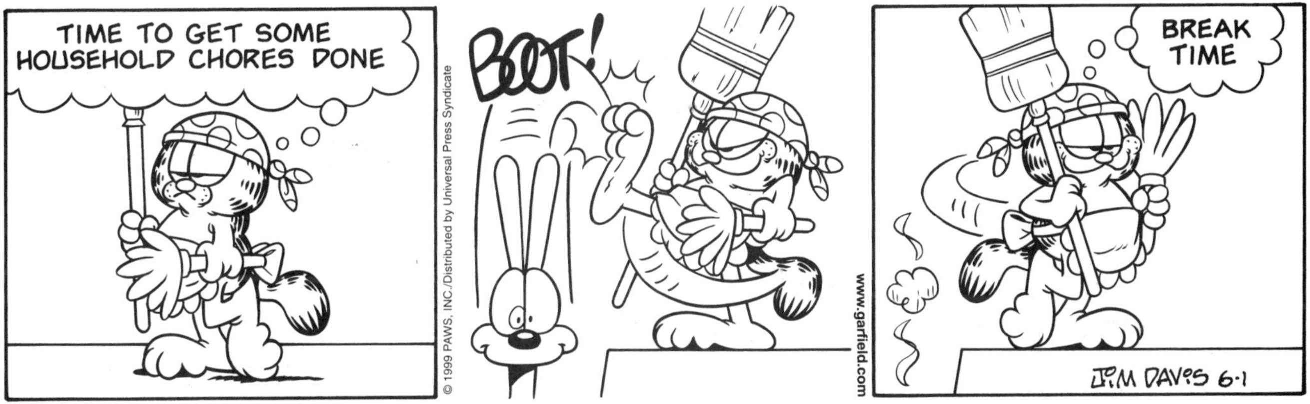
TIME TO GET SOME HOUSEHOLD CHORES DONE
BOOT!
BREAK TIME
JIM DAVIS 6-1
© 1999 PAWS, INC./Distributed by Universal Press Syndicate
www.garfield.com

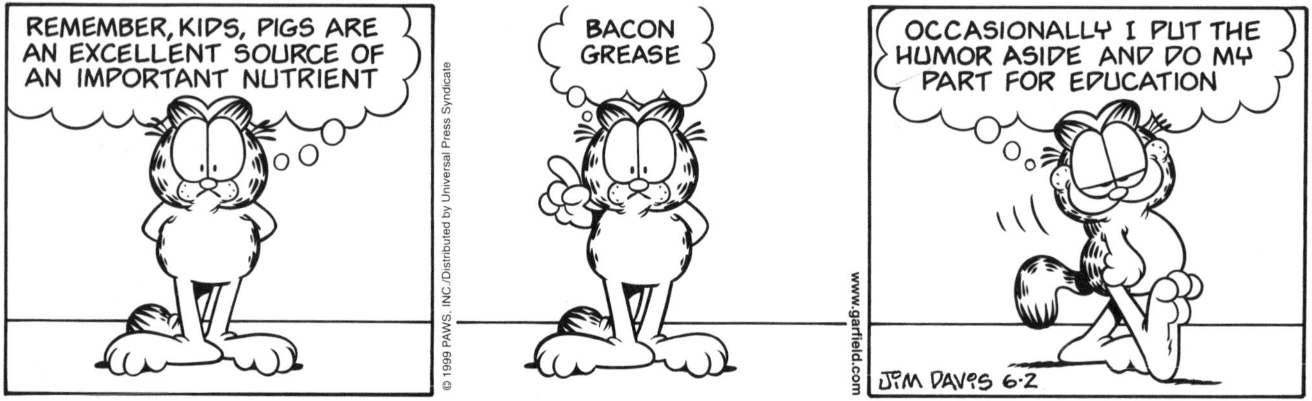
REMEMBER, KIDS, PIGS ARE AN EXCELLENT SOURCE OF AN IMPORTANT NUTRIENT
BACON GREASE
OCCASIONALLY I PUT THE HUMOR ASIDE AND DO MY PART FOR EDUCATION
JIM DAVIS 6-2

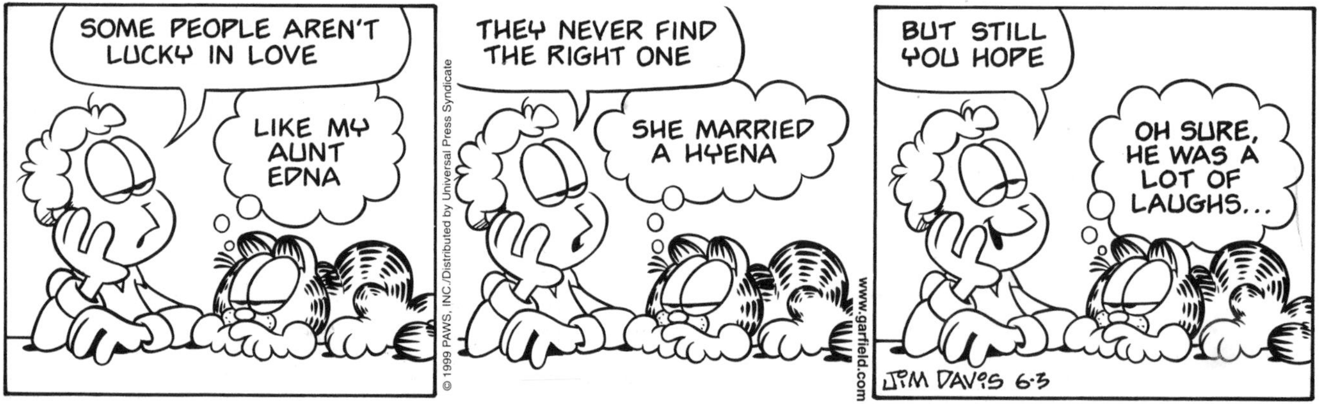
SOME PEOPLE AREN'T LUCKY IN LOVE
LIKE MY AUNT EDNA
THEY NEVER FIND THE RIGHT ONE
SHE MARRIED A HYENA
BUT STILL YOU HOPE
OH SURE, HE WAS A LOT OF LAUGHS...
JIM DAVIS 6-3

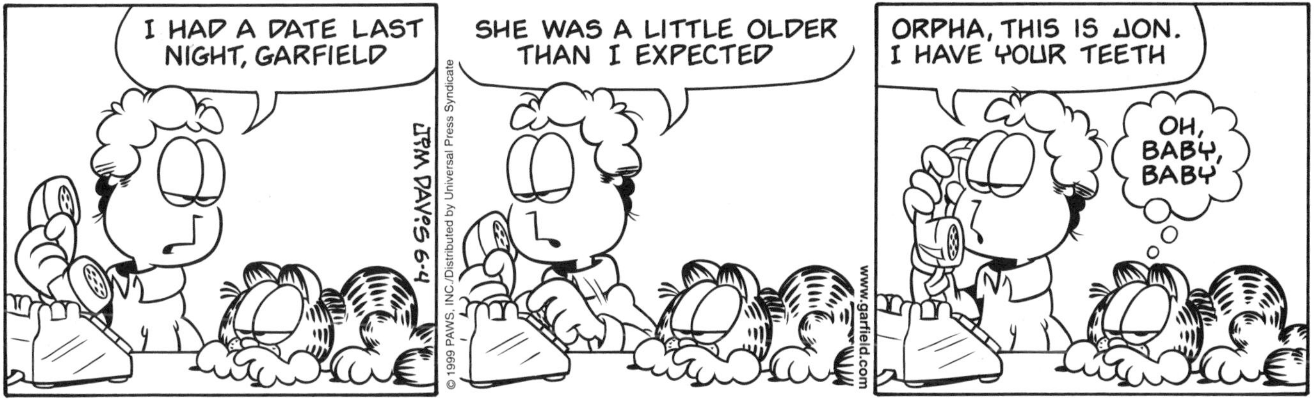
I HAD A DATE LAST NIGHT, GARFIELD
SHE WAS A LITTLE OLDER THAN I EXPECTED
ORPHA, THIS IS JON. I HAVE YOUR TEETH
OH, BABY, BABY
JIM DAVIS 6-4

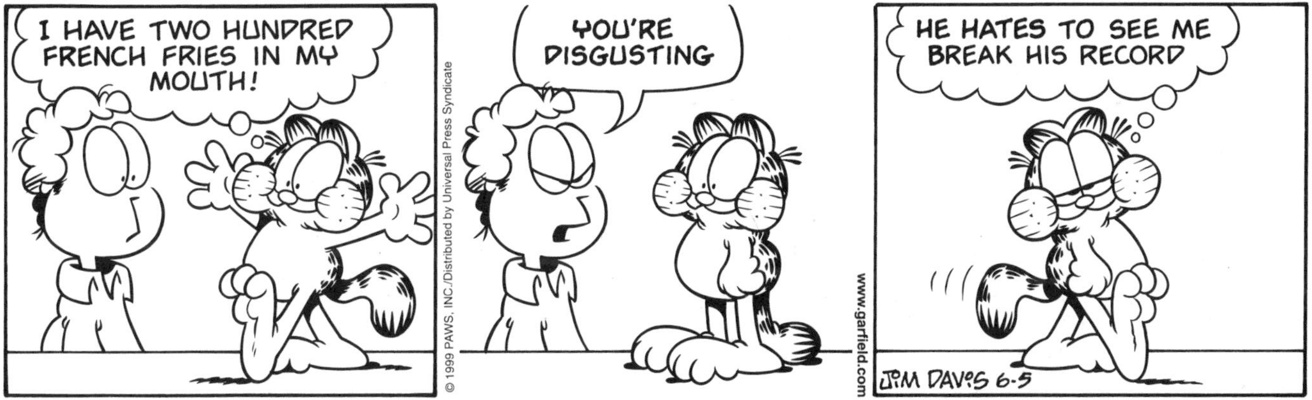
I HAVE TWO HUNDRED FRENCH FRIES IN MY MOUTH!
YOU'RE DISGUSTING
HE HATES TO SEE ME BREAK HIS RECORD
JIM DAVIS 6-5

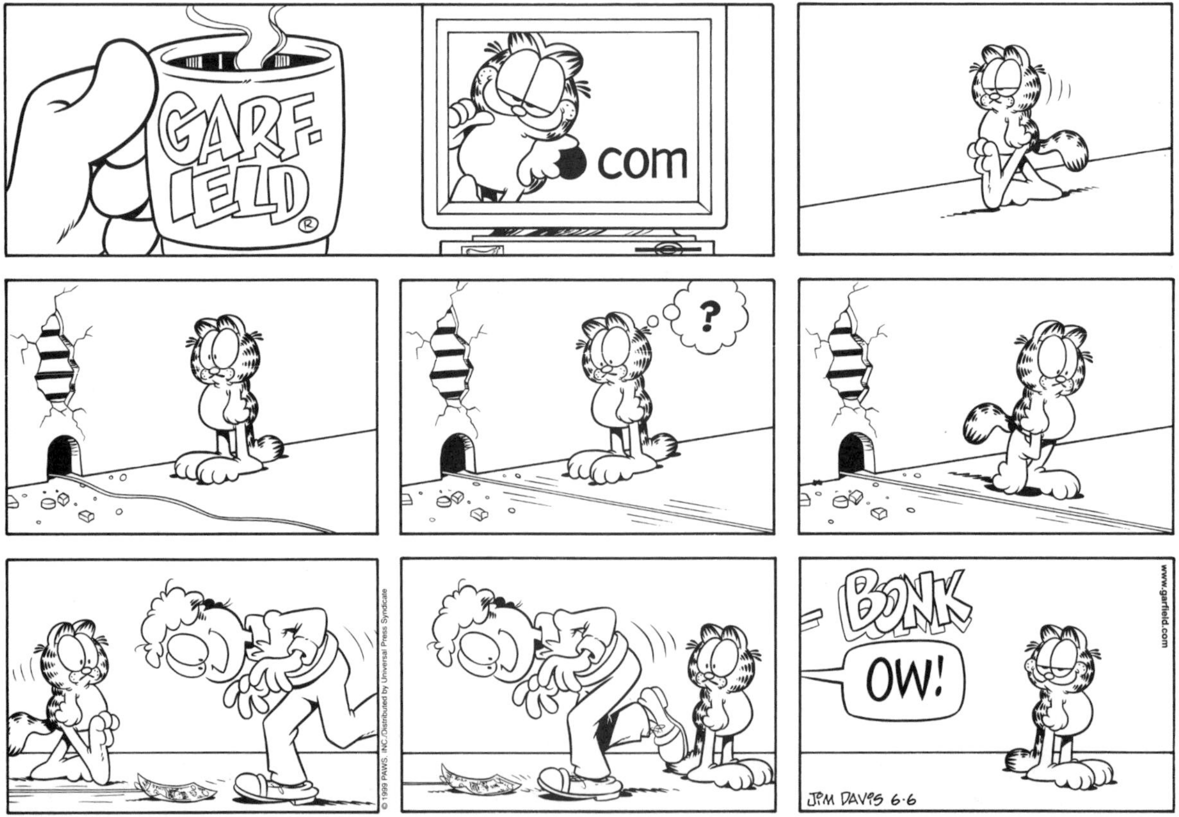
GARF-IELD
com
?
© 1999 PAWS, INC./Distributed by Universal Press Syndicate
BONK
OW!
www.garfield.com
JIM DAVIS 6·6

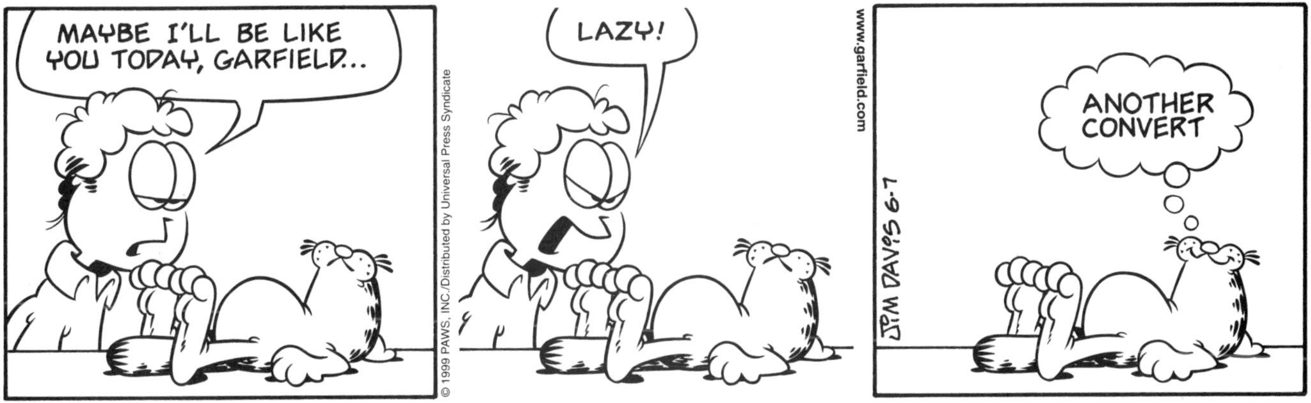
MAYBE I'LL BE LIKE YOU TODAY, GARFIELD...
LAZY!
ANOTHER CONVERT
© 1999 PAWS, INC./Distributed by Universal Press Syndicate
www.garfield.com
JIM DAVIS 6-7

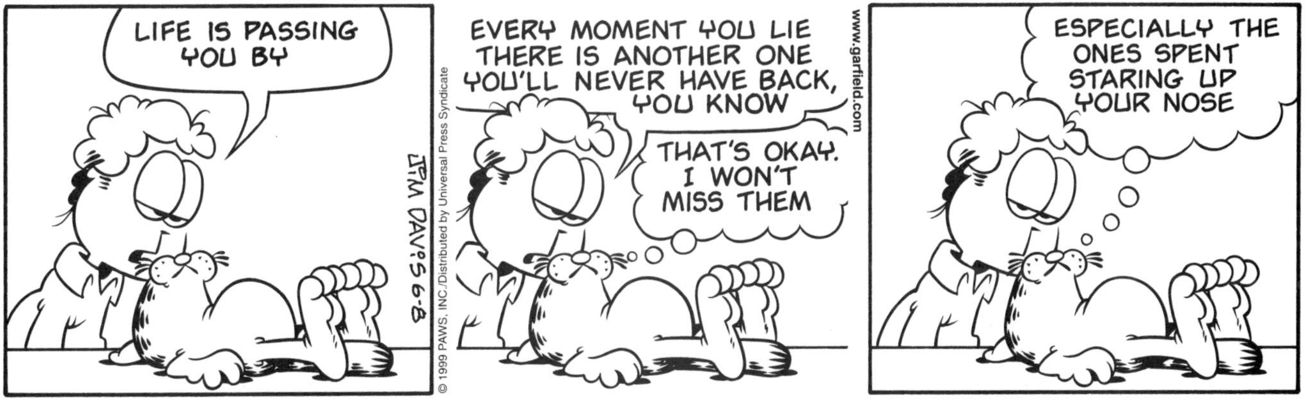
LIFE IS PASSING YOU BY
EVERY MOMENT YOU LIE THERE IS ANOTHER ONE YOU'LL NEVER HAVE BACK, YOU KNOW
THAT'S OKAY. I WON'T MISS THEM
ESPECIALLY THE ONES SPENT STARING UP YOUR NOSE
© 1999 PAWS, INC./Distributed by Universal Press Syndicate
www.garfield.com
JIM DAVIS 6-8

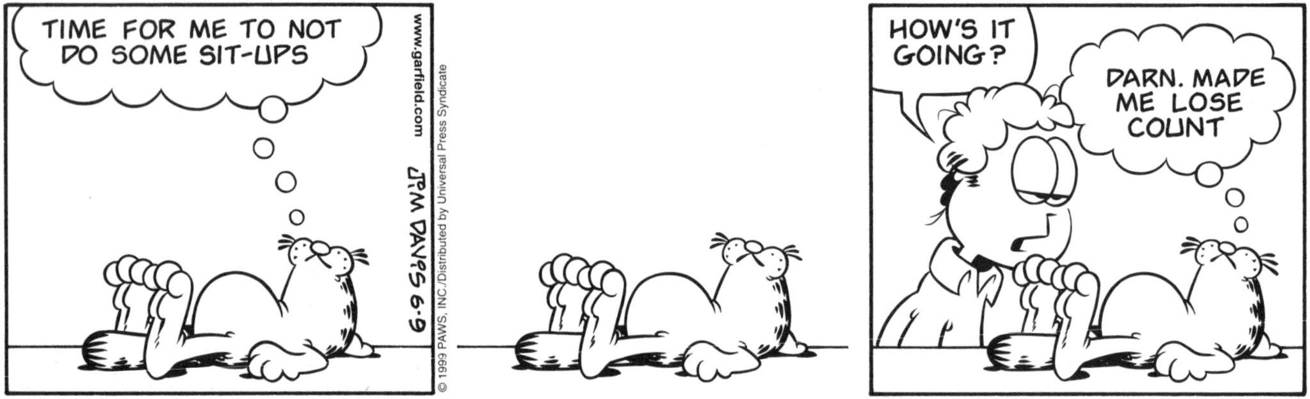
TIME FOR ME TO NOT DO SOME SIT-UPS
www.garfield.com
JIM DAVIS 6-9
© 1999 PAWS, INC./Distributed by Universal Press Syndicate
HOW'S IT GOING?
DARN. MADE ME LOSE COUNT

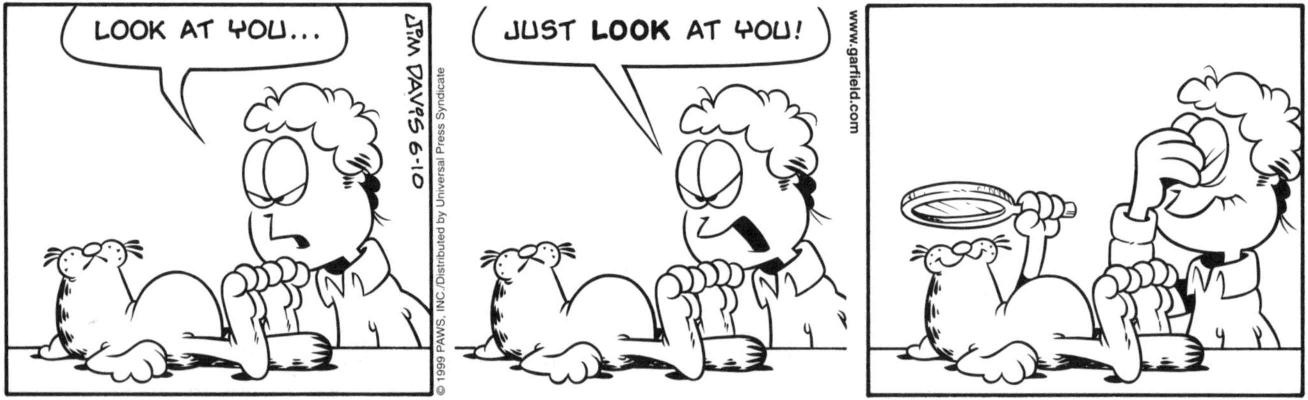
LOOK AT YOU...
JIM DAVIS 6-10
© 1999 PAWS, INC./Distributed by Universal Press Syndicate
JUST **LOOK** AT YOU!
www.garfield.com

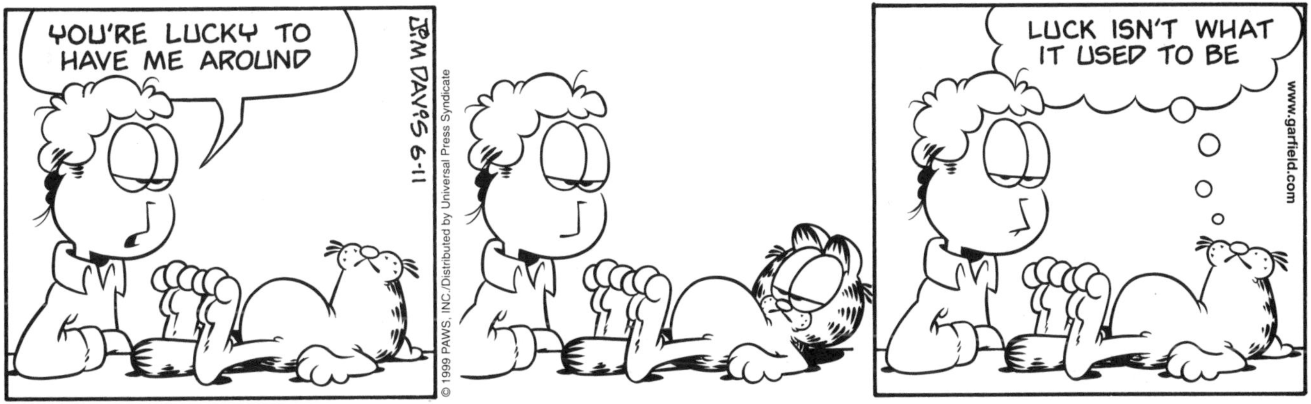
YOU'RE LUCKY TO HAVE ME AROUND
JIM DAVIS 6-11
© 1999 PAWS, INC./Distributed by Universal Press Syndicate
LUCK ISN'T WHAT IT USED TO BE
www.garfield.com

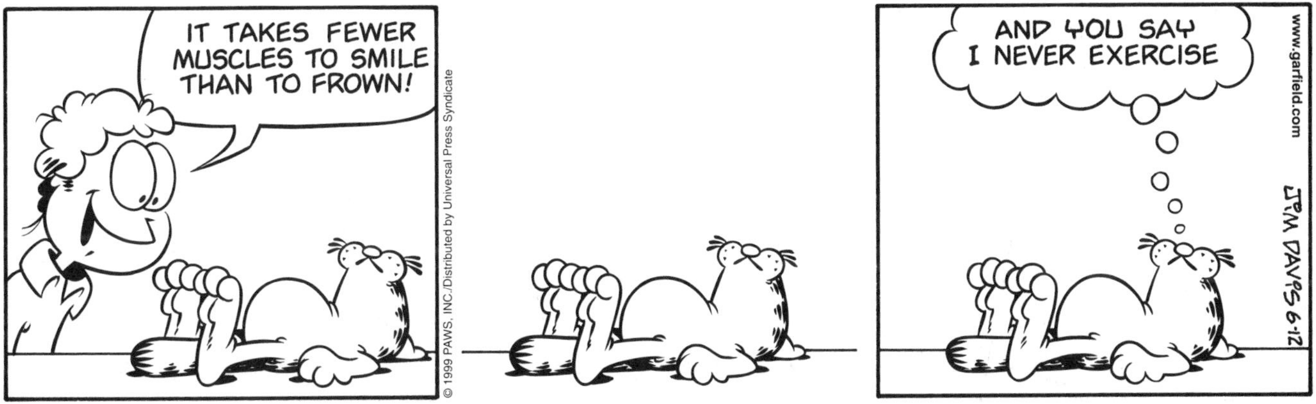
IT TAKES FEWER MUSCLES TO SMILE THAN TO FROWN!
© 1999 PAWS, INC./Distributed by Universal Press Syndicate
AND YOU SAY I NEVER EXERCISE
www.garfield.com
JIM DAVIS 6-12

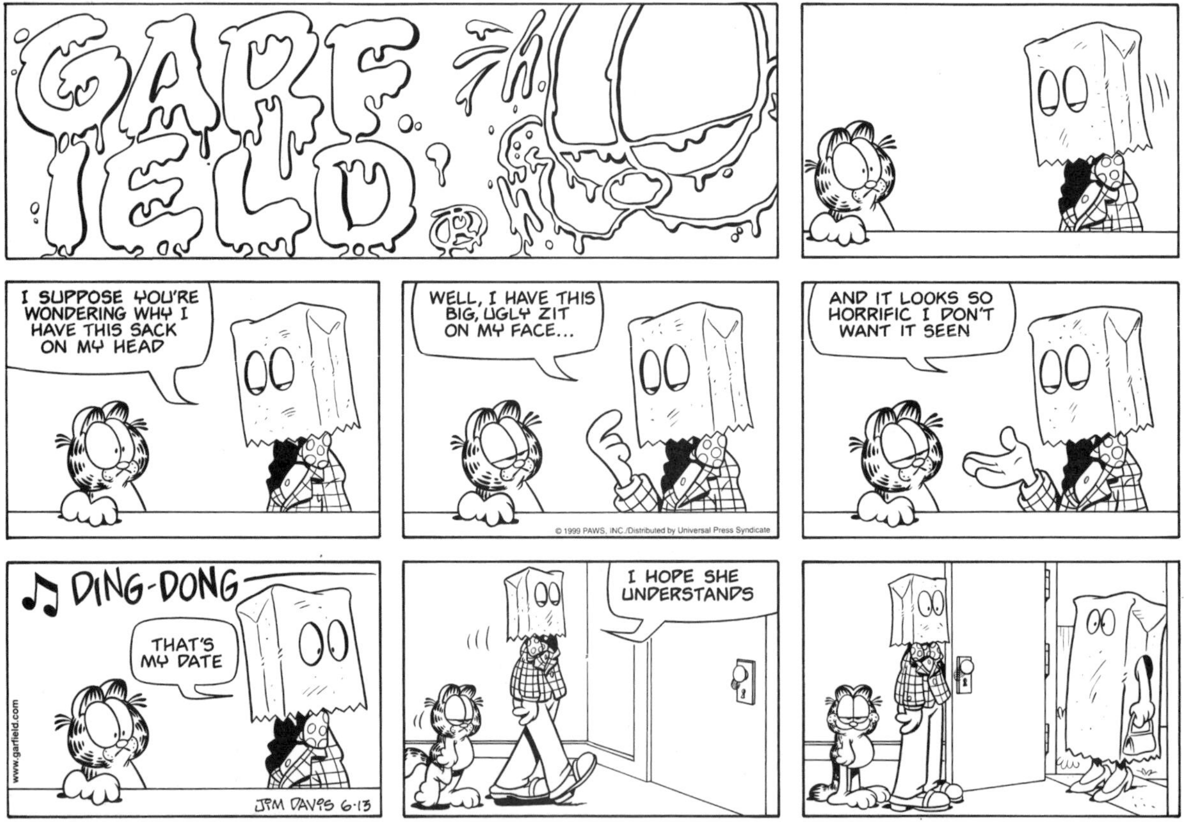
GARFIELD
I SUPPOSE YOU'RE WONDERING WHY I HAVE THIS SACK ON MY HEAD
WELL, I HAVE THIS BIG, UGLY ZIT ON MY FACE...
© 1999 PAWS, INC./Distributed by Universal Press Syndicate
AND IT LOOKS SO HORRIFIC I DON'T WANT IT SEEN
DING-DONG
THAT'S MY DATE
www.garfield.com
JIM DAVIS 6·13
I HOPE SHE UNDERSTANDS

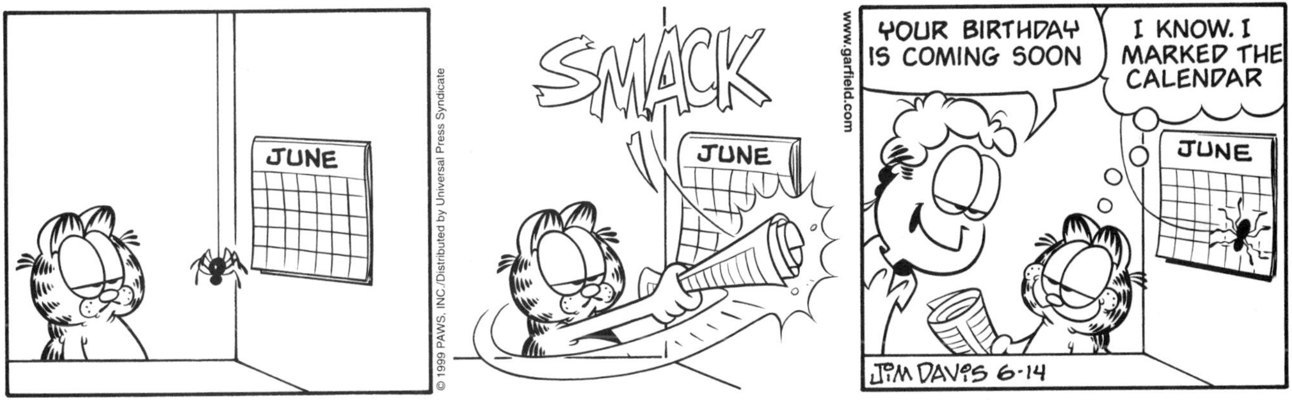
JUNE
© 1999 PAWS, INC./Distributed by Universal Press Syndicate
SMACK
JUNE
www.garfield.com
YOUR BIRTHDAY IS COMING SOON
I KNOW. I MARKED THE CALENDAR
JUNE
JIM DAVIS 6-14

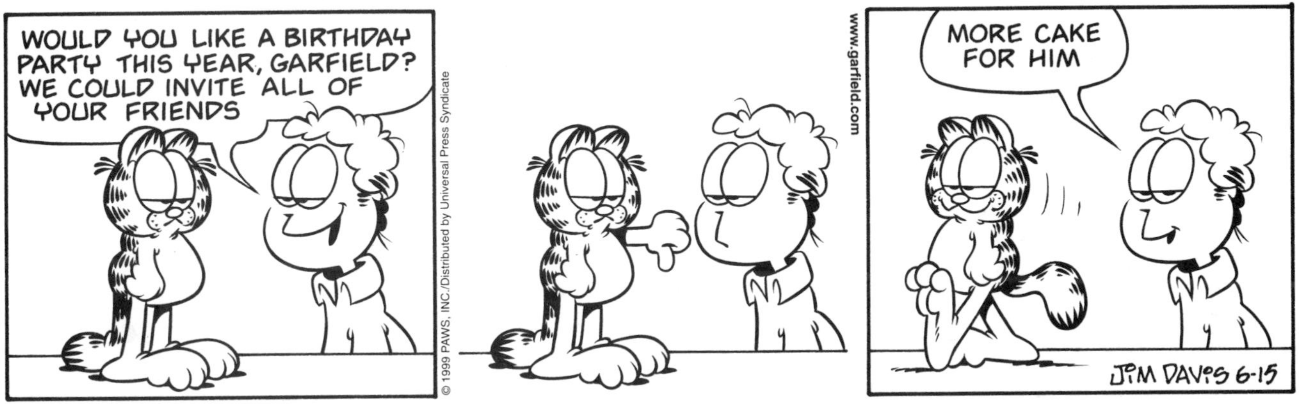
WOULD YOU LIKE A BIRTHDAY PARTY THIS YEAR, GARFIELD? WE COULD INVITE ALL OF YOUR FRIENDS
© 1999 PAWS, INC./Distributed by Universal Press Syndicate
www.garfield.com
MORE CAKE FOR HIM
JIM DAVIS 6-15

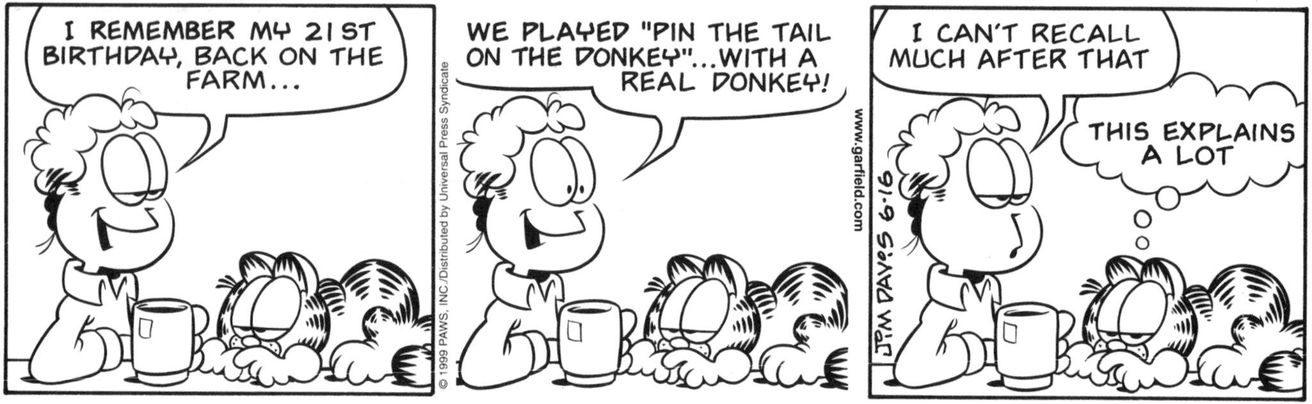
I REMEMBER MY 21 ST BIRTHDAY, BACK ON THE FARM...
WE PLAYED "PIN THE TAIL ON THE DONKEY"...WITH A REAL DONKEY!
I CAN'T RECALL MUCH AFTER THAT
THIS EXPLAINS A LOT
JIM DAVIS 6·16

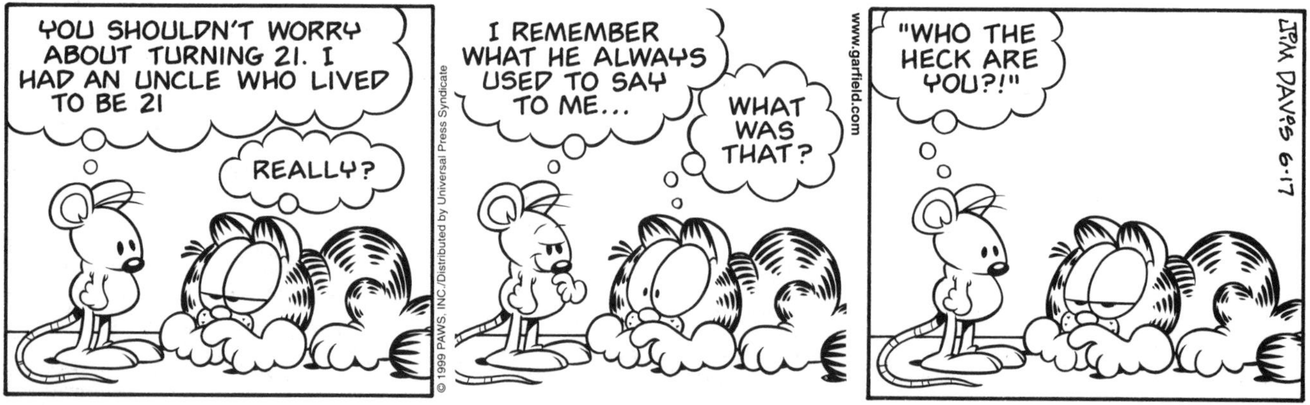
YOU SHOULDN'T WORRY ABOUT TURNING 21. I HAD AN UNCLE WHO LIVED TO BE 21
REALLY?
I REMEMBER WHAT HE ALWAYS USED TO SAY TO ME...
WHAT WAS THAT?
"WHO THE HECK ARE YOU?!"
JIM DAVIS 6·17

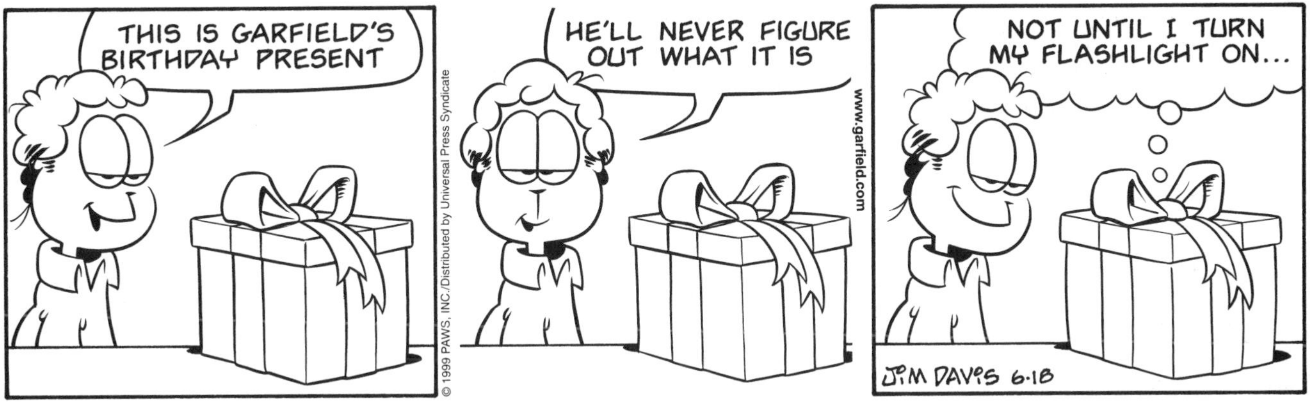
THIS IS GARFIELD'S BIRTHDAY PRESENT
HE'LL NEVER FIGURE OUT WHAT IT IS
NOT UNTIL I TURN MY FLASHLIGHT ON...
www.garfield.com
JIM DAVIS 6·18

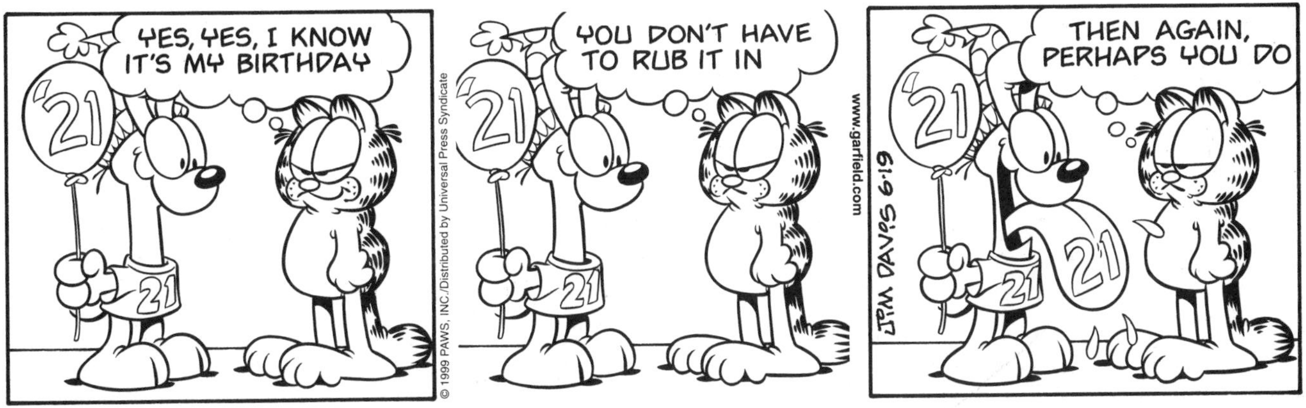
YES, YES, I KNOW IT'S MY BIRTHDAY
YOU DON'T HAVE TO RUB IT IN
THEN AGAIN, PERHAPS YOU DO
21
www.garfield.com
JIM DAVIS 6·19

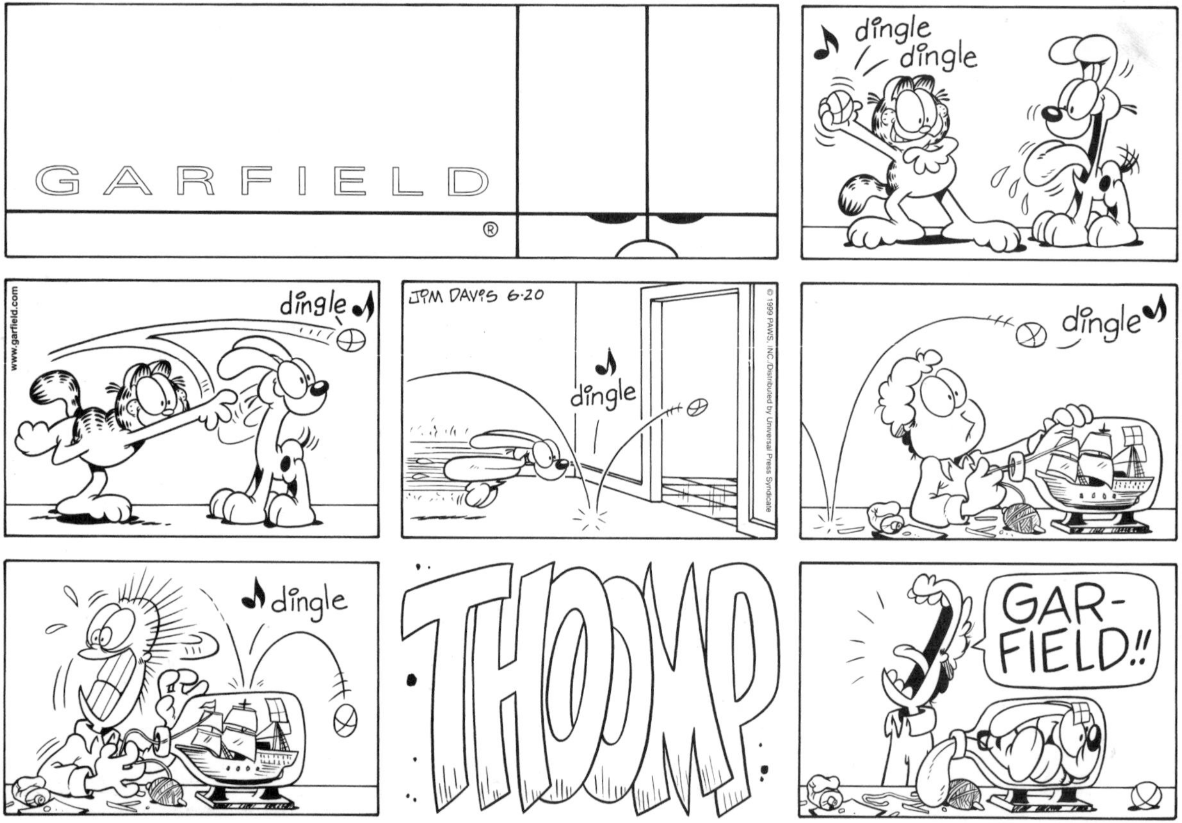
GARFIELD
dingle dingle
dingle
www.garfield.com
JIM DAVIS 6-20
dingle
© 1999 PAWS, INC./Distributed by Universal Press Syndicate
dingle
dingle
THOOMP
GAR-FIELD!!

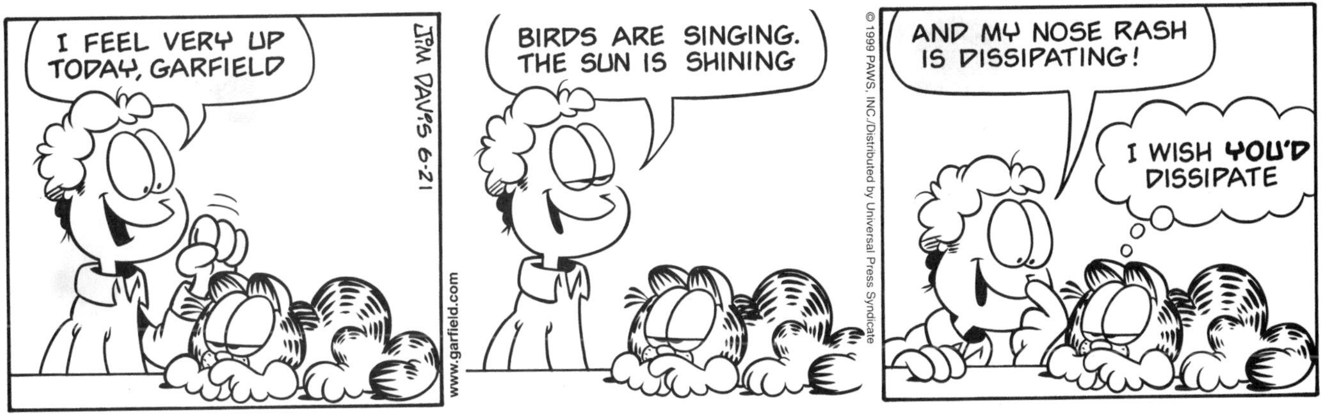
I FEEL VERY UP TODAY, GARFIELD
JIM DAVIS 6-21
www.garfield.com
BIRDS ARE SINGING. THE SUN IS SHINING
© 1999 PAWS, INC./Distributed by Universal Press Syndicate
AND MY NOSE RASH IS DISSIPATING!
I WISH **YOU'D** DISSIPATE

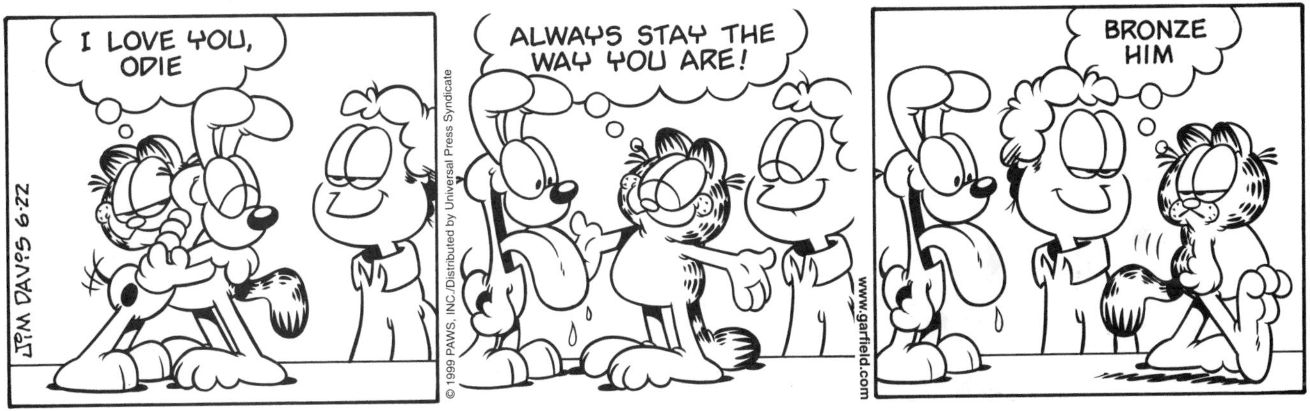
I LOVE YOU, ODIE
JIM DAVIS 6-22
© 1999 PAWS, INC./Distributed by Universal Press Syndicate
ALWAYS STAY THE WAY YOU ARE!
www.garfield.com
BRONZE HIM

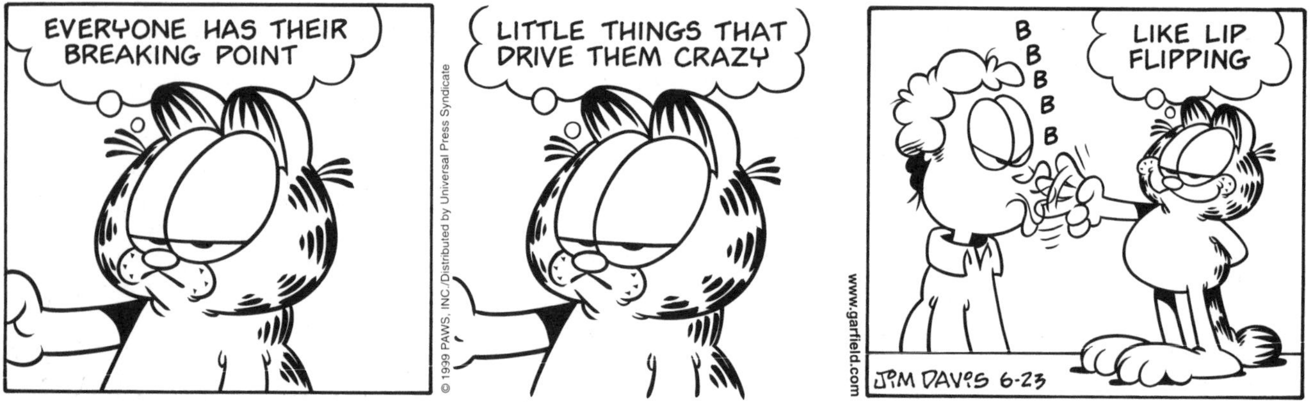
EVERYONE HAS THEIR BREAKING POINT
LITTLE THINGS THAT DRIVE THEM CRAZY
B B B B B
LIKE LIP FLIPPING
JIM DAVIS 6-23
www.garfield.com

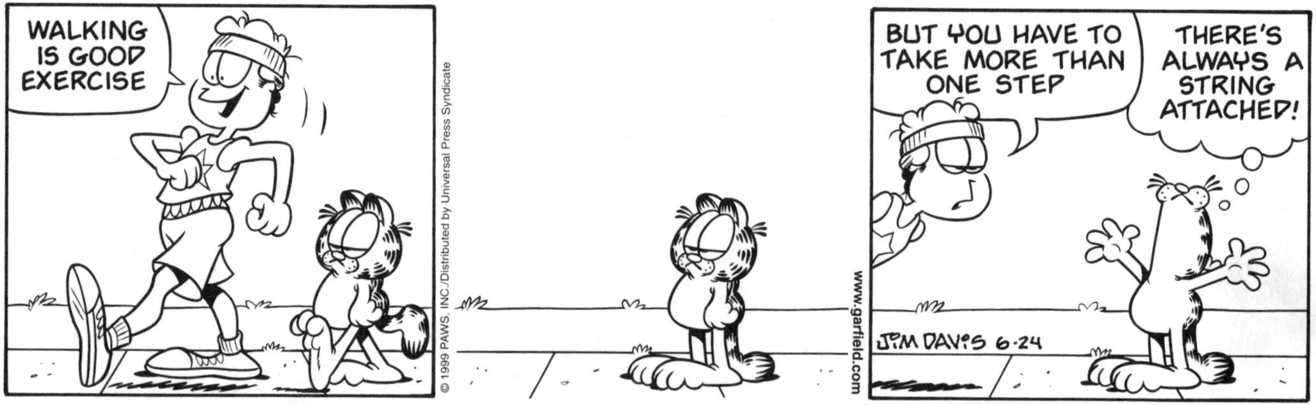
WALKING IS GOOD EXERCISE
BUT YOU HAVE TO TAKE MORE THAN ONE STEP
THERE'S ALWAYS A STRING ATTACHED!
JIM DAVIS 6-24
www.garfield.com

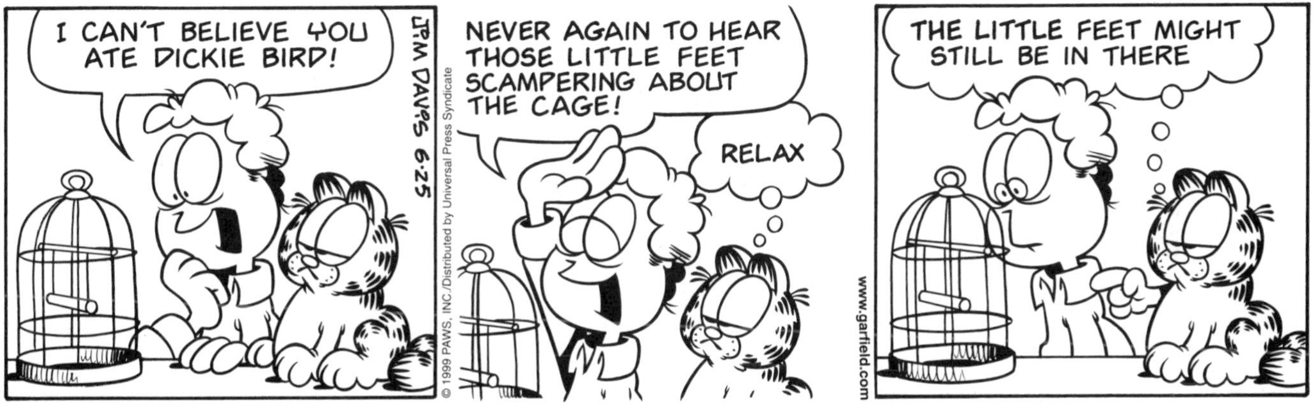
I CAN'T BELIEVE YOU ATE DICKIE BIRD!
JIM DAVIS 6-25
NEVER AGAIN TO HEAR THOSE LITTLE FEET SCAMPERING ABOUT THE CAGE!
RELAX
THE LITTLE FEET MIGHT STILL BE IN THERE
© 1999 PAWS, INC./Distributed by Universal Press Syndicate
www.garfield.com

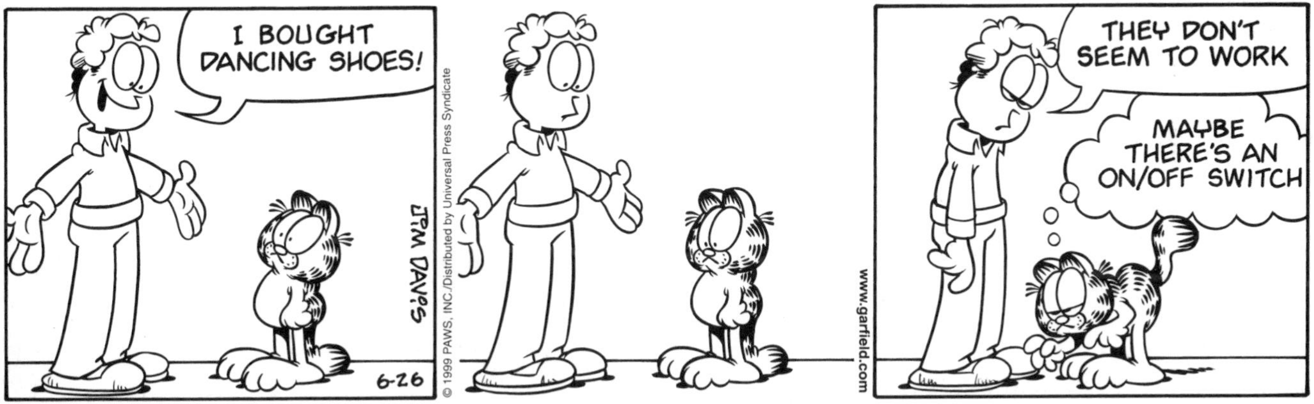
I BOUGHT DANCING SHOES!
JIM DAVIS
6-26
THEY DON'T SEEM TO WORK
MAYBE THERE'S AN ON/OFF SWITCH
© 1999 PAWS, INC./Distributed by Universal Press Syndicate
www.garfield.com

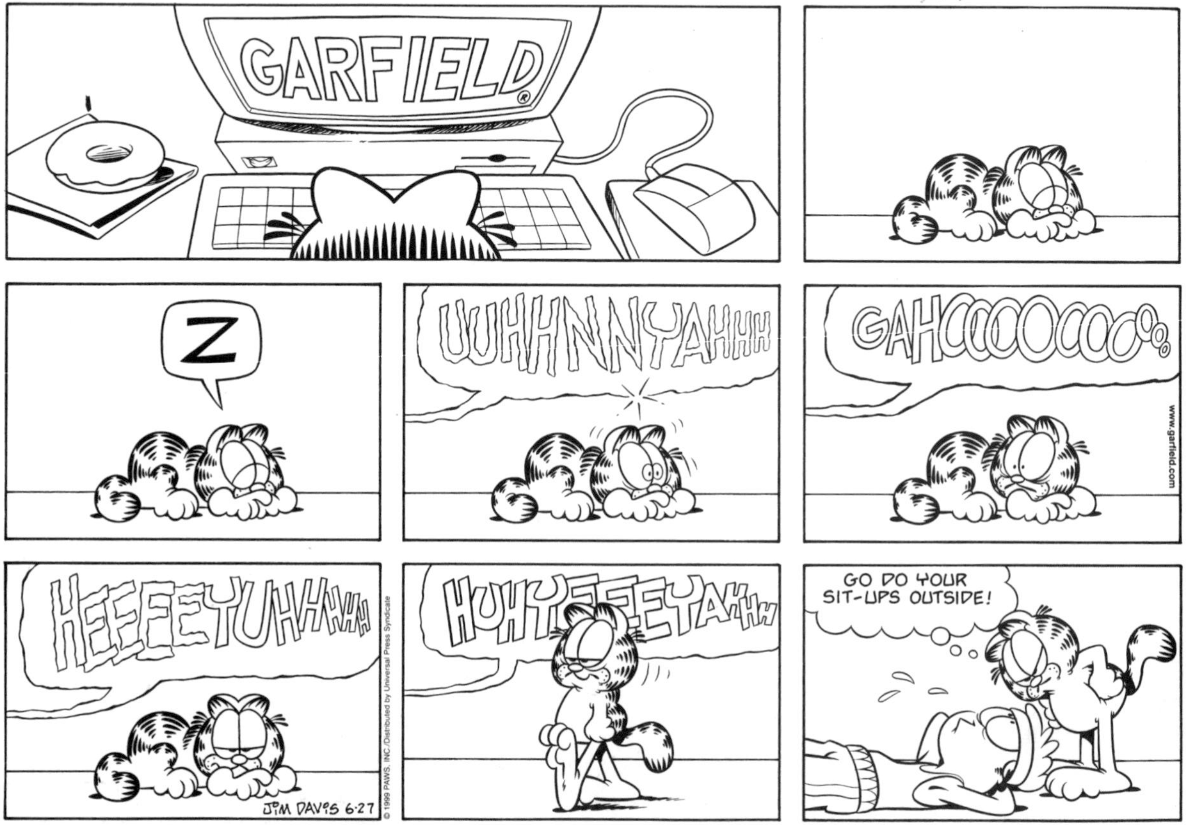
GARFIELD
Z
UUHHNNYAHHH
GAHOOOOOOOO
HEEEEEYUHHHHH
JIM DAVIS 6-27
© 1999 PAWS, INC./Distributed by Universal Press Syndicate
www.garfield.com
HUHYEEEEYAHHH
GO DO YOUR SIT-UPS OUTSIDE!

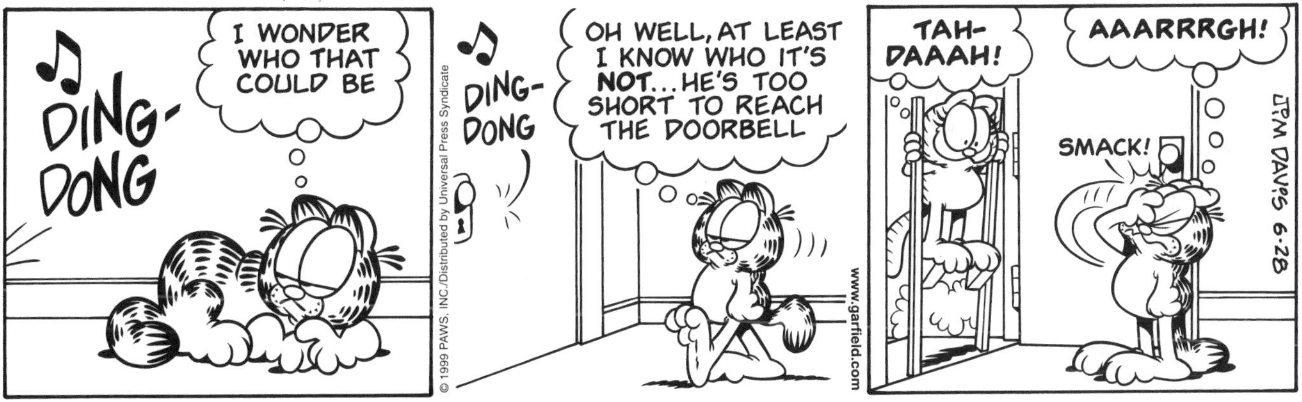
DING-DONG
I WONDER WHO THAT COULD BE
© 1999 PAWS, INC./Distributed by Universal Press Syndicate
DING-DONG
OH WELL, AT LEAST I KNOW WHO IT'S NOT... HE'S TOO SHORT TO REACH THE DOORBELL
www.garfield.com
TAH-DAAAH!
AAARRRGH!
SMACK!
JPM DAV95 6-28

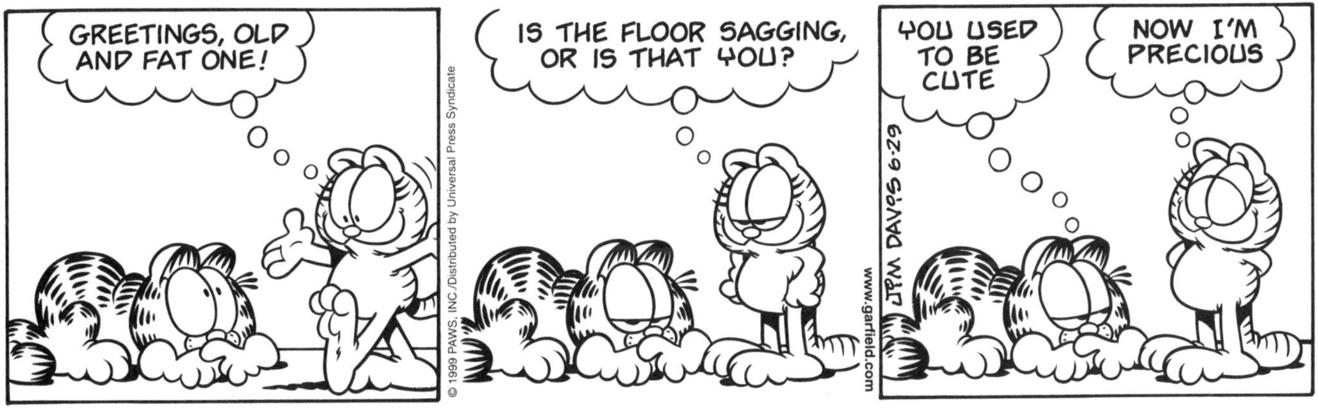
GREETINGS, OLD AND FAT ONE!
© 1999 PAWS, INC./Distributed by Universal Press Syndicate
IS THE FLOOR SAGGING, OR IS THAT YOU?
www.garfield.com
JPM DAV95 6-29
YOU USED TO BE CUTE
NOW I'M PRECIOUS

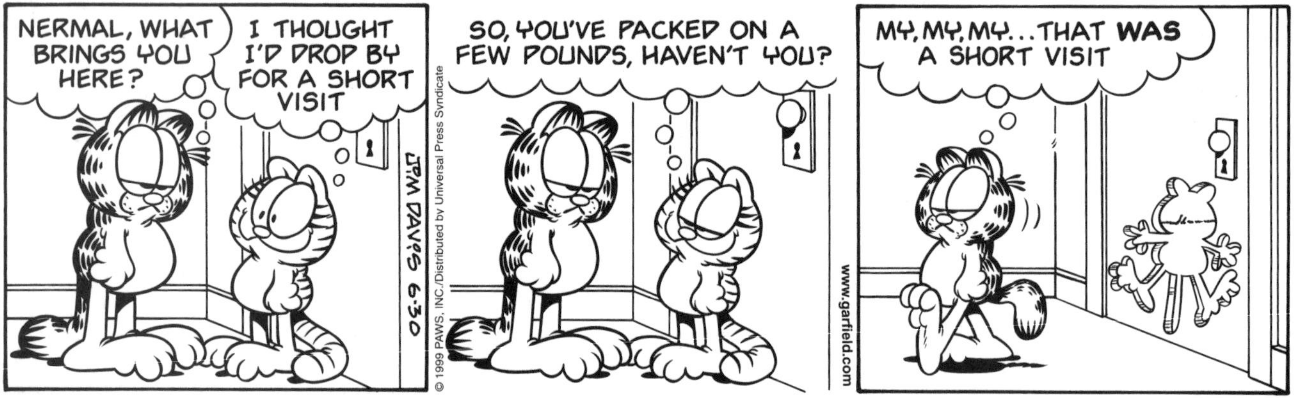
NERMAL, WHAT BRINGS YOU HERE?
I THOUGHT I'D DROP BY FOR A SHORT VISIT
JPM DAVIS 6-30
SO, YOU'VE PACKED ON A FEW POUNDS, HAVEN'T YOU?
MY, MY, MY... THAT **WAS** A SHORT VISIT
www.garfield.com

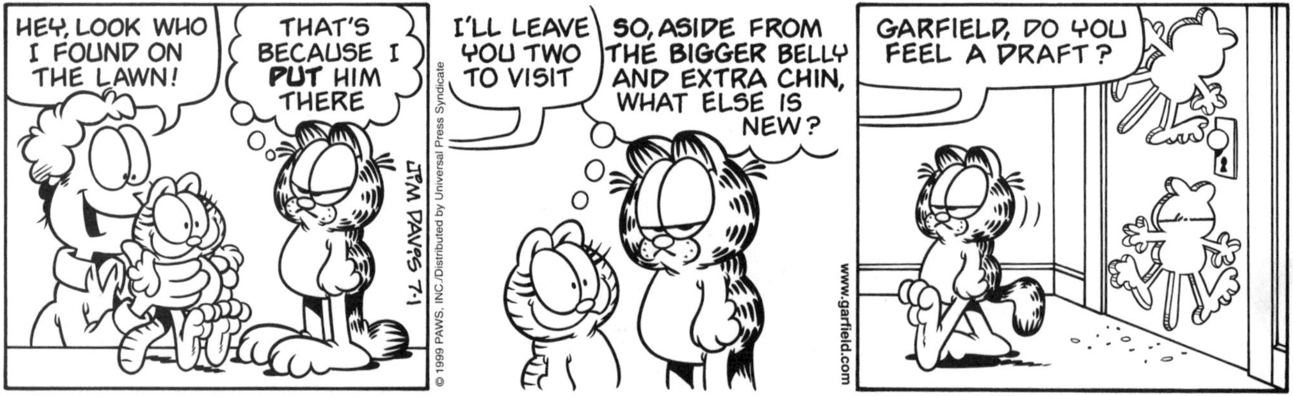
HEY, LOOK WHO I FOUND ON THE LAWN!
THAT'S BECAUSE I **PUT** HIM THERE
JPM DAVIS 7-1
I'LL LEAVE YOU TWO TO VISIT
SO, ASIDE FROM THE BIGGER BELLY AND EXTRA CHIN, WHAT ELSE IS NEW?
GARFIELD, DO YOU FEEL A DRAFT?
www.garfield.com

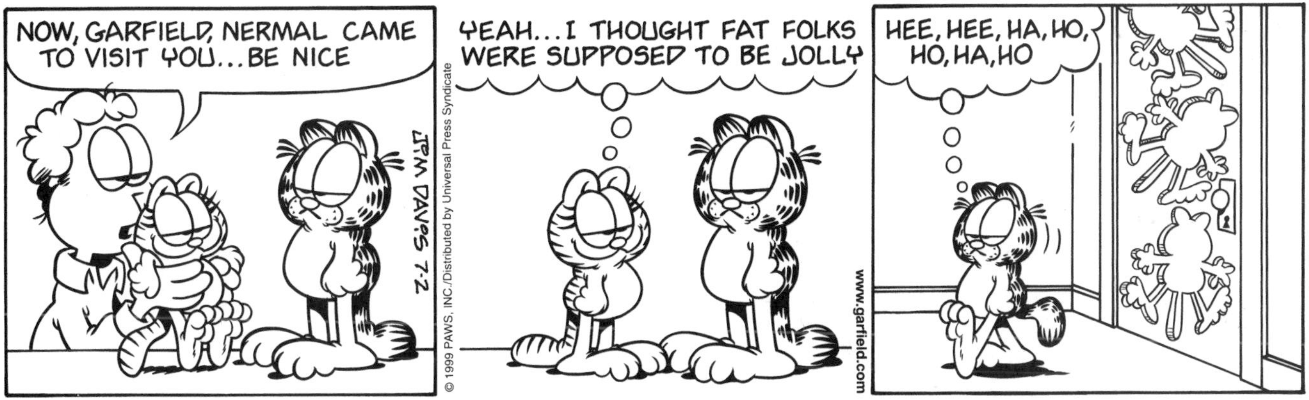
NOW, GARFIELD, NERMAL CAME TO VISIT YOU...BE NICE
JIM DAVIS 7-2
© 1999 PAWS, INC./Distributed by Universal Press Syndicate
YEAH...I THOUGHT FAT FOLKS WERE SUPPOSED TO BE JOLLY
www.garfield.com
HEE, HEE, HA, HO, HO, HA, HO

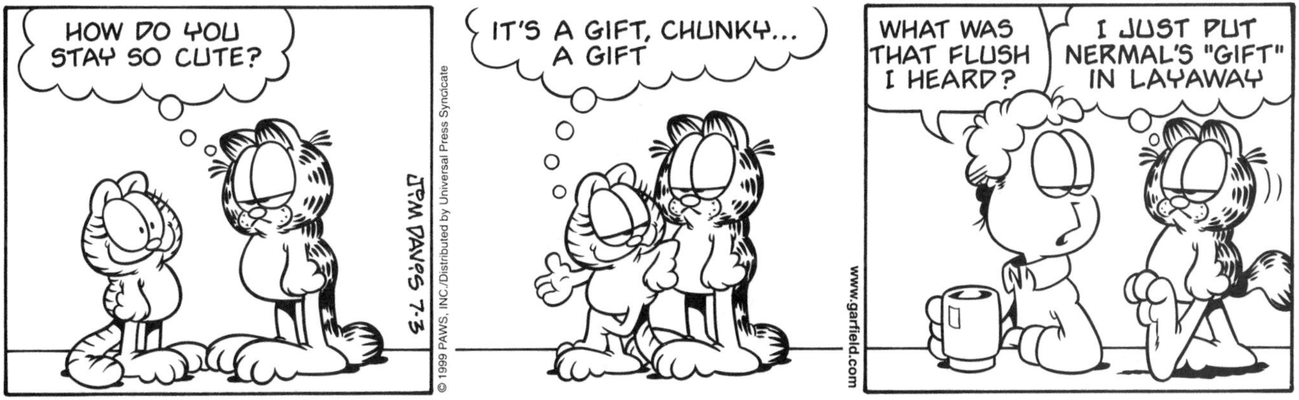
HOW DO YOU STAY SO CUTE?
JIM DAVIS 7-3
© 1999 PAWS, INC./Distributed by Universal Press Syndicate
IT'S A GIFT, CHUNKY... A GIFT
www.garfield.com
WHAT WAS THAT FLUSH I HEARD?
I JUST PUT NERMAL'S "GIFT" IN LAYAWAY

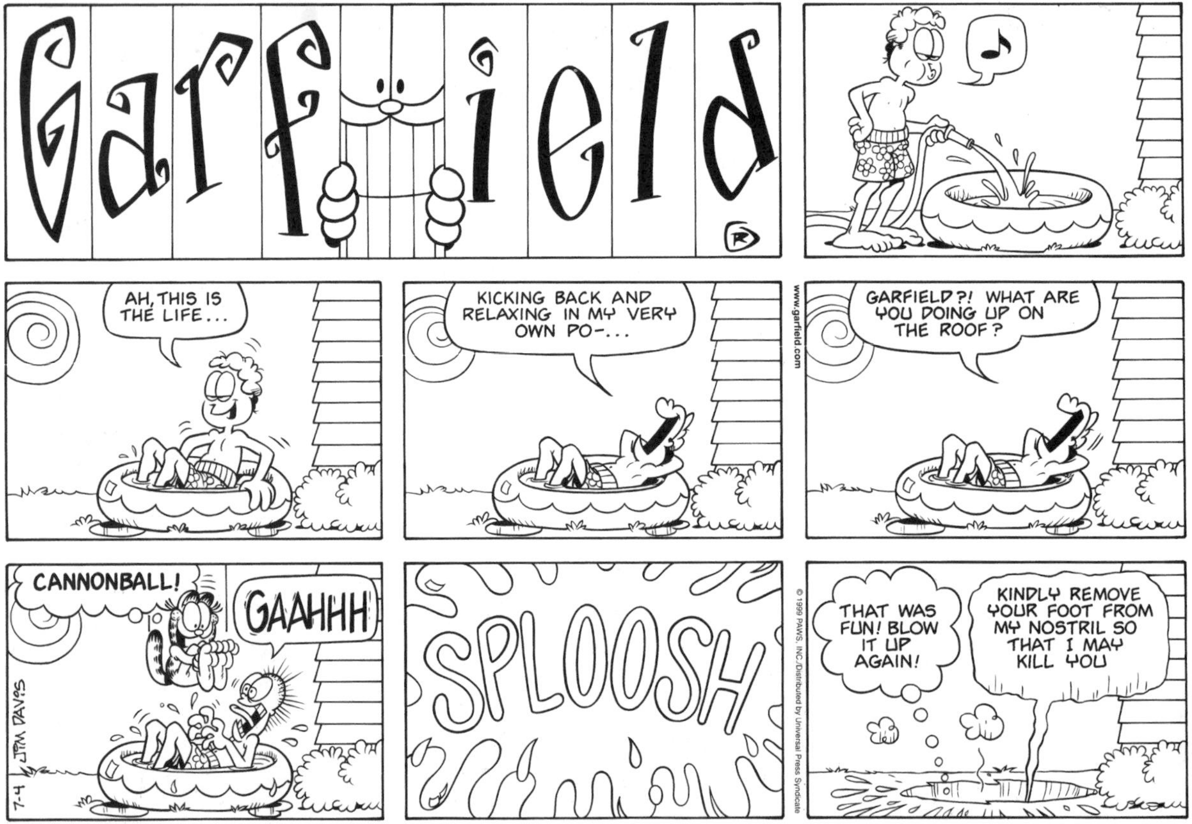
Garfield
AH, THIS IS THE LIFE...
KICKING BACK AND RELAXING IN MY VERY OWN PO-...
GARFIELD?! WHAT ARE YOU DOING UP ON THE ROOF?
CANNONBALL!
GAAHHH
SPLOOSH
THAT WAS FUN! BLOW IT UP AGAIN!
KINDLY REMOVE YOUR FOOT FROM MY NOSTRIL SO THAT I MAY KILL YOU
www.garfield.com
© 1999 PAWS, INC./Distributed by Universal Press Syndicate
JPM DAVIS 7-4

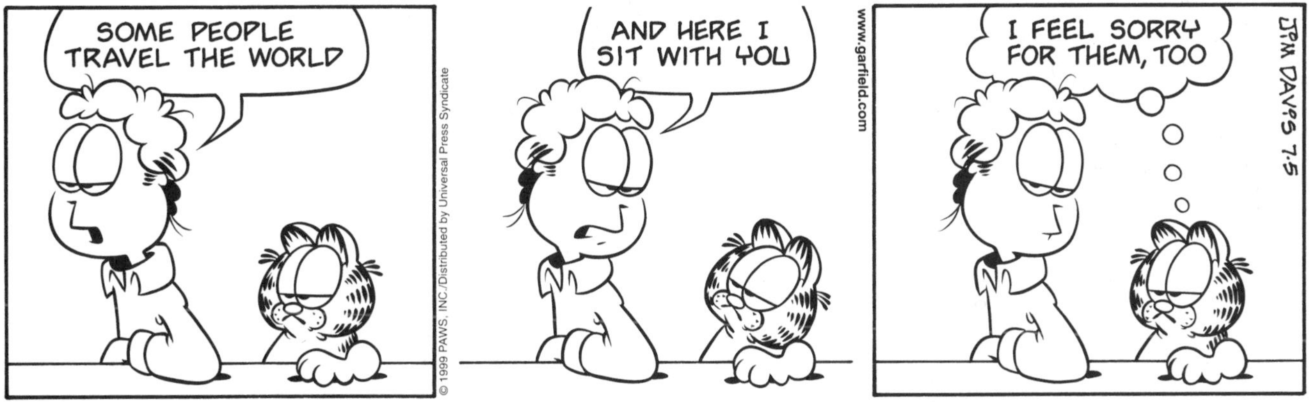
SOME PEOPLE TRAVEL THE WORLD
AND HERE I SIT WITH YOU
I FEEL SORRY FOR THEM, TOO
JIM DAVIS 7-5
© 1999 PAWS, INC./Distributed by Universal Press Syndicate
www.garfield.com

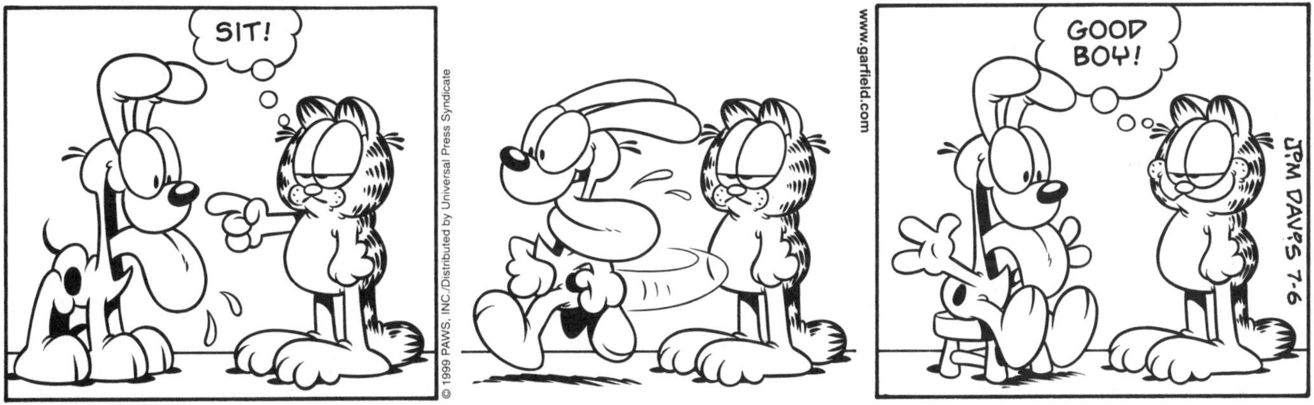
SIT!
GOOD BOY!
JIM DAVIS 7-6
© 1999 PAWS, INC./Distributed by Universal Press Syndicate
www.garfield.com

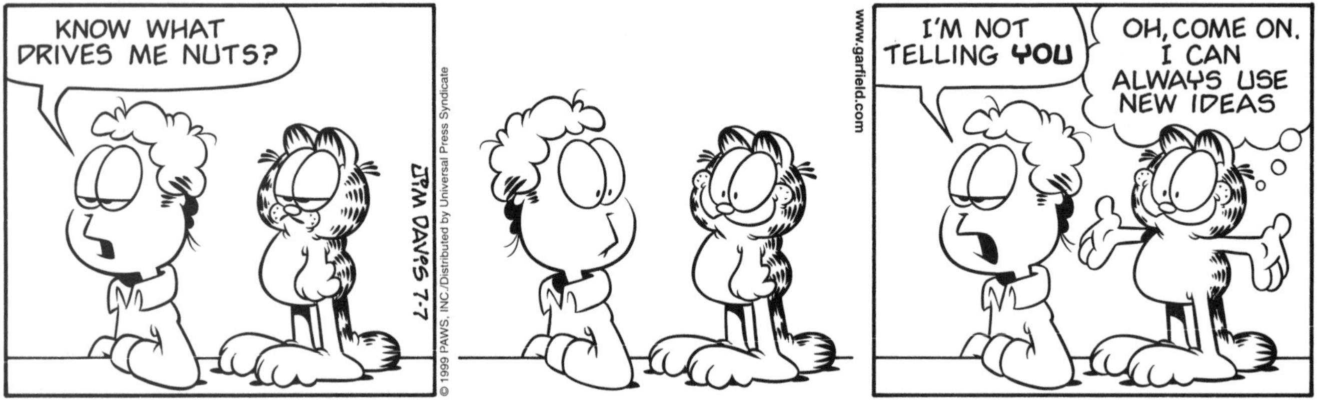
KNOW WHAT DRIVES ME NUTS?
JIM DAVIS 7-7
© 1999 PAWS, INC./Distributed by Universal Press Syndicate
www.garfield.com
I'M NOT TELLING **YOU**
OH, COME ON. I CAN ALWAYS USE NEW IDEAS

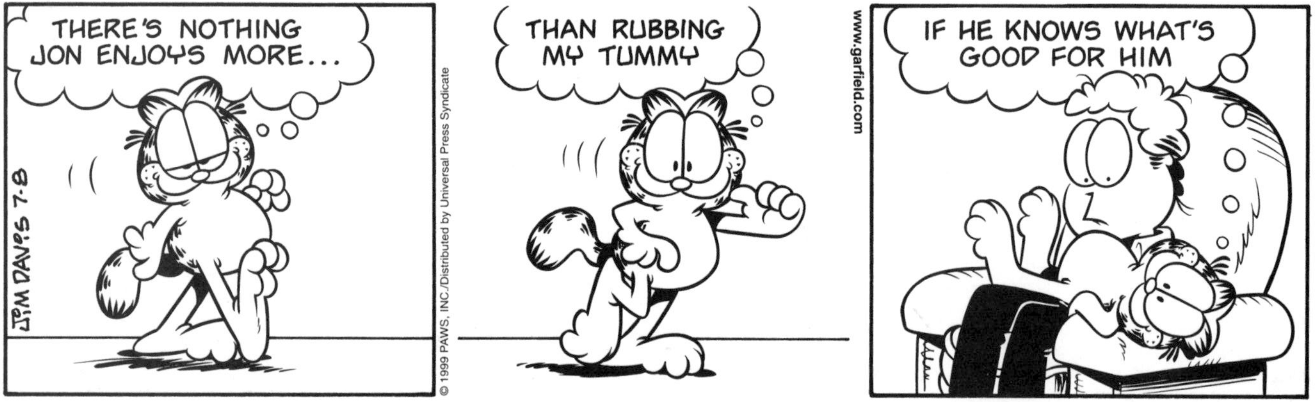
THERE'S NOTHING JON ENJOYS MORE...
JIM DAVIS 7-8
© 1999 PAWS, INC./Distributed by Universal Press Syndicate
THAN RUBBING MY TUMMY
www.garfield.com
IF HE KNOWS WHAT'S GOOD FOR HIM

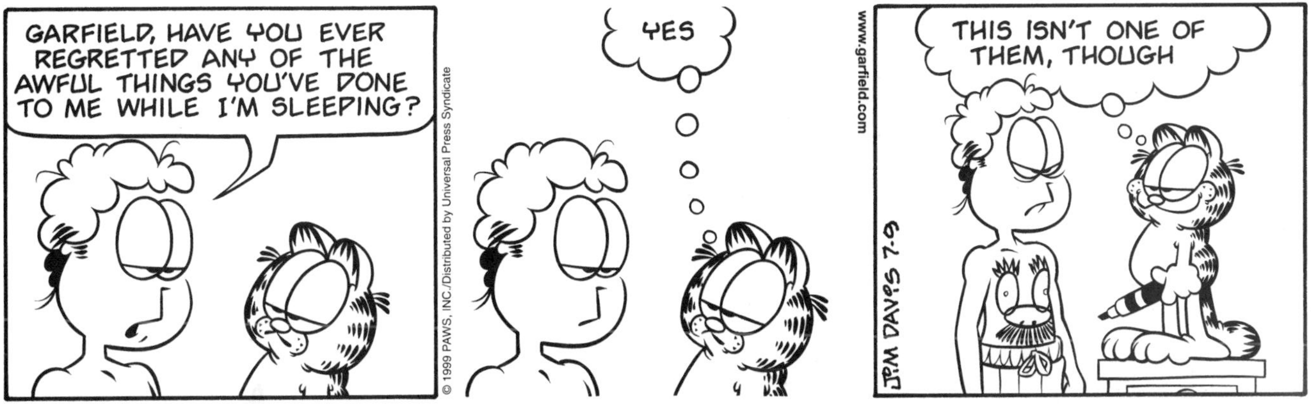
GARFIELD, HAVE YOU EVER REGRETTED ANY OF THE AWFUL THINGS YOU'VE DONE TO ME WHILE I'M SLEEPING?
YES
THIS ISN'T ONE OF THEM, THOUGH
JIM DAVIS 7-9
www.garfield.com
© 1999 PAWS, INC./Distributed by Universal Press Syndicate

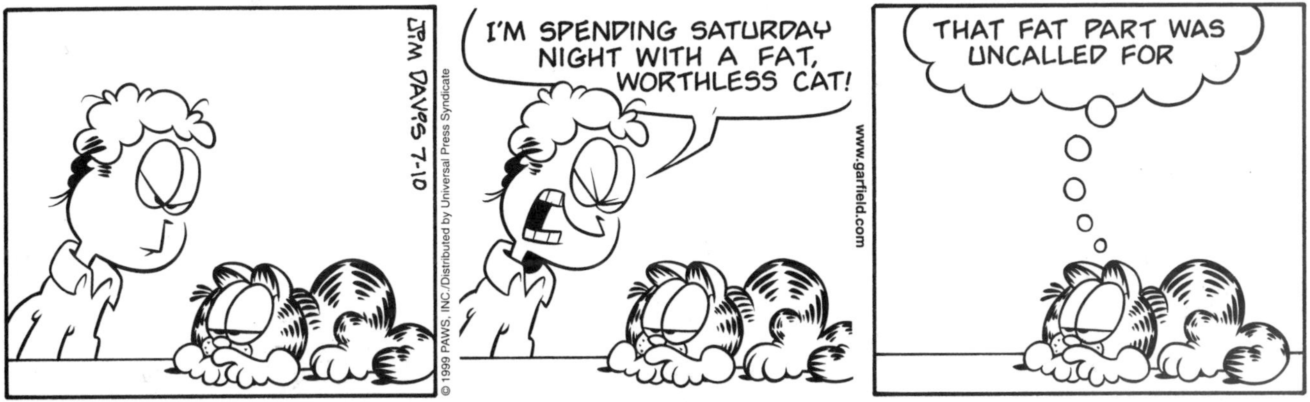
JIM DAVIS 7-10
I'M SPENDING SATURDAY NIGHT WITH A FAT, WORTHLESS CAT!
THAT FAT PART WAS UNCALLED FOR
www.garfield.com
© 1999 PAWS, INC./Distributed by Universal Press Syndicate

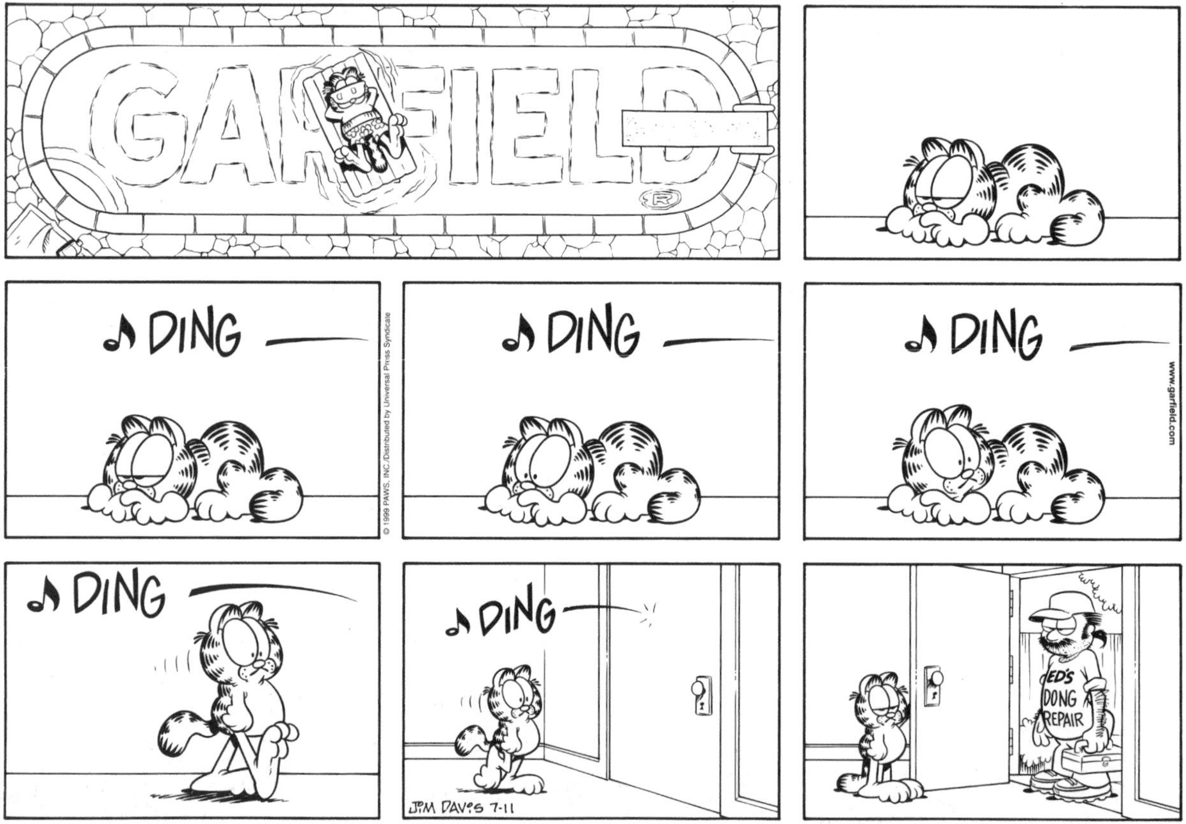
GARFIELD
DING
DING
DING
DING
DING
ED'S DONG REPAIR
JIM DAVIS 7-11
© 1999 PAWS, INC./Distributed by Universal Press Syndicate
www.garfield.com

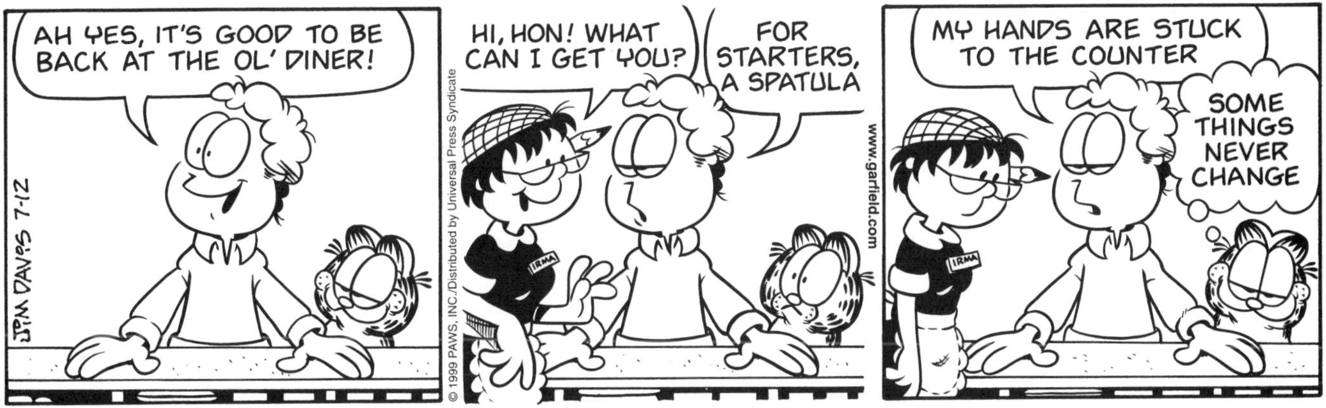
AH YES, IT'S GOOD TO BE BACK AT THE OL' DINER!
JIM DAVIS 7-12
© 1999 PAWS, INC./Distributed by Universal Press Syndicate
HI, HON! WHAT CAN I GET YOU?
FOR STARTERS, A SPATULA
IRMA
www.garfield.com
MY HANDS ARE STUCK TO THE COUNTER
SOME THINGS NEVER CHANGE

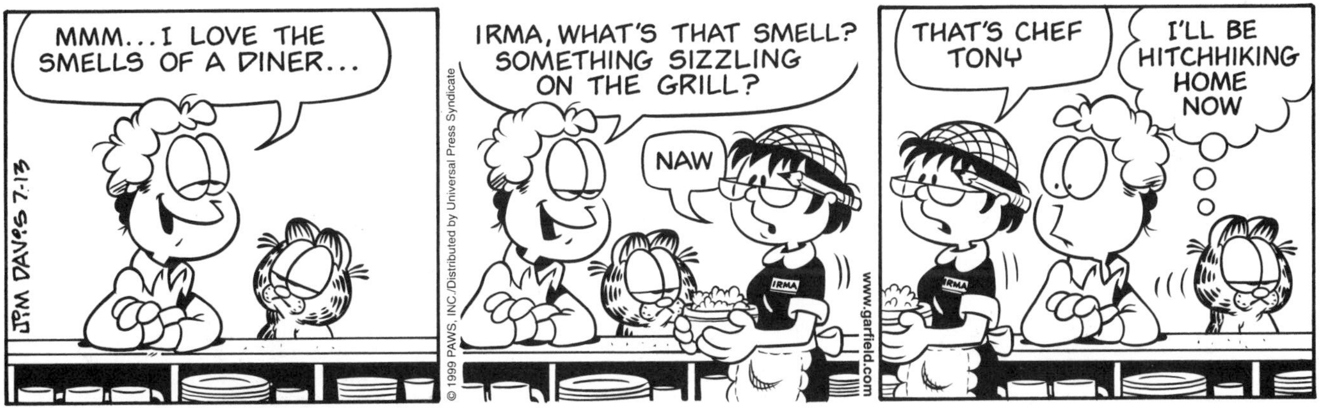
MMM... I LOVE THE SMELLS OF A DINER...
JIM DAVIS 7-13
© 1999 PAWS, INC./Distributed by Universal Press Syndicate
IRMA, WHAT'S THAT SMELL? SOMETHING SIZZLING ON THE GRILL?
NAW
IRMA
www.garfield.com
THAT'S CHEF TONY
I'LL BE HITCHHIKING HOME NOW

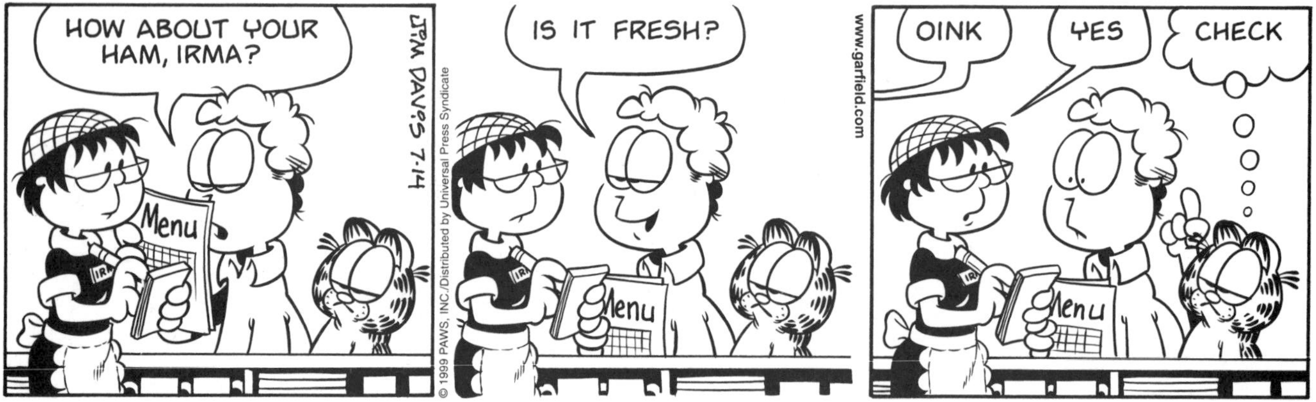
HOW ABOUT YOUR HAM, IRMA?
JPM DAVPS 7-14
© 1999 PAWS, INC./Distributed by Universal Press Syndicate
IS IT FRESH?
www.garfield.com
OINK
YES
CHECK
Menu
IRMA

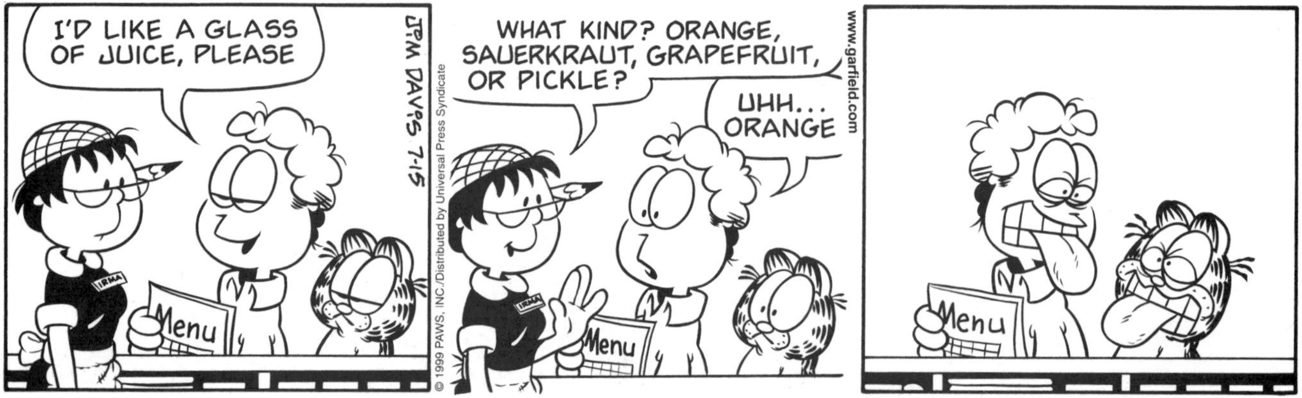
I'D LIKE A GLASS OF JUICE, PLEASE
JPM DAVPS 7-15
© 1999 PAWS, INC./Distributed by Universal Press Syndicate
WHAT KIND? ORANGE, SAUERKRAUT, GRAPEFRUIT, OR PICKLE?
UHH... ORANGE
www.garfield.com
Menu
IRMA

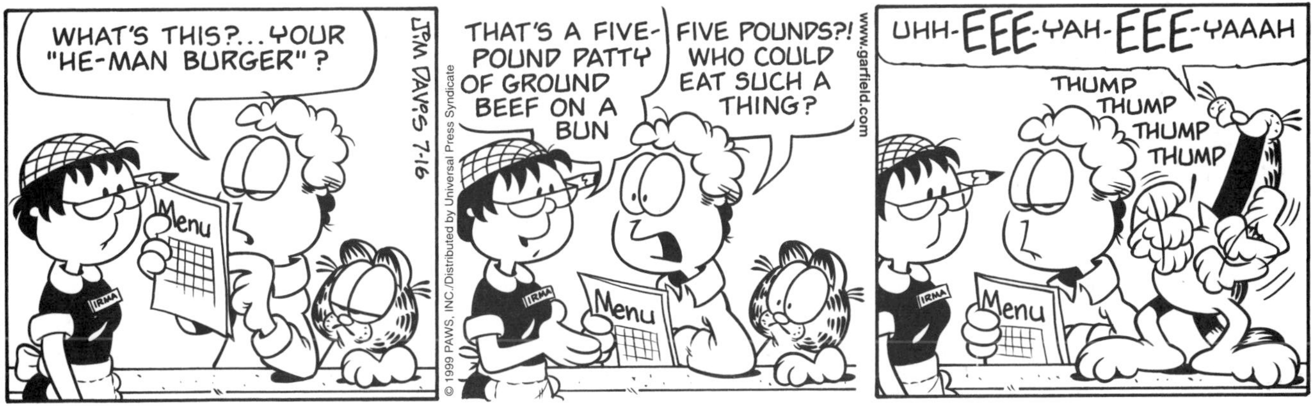
WHAT'S THIS?... YOUR "HE-MAN BURGER"?
JPM DAVPS 7-16
Menu
IRMA
THAT'S A FIVE-POUND PATTY OF GROUND BEEF ON A BUN
FIVE POUNDS?! WHO COULD EAT SUCH A THING?
© 1999 PAWS, INC./Distributed by Universal Press Syndicate
www.garfield.com
UHH-EEE-YAH-EEE-YAAAH
THUMP THUMP THUMP THUMP

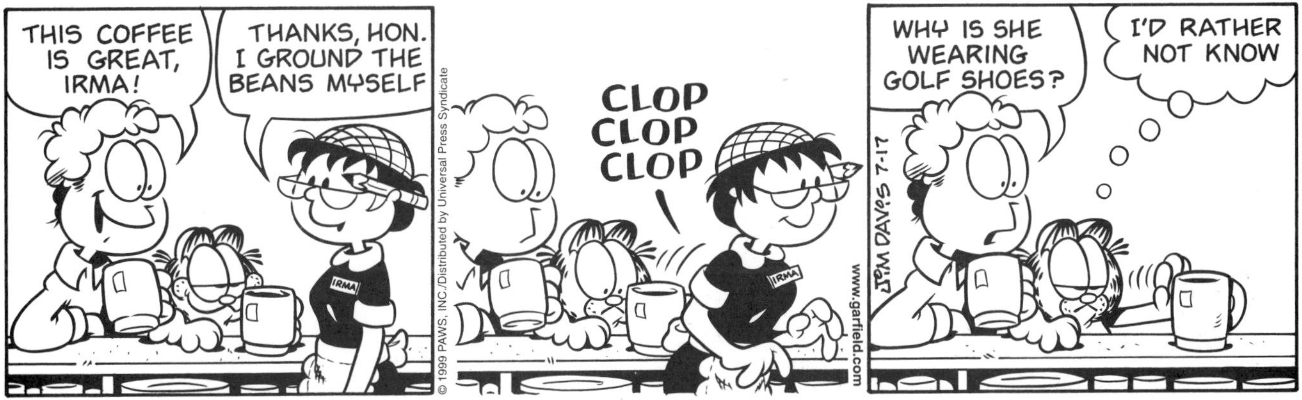
THIS COFFEE IS GREAT, IRMA!
THANKS, HON. I GROUND THE BEANS MYSELF
IRMA
© 1999 PAWS, INC./Distributed by Universal Press Syndicate
CLOP CLOP CLOP
www.garfield.com
JPM DAVPS 7-17
WHY IS SHE WEARING GOLF SHOES?
I'D RATHER NOT KNOW

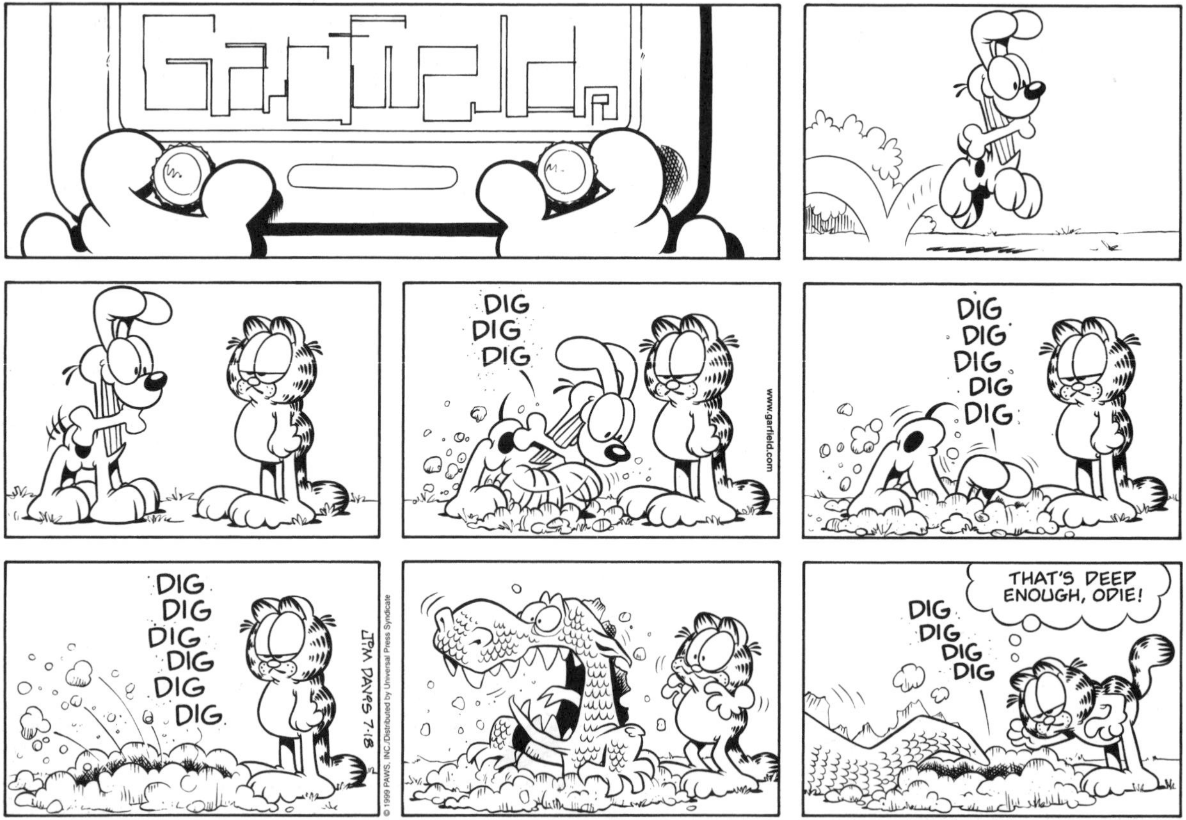
GARFIELD
DIG DIG DIG
www.garfield.com
DIG DIG DIG DIG DIG
DIG DIG DIG DIG DIG DIG
JPM DAVIS 7-18
© 1999 PAWS, INC./Distributed by Universal Press Syndicate
DIG DIG DIG DIG
THAT'S DEEP ENOUGH, ODIE!

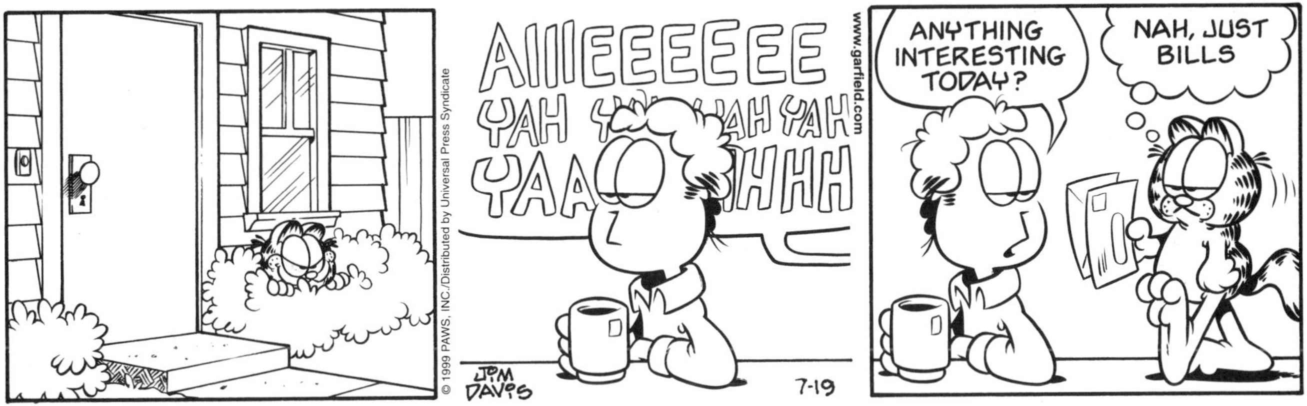
AIIIEEEEEE
YAH YAH YAH YAH
YAA HHH
JIM DAVIS
7-19
www.garfield.com
ANYTHING INTERESTING TODAY?
NAH, JUST BILLS

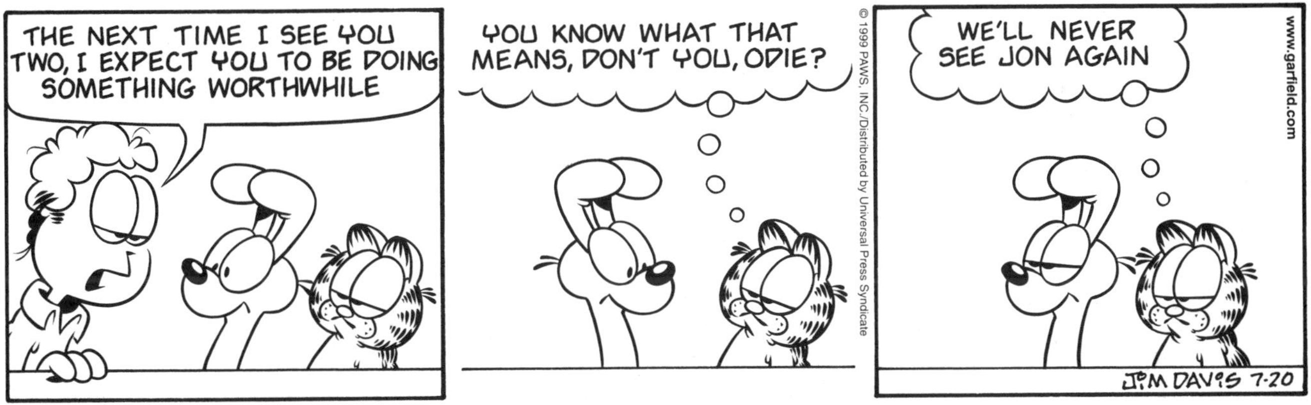
THE NEXT TIME I SEE YOU TWO, I EXPECT YOU TO BE DOING SOMETHING WORTHWHILE
YOU KNOW WHAT THAT MEANS, DON'T YOU, ODIE?
WE'LL NEVER SEE JON AGAIN
www.garfield.com
JIM DAVIS 7-20

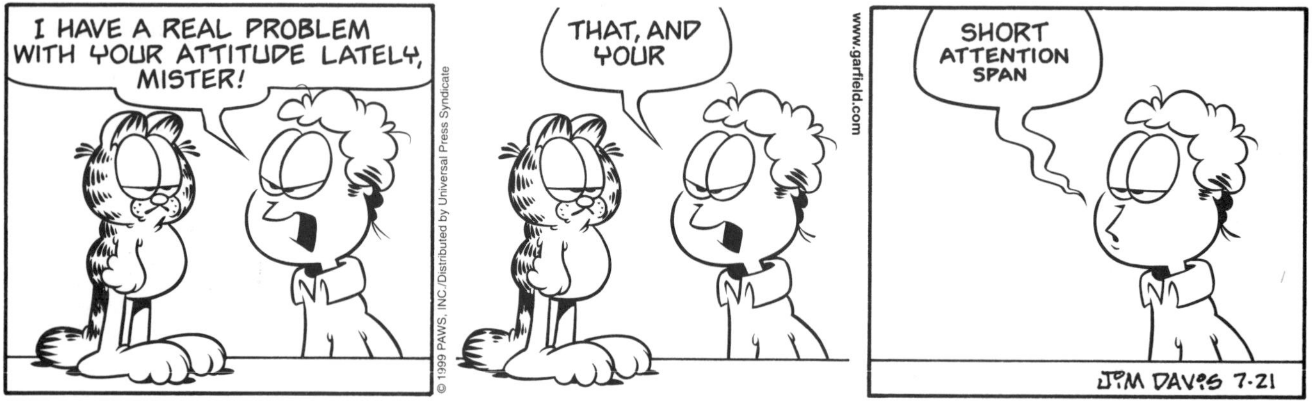
I HAVE A REAL PROBLEM WITH YOUR ATTITUDE LATELY, MISTER!
THAT, AND YOUR
SHORT ATTENTION SPAN
JIM DAVIS 7-21

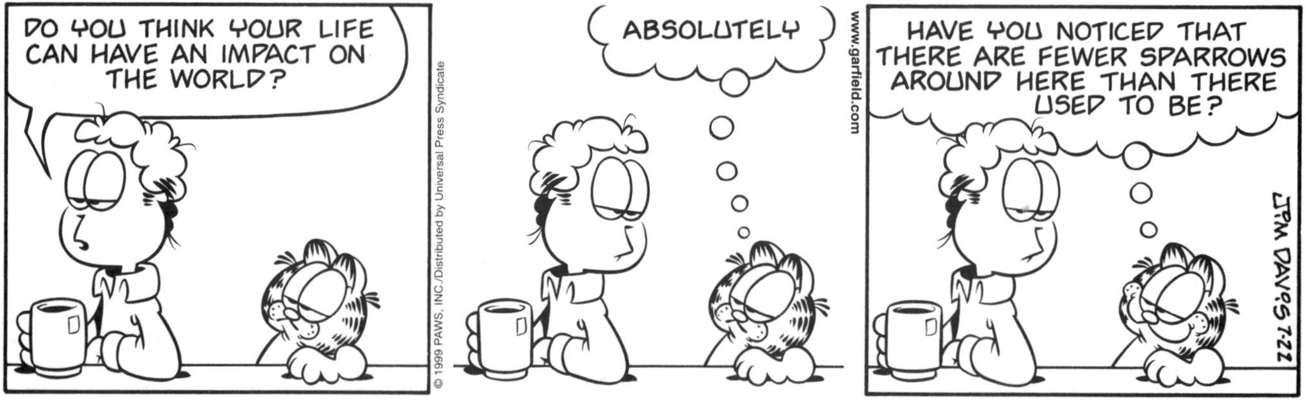
DO YOU THINK YOUR LIFE CAN HAVE AN IMPACT ON THE WORLD?
ABSOLUTELY
HAVE YOU NOTICED THAT THERE ARE FEWER SPARROWS AROUND HERE THAN THERE USED TO BE?
JIM DAVIS 7-22

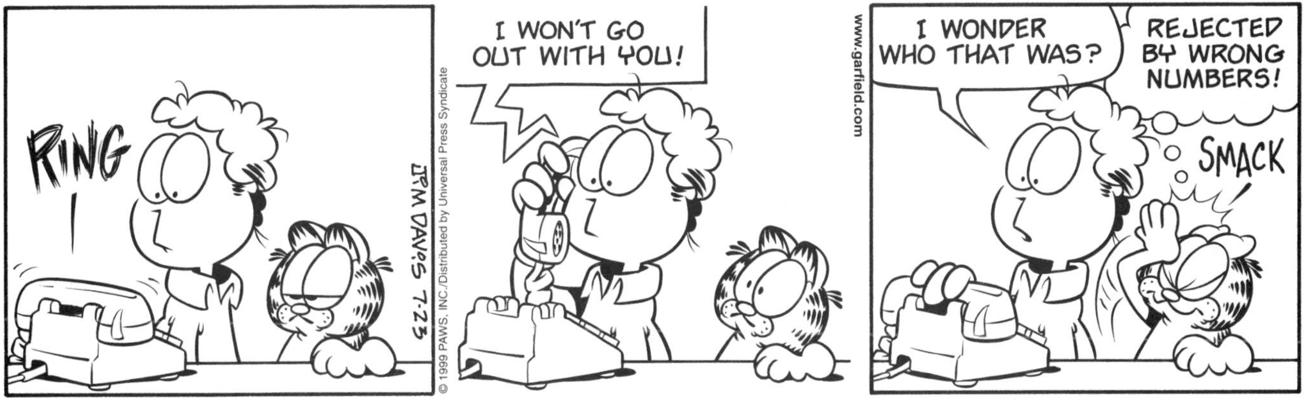
RING
JIM DAVIS 7-23
© 1999 PAWS, INC./Distributed by Universal Press Syndicate
I WON'T GO OUT WITH YOU!
www.garfield.com
I WONDER WHO THAT WAS?
REJECTED BY WRONG NUMBERS!
SMACK

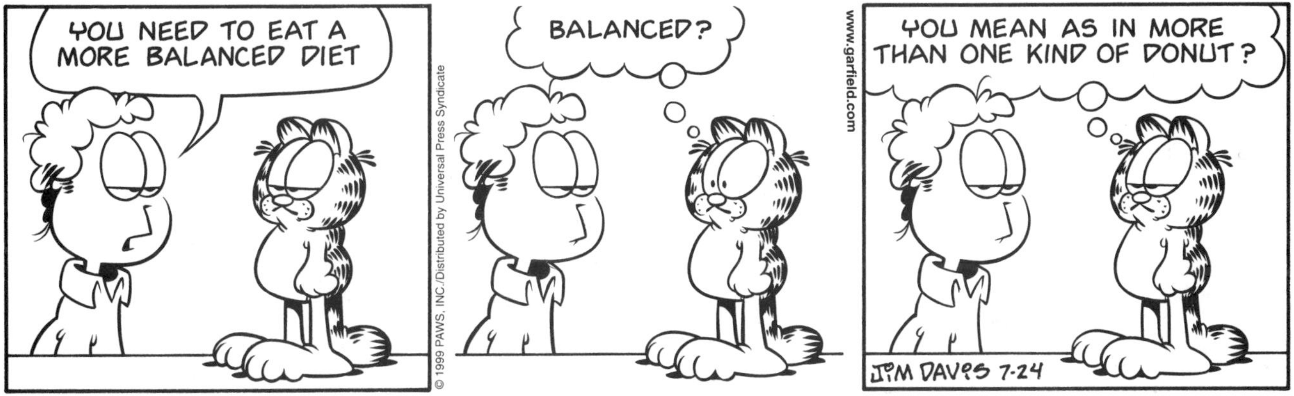
YOU NEED TO EAT A MORE BALANCED DIET
© 1999 PAWS, INC./Distributed by Universal Press Syndicate
BALANCED?
www.garfield.com
YOU MEAN AS IN MORE THAN ONE KIND OF DONUT?
JIM DAVIS 7-24

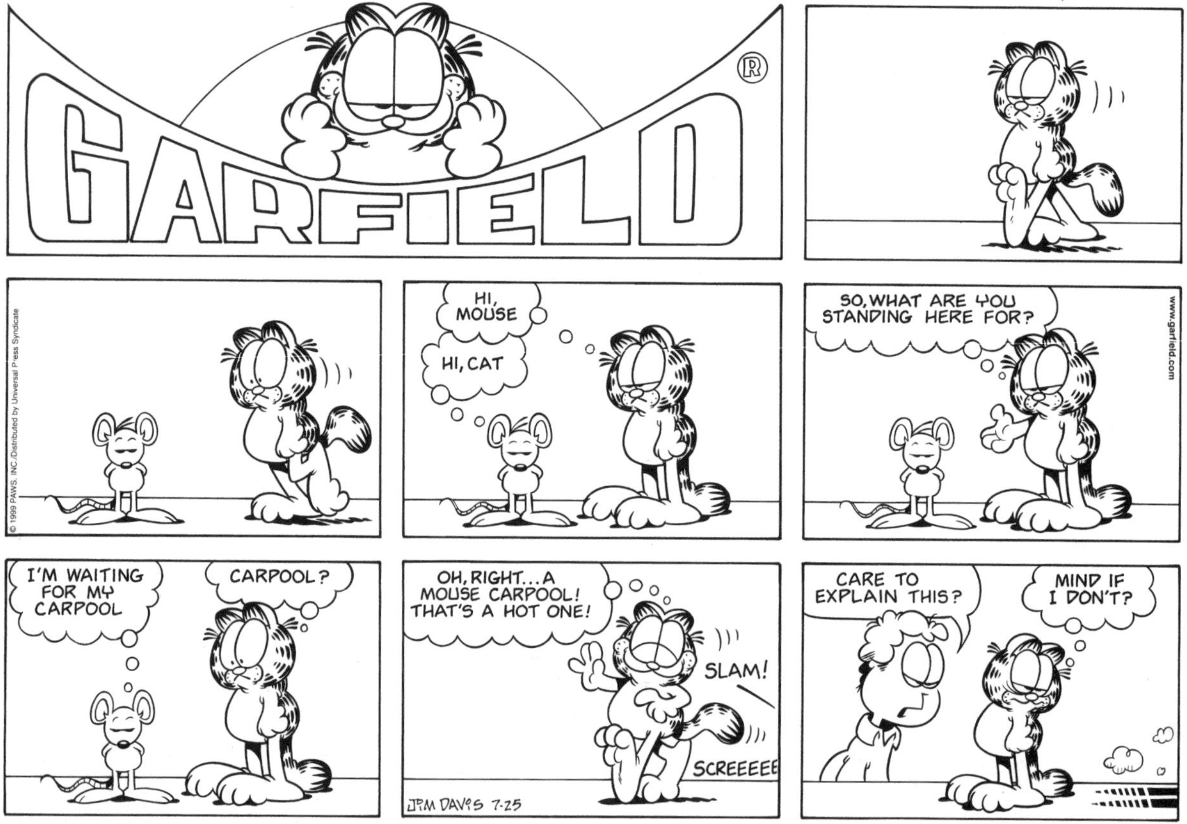
GARFIELD
© 1999 PAWS, INC./Distributed by Universal Press Syndicate
HI, MOUSE
HI, CAT
SO, WHAT ARE YOU STANDING HERE FOR?
www.garfield.com
I'M WAITING FOR MY CARPOOL
CARPOOL?
OH, RIGHT... A MOUSE CARPOOL! THAT'S A HOT ONE!
SLAM!
SCREEEEE
JIM DAVIS 7-25
CARE TO EXPLAIN THIS?
MIND IF I DON'T?

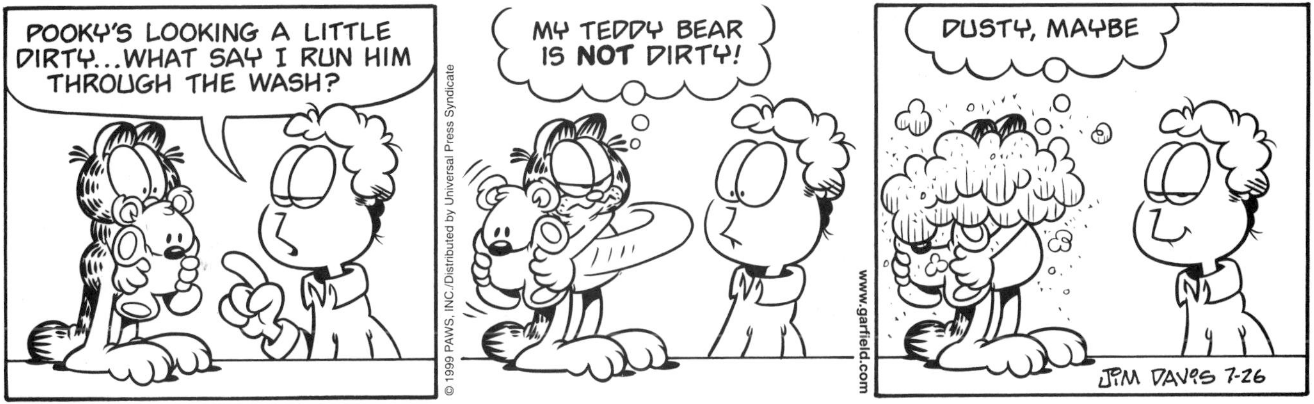
POOKY'S LOOKING A LITTLE DIRTY...WHAT SAY I RUN HIM THROUGH THE WASH?
MY TEDDY BEAR IS **NOT** DIRTY!
DUSTY, MAYBE
JIM DAVIS 7-26
© 1999 PAWS, INC./Distributed by Universal Press Syndicate
www.garfield.com

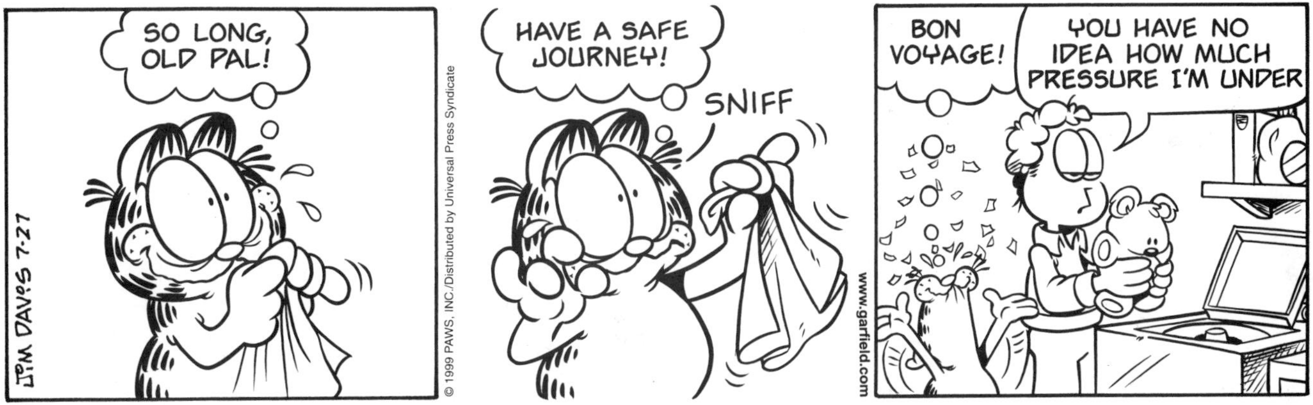
SO LONG, OLD PAL!
JIM DAVIS 7-27
HAVE A SAFE JOURNEY!
SNIFF
BON VOYAGE!
YOU HAVE NO IDEA HOW MUCH PRESSURE I'M UNDER
© 1999 PAWS, INC./Distributed by Universal Press Syndicate
www.garfield.com

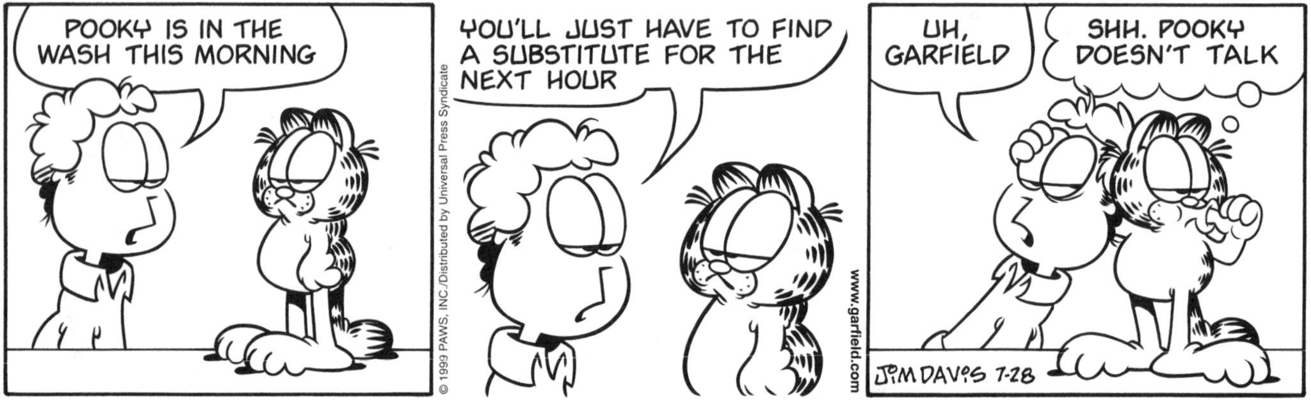
POOKY IS IN THE WASH THIS MORNING
YOU'LL JUST HAVE TO FIND A SUBSTITUTE FOR THE NEXT HOUR
UH, GARFIELD
SHH. POOKY DOESN'T TALK
© 1999 PAWS, INC./Distributed by Universal Press Syndicate
www.garfield.com
JIM DAVIS 7-28

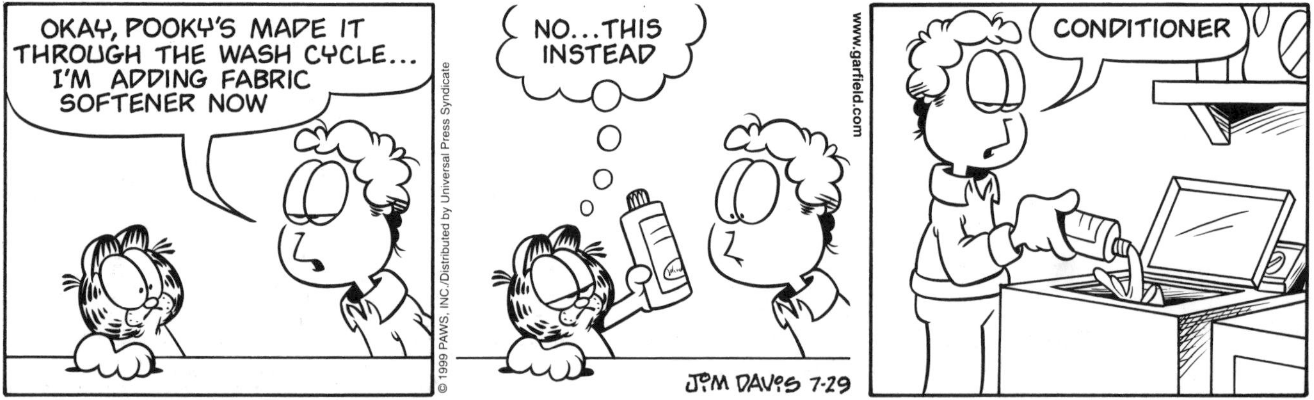
OKAY, POOKY'S MADE IT THROUGH THE WASH CYCLE... I'M ADDING FABRIC SOFTENER NOW
NO...THIS INSTEAD
CONDITIONER
© 1999 PAWS, INC./Distributed by Universal Press Syndicate
www.garfield.com
JIM DAVIS 7-29

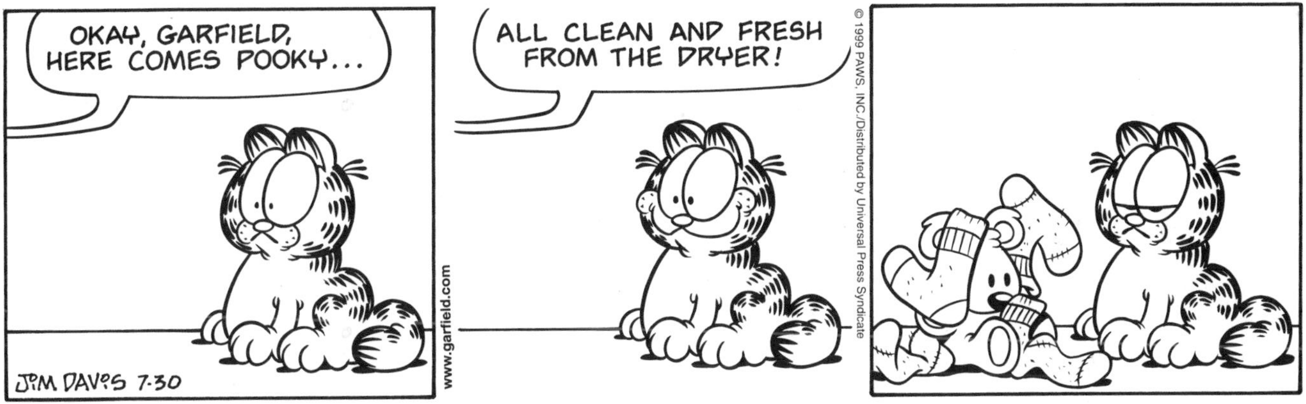
OKAY, GARFIELD, HERE COMES POOKY...
ALL CLEAN AND FRESH FROM THE DRYER!
JIM DAVIS 7-30
www.garfield.com
© 1999 PAWS, INC./Distributed by Universal Press Syndicate

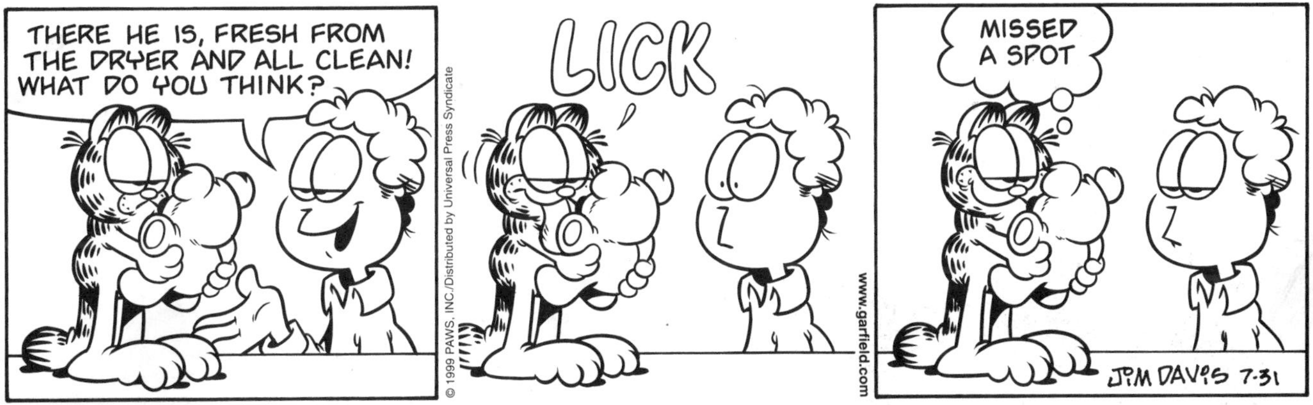
THERE HE IS, FRESH FROM THE DRYER AND ALL CLEAN! WHAT DO YOU THINK?
LICK
MISSED A SPOT
JIM DAVIS 7-31
© 1999 PAWS, INC./Distributed by Universal Press Syndicate
www.garfield.com

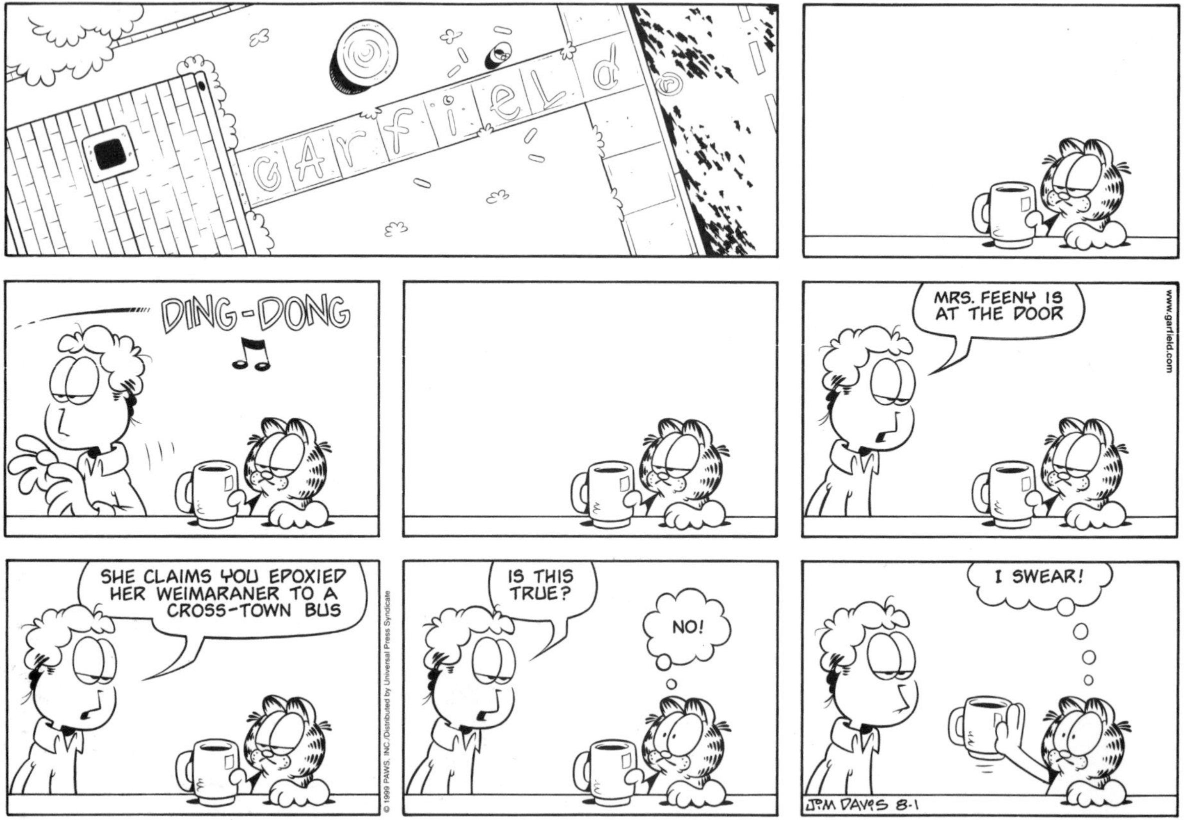
garfield
DING-DONG
MRS. FEENY IS AT THE DOOR
www.garfield.com
SHE CLAIMS YOU EPOXIED HER WEIMARANER TO A CROSS-TOWN BUS
© 1999 PAWS, INC./Distributed by Universal Press Syndicate
IS THIS TRUE?
NO!
I SWEAR!
JIM DAVIS 8-1

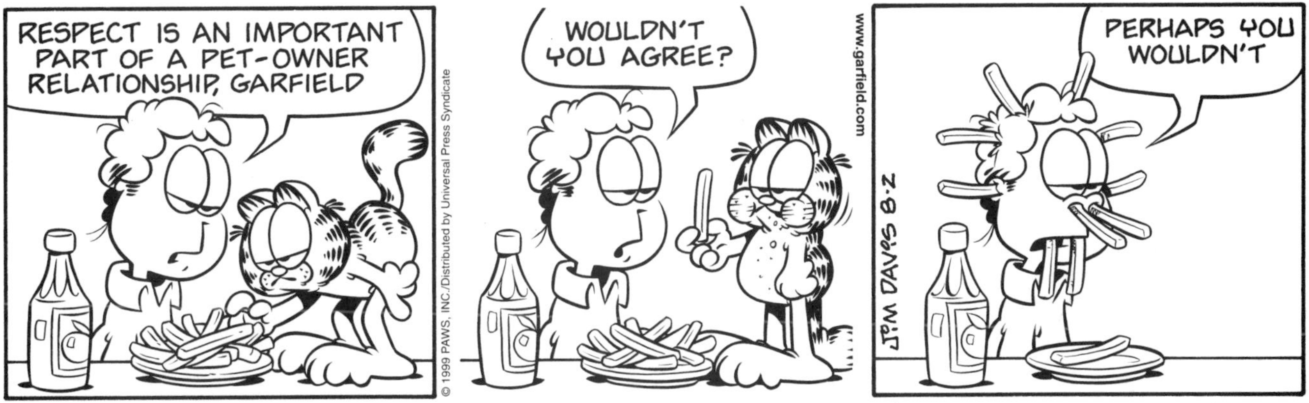
RESPECT IS AN IMPORTANT PART OF A PET-OWNER RELATIONSHIP, GARFIELD
© 1999 PAWS, INC./Distributed by Universal Press Syndicate
WOULDN'T YOU AGREE?
www.garfield.com
JIM DAVIS 8-2
PERHAPS YOU WOULDN'T

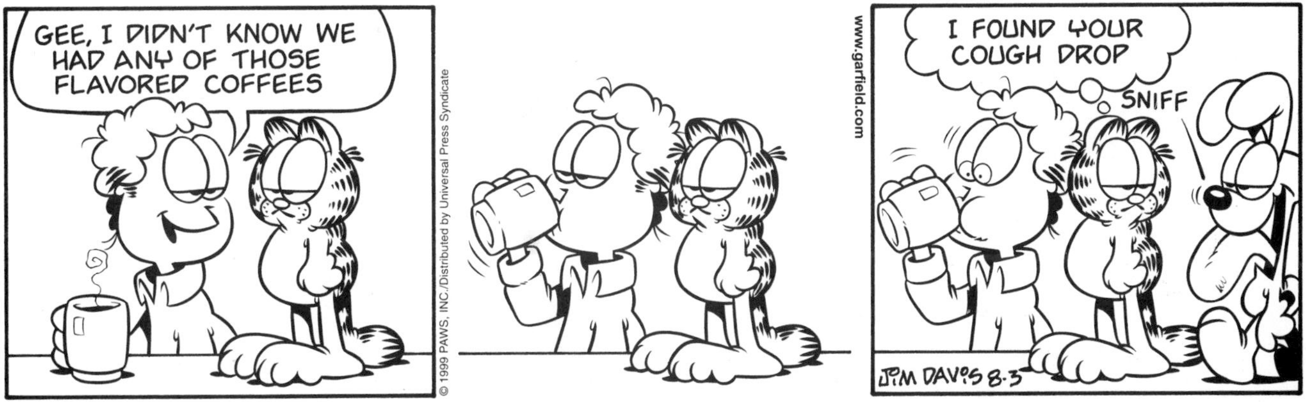
GEE, I DIDN'T KNOW WE HAD ANY OF THOSE FLAVORED COFFEES
© 1999 PAWS, INC./Distributed by Universal Press Syndicate
www.garfield.com
I FOUND YOUR COUGH DROP
SNIFF
JIM DAVIS 8-3

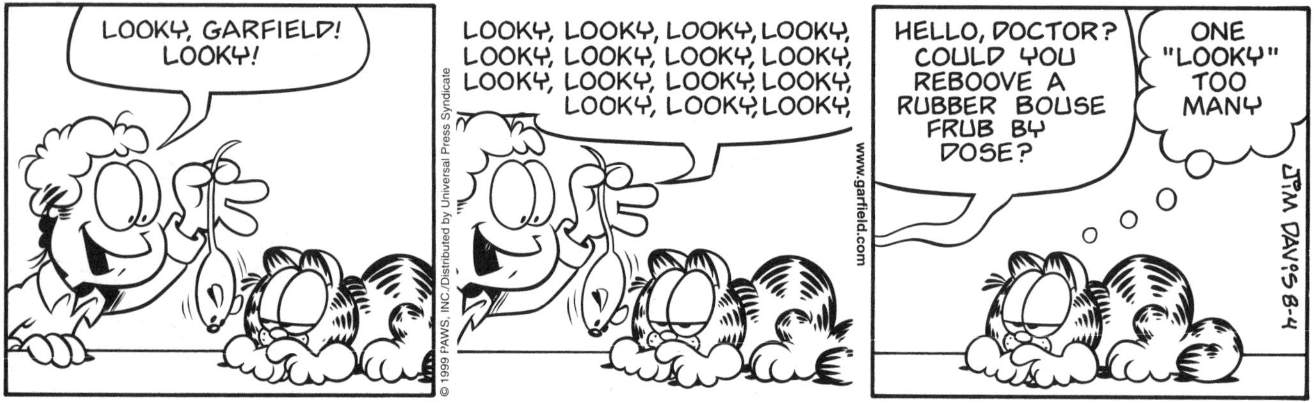
LOOKY, GARFIELD! LOOKY!
© 1999 PAWS, INC./Distributed by Universal Press Syndicate
LOOKY, LOOKY, LOOKY, LOOKY, LOOKY, LOOKY, LOOKY, LOOKY, LOOKY, LOOKY, LOOKY, LOOKY, LOOKY, LOOKY, LOOKY,
www.garfield.com
HELLO, DOCTOR? COULD YOU REBOOVE A RUBBER BOUSE FRUB BY DOSE?
ONE "LOOKY" TOO MANY
JIM DAVIS 8-4

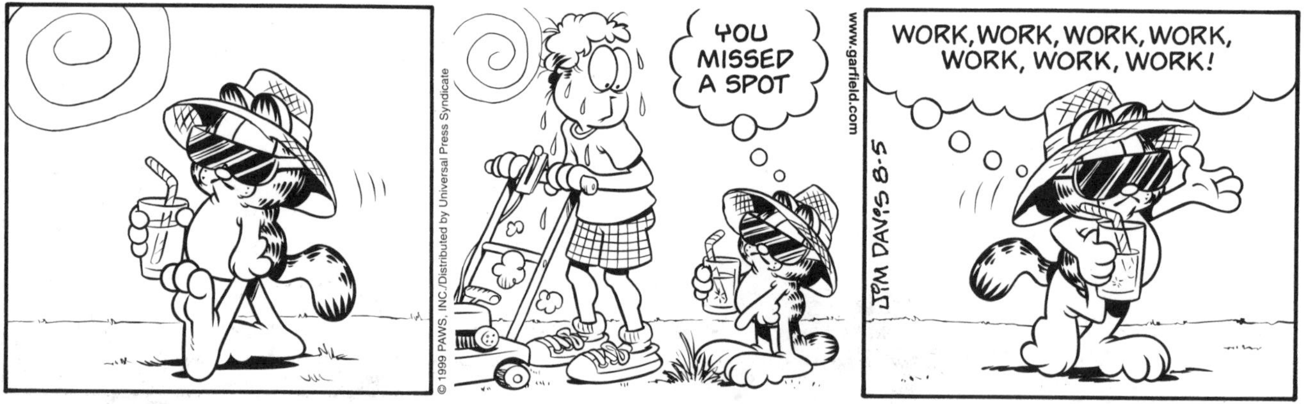
© 1999 PAWS, INC./Distributed by Universal Press Syndicate
YOU MISSED A SPOT
www.garfield.com
JIM DAVIS 8-5
WORK, WORK, WORK, WORK, WORK, WORK, WORK!

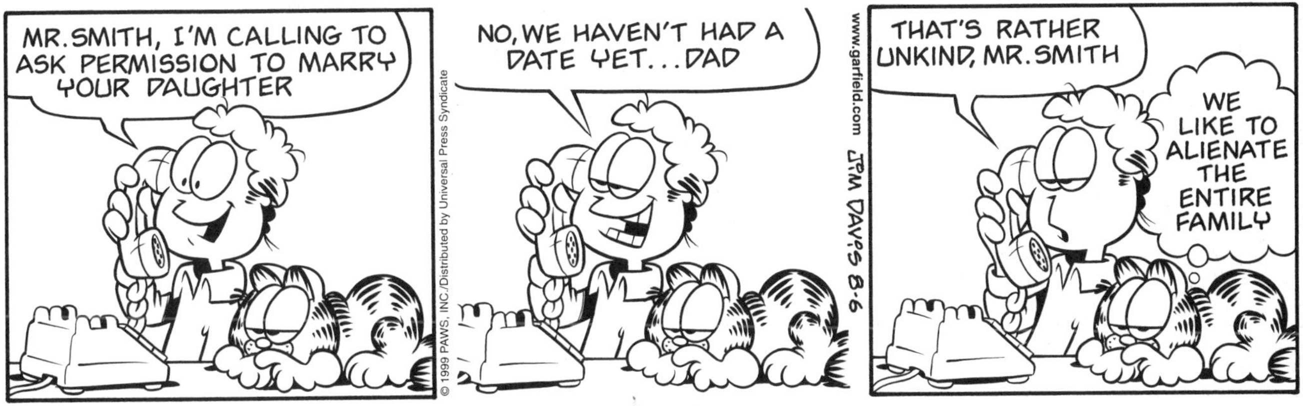
MR. SMITH, I'M CALLING TO ASK PERMISSION TO MARRY YOUR DAUGHTER
NO, WE HAVEN'T HAD A DATE YET. . . DAD
THAT'S RATHER UNKIND, MR. SMITH
WE LIKE TO ALIENATE THE ENTIRE FAMILY
© 1999 PAWS, INC./Distributed by Universal Press Syndicate
www.garfield.com
JPM DAVPS 8-6

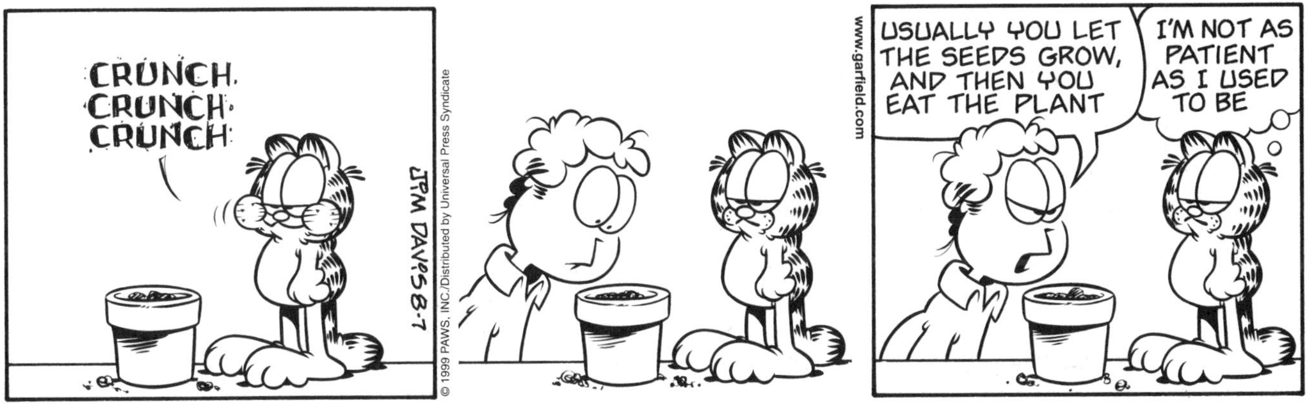
CRUNCH CRUNCH CRUNCH
USUALLY YOU LET THE SEEDS GROW, AND THEN YOU EAT THE PLANT
I'M NOT AS PATIENT AS I USED TO BE
© 1999 PAWS, INC./Distributed by Universal Press Syndicate
www.garfield.com
JPM DAVPS 8-7

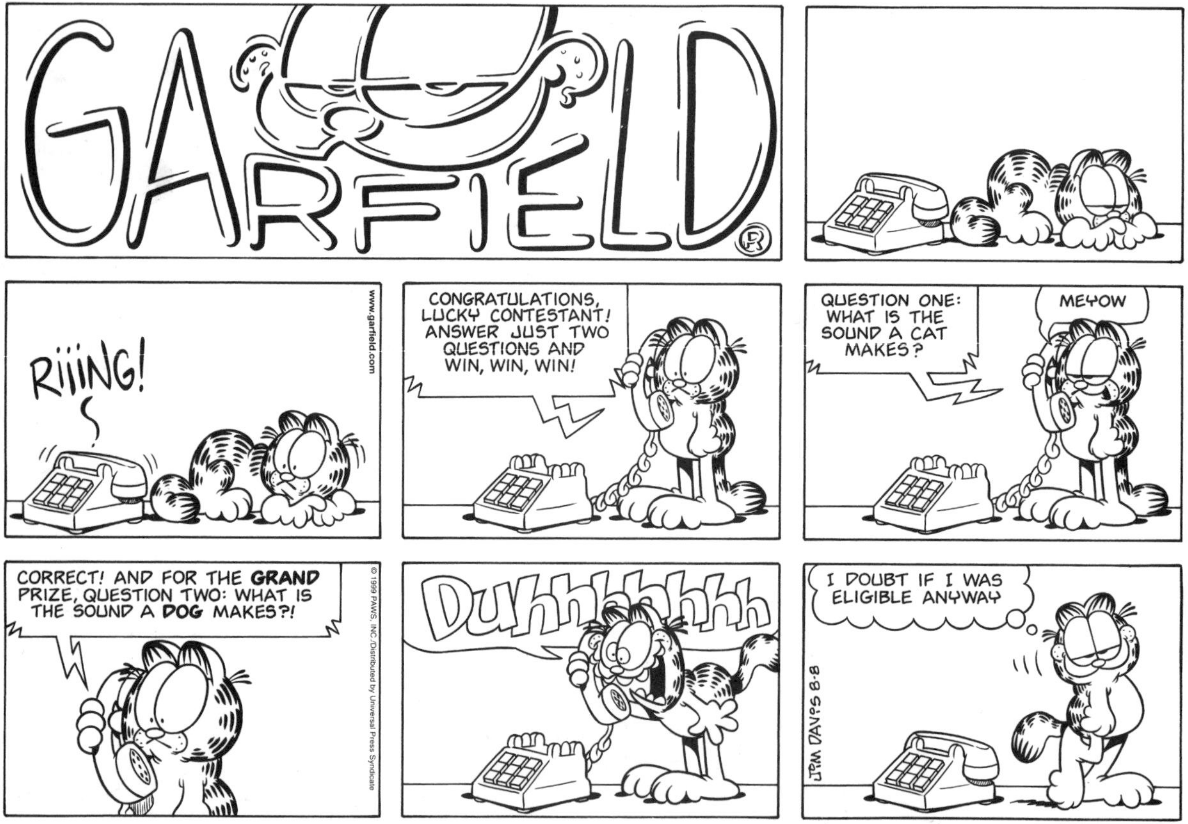
GARFIELD®
www.garfield.com
RIIING!
CONGRATULATIONS, LUCKY CONTESTANT! ANSWER JUST TWO QUESTIONS AND WIN, WIN, WIN!
QUESTION ONE: WHAT IS THE SOUND A CAT MAKES?
MEYOW
CORRECT! AND FOR THE GRAND PRIZE, QUESTION TWO: WHAT IS THE SOUND A DOG MAKES?!
© 1999 PAWS, INC./Distributed by Universal Press Syndicate
Duhhhhhhh
JPM DAVPS 8-8
I DOUBT IF I WAS ELIGIBLE ANYWAY

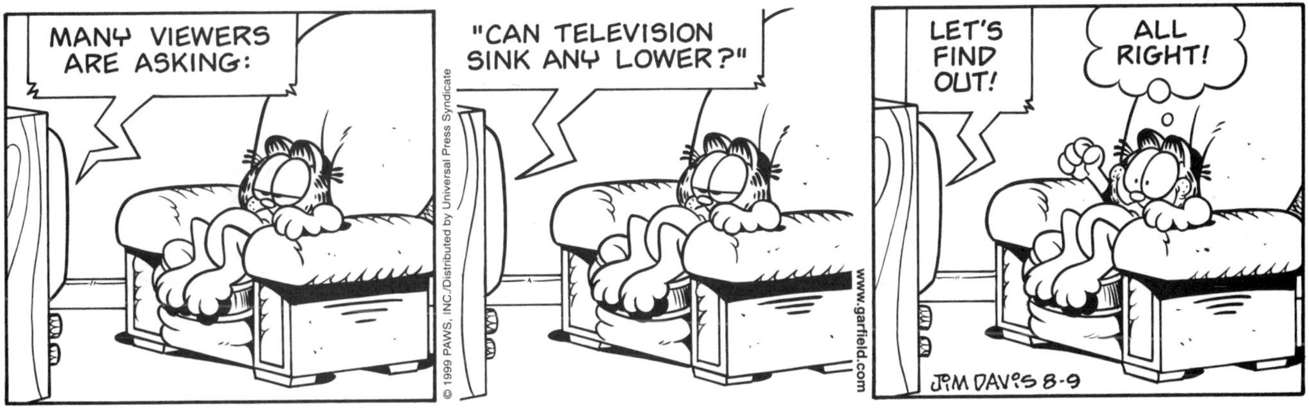
MANY VIEWERS ARE ASKING:
"CAN TELEVISION SINK ANY LOWER?"
LET'S FIND OUT!
ALL RIGHT!
www.garfield.com
JIM DAVIS 8-9

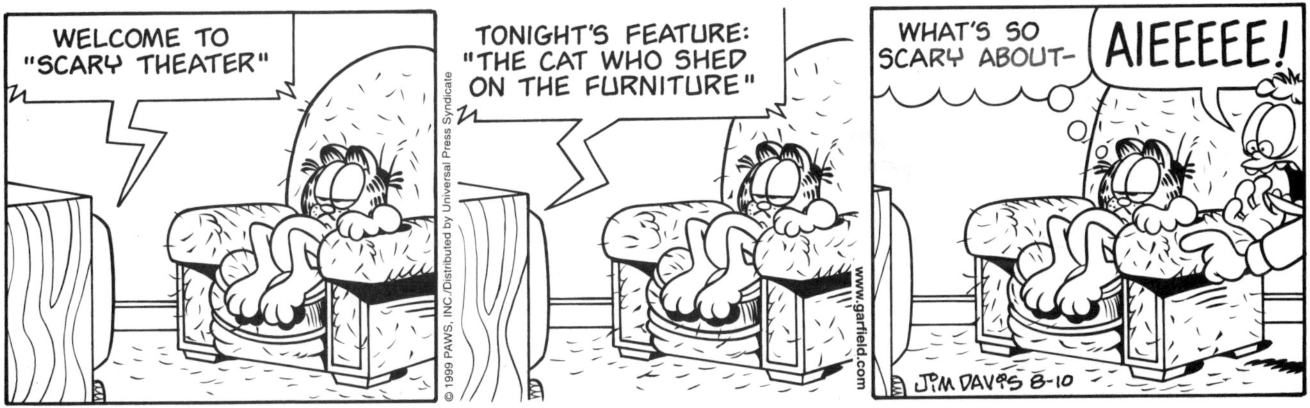
WELCOME TO "SCARY THEATER"
TONIGHT'S FEATURE: "THE CAT WHO SHED ON THE FURNITURE"
WHAT'S SO SCARY ABOUT-
AIEEEEE!
www.garfield.com
JIM DAVIS 8-10

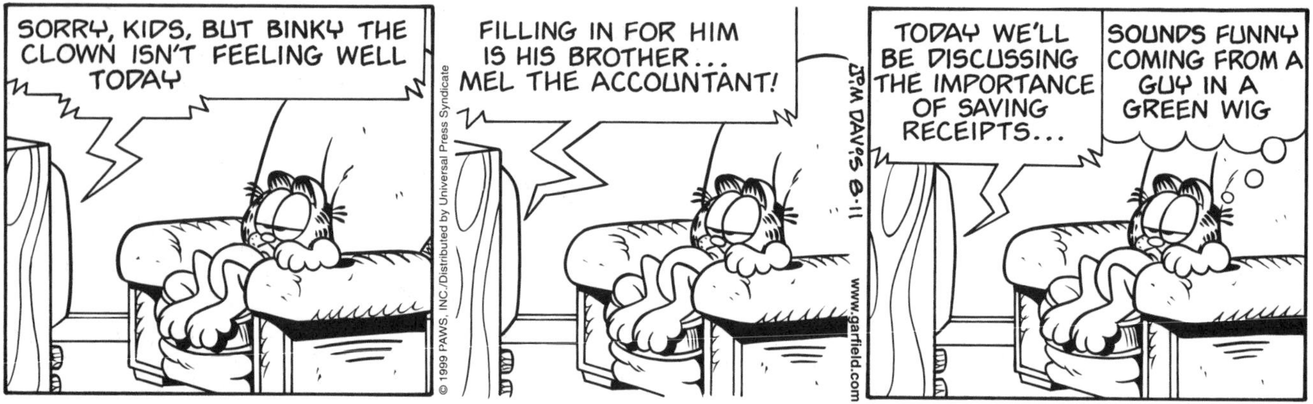
SORRY, KIDS, BUT BINKY THE CLOWN ISN'T FEELING WELL TODAY
FILLING IN FOR HIM IS HIS BROTHER... MEL THE ACCOUNTANT!
TODAY WE'LL BE DISCUSSING THE IMPORTANCE OF SAVING RECEIPTS...
SOUNDS FUNNY COMING FROM A GUY IN A GREEN WIG
© 1999 PAWS, INC./Distributed by Universal Press Syndicate
JIM DAVIS 8-11
www.garfield.com

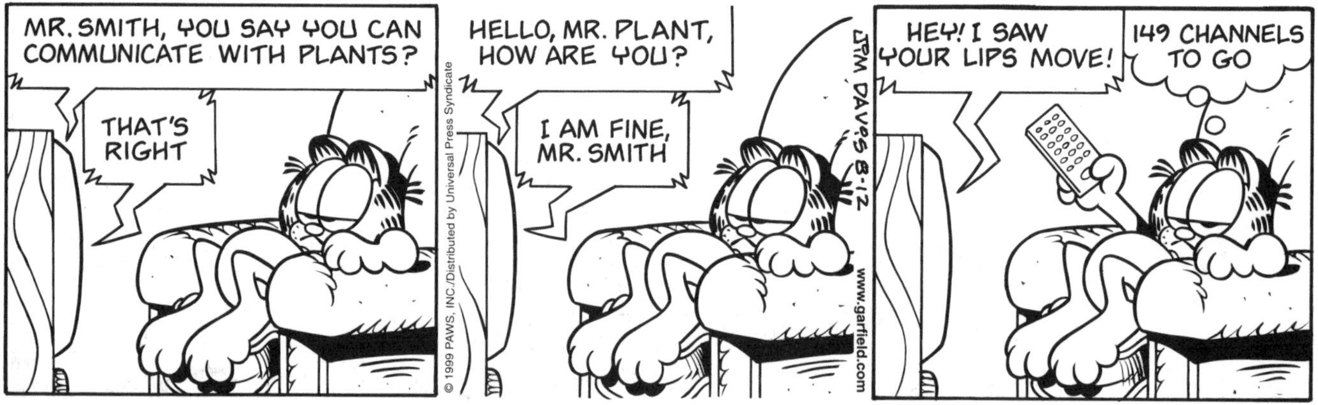
MR. SMITH, YOU SAY YOU CAN COMMUNICATE WITH PLANTS?
THAT'S RIGHT
HELLO, MR. PLANT, HOW ARE YOU?
I AM FINE, MR. SMITH
HEY! I SAW YOUR LIPS MOVE!
149 CHANNELS TO GO
© 1999 PAWS, INC./Distributed by Universal Press Syndicate
JIM DAVIS 8-12
www.garfield.com

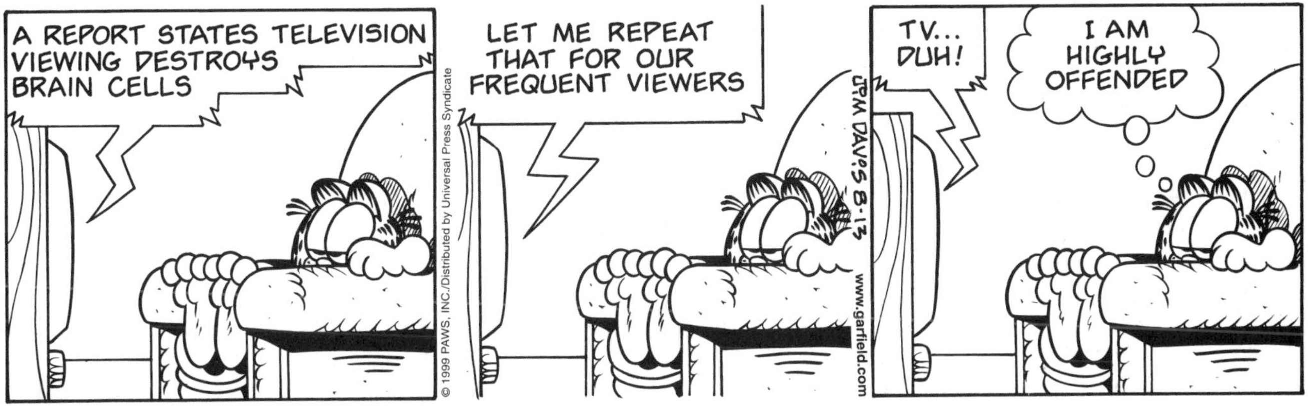
A REPORT STATES TELEVISION VIEWING DESTROYS BRAIN CELLS
© 1999 PAWS, INC./Distributed by Universal Press Syndicate
LET ME REPEAT THAT FOR OUR FREQUENT VIEWERS
JIM DAVIS 8-13
www.garfield.com
TV... DUH!
I AM HIGHLY OFFENDED

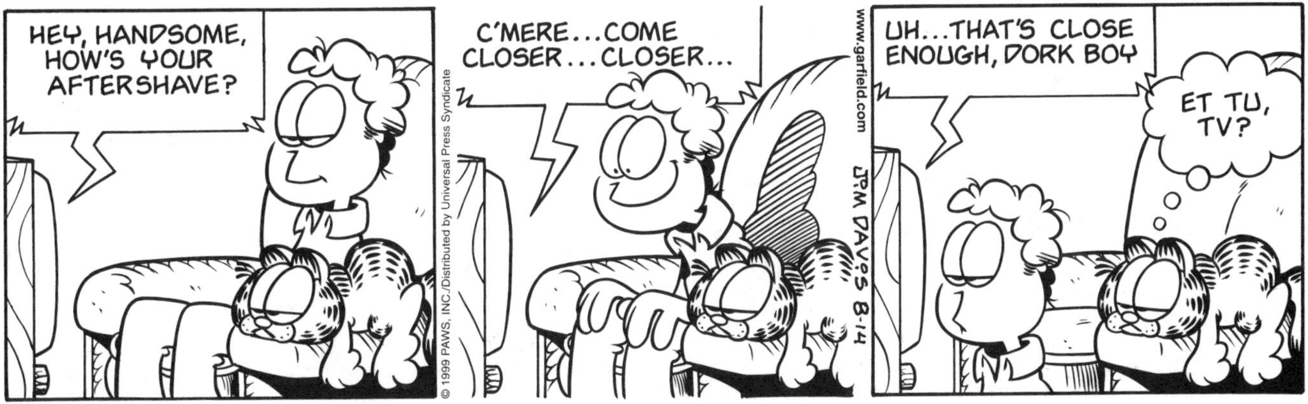
HEY, HANDSOME, HOW'S YOUR AFTERSHAVE?
© 1999 PAWS, INC./Distributed by Universal Press Syndicate
C'MERE...COME CLOSER...CLOSER...
www.garfield.com
JIM DAVIS 8-14
UH...THAT'S CLOSE ENOUGH, DORK BOY
ET TU, TV?

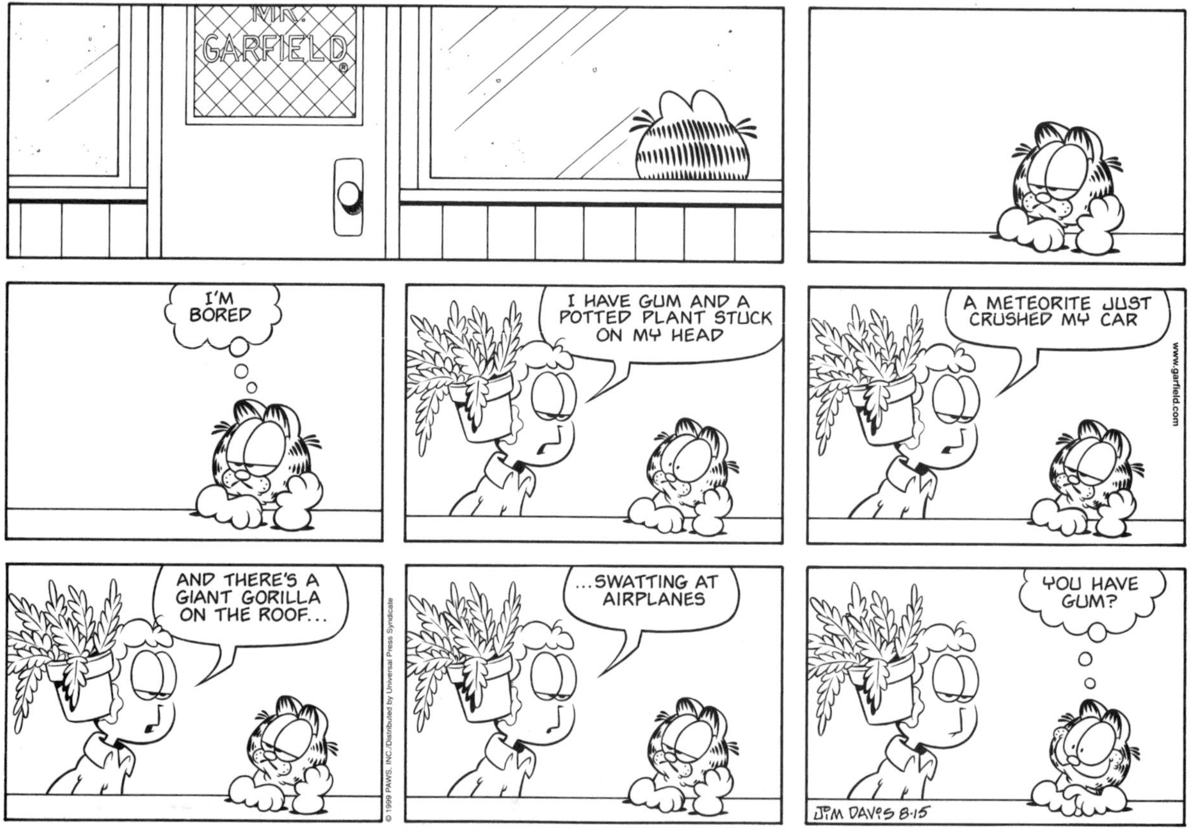
MR. GARFIELD®
I'M BORED
I HAVE GUM AND A POTTED PLANT STUCK ON MY HEAD
A METEORITE JUST CRUSHED MY CAR
www.garfield.com
AND THERE'S A GIANT GORILLA ON THE ROOF...
...SWATTING AT AIRPLANES
YOU HAVE GUM?
JIM DAVIS 8-15
© 1999 PAWS, INC./Distributed by Universal Press Syndicate

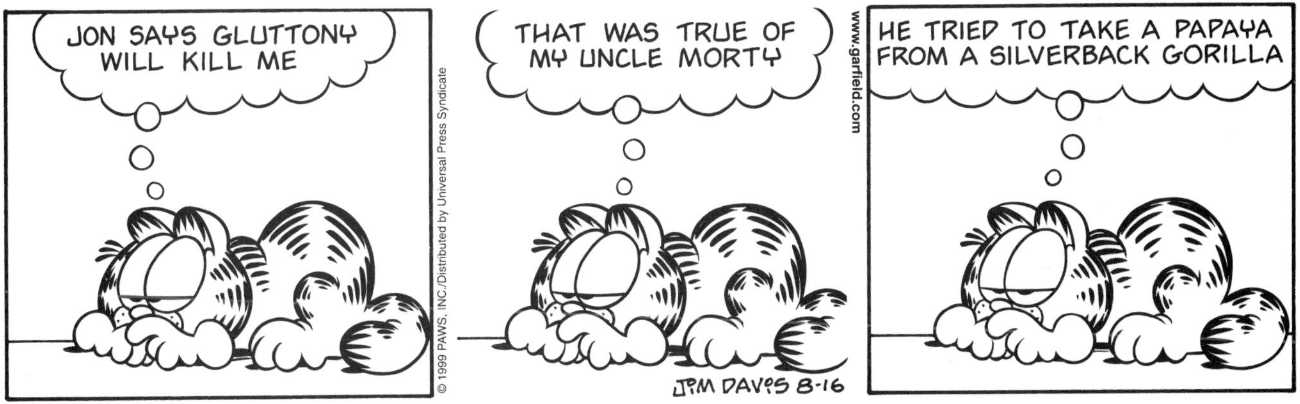
JON SAYS GLUTTONY WILL KILL ME
© 1999 PAWS, INC./Distributed by Universal Press Syndicate
THAT WAS TRUE OF MY UNCLE MORTY
JIM DAVIS 8-16
www.garfield.com
HE TRIED TO TAKE A PAPAYA FROM A SILVERBACK GORILLA

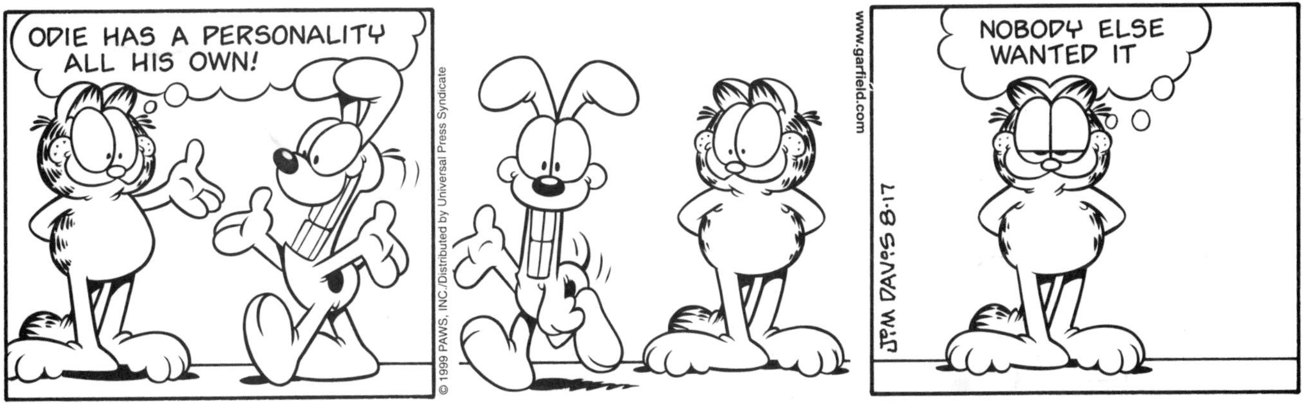
ODIE HAS A PERSONALITY ALL HIS OWN!
© 1999 PAWS, INC./Distributed by Universal Press Syndicate
JIM DAVIS 8-17
www.garfield.com
NOBODY ELSE WANTED IT

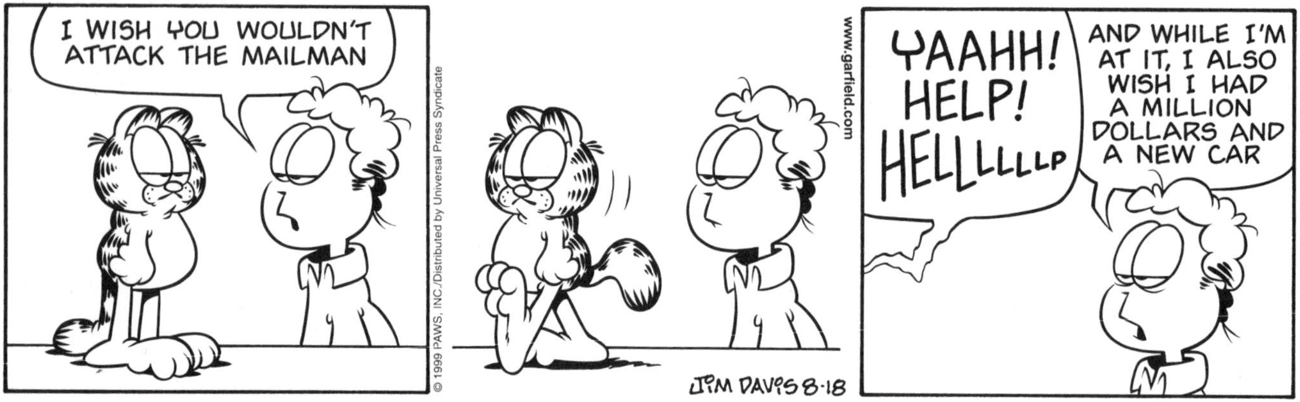
I WISH YOU WOULDN'T ATTACK THE MAILMAN
YAAHH! HELP! HELLLLLLLP
AND WHILE I'M AT IT, I ALSO WISH I HAD A MILLION DOLLARS AND A NEW CAR
© 1999 PAWS, INC./Distributed by Universal Press Syndicate
www.garfield.com
JIM DAVIS 8-18

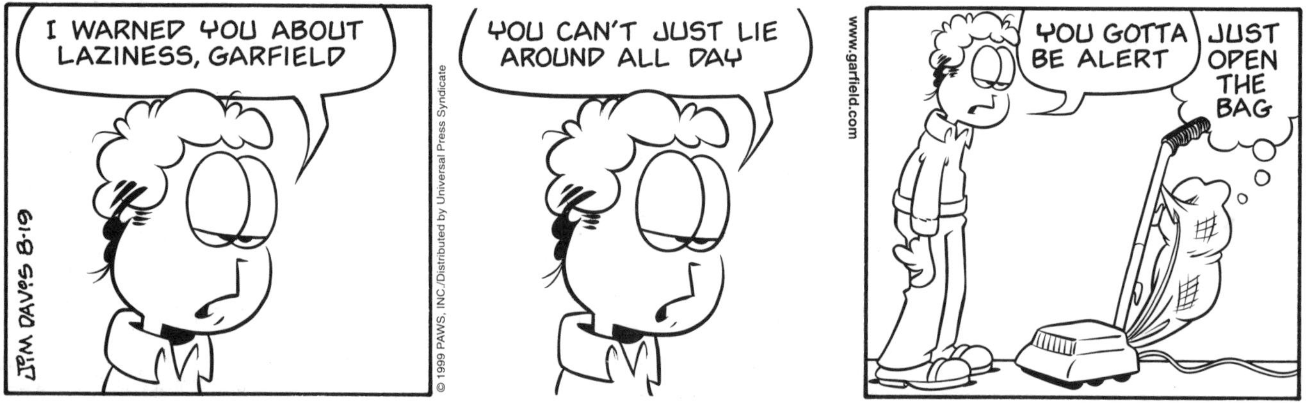
I WARNED YOU ABOUT LAZINESS, GARFIELD
YOU CAN'T JUST LIE AROUND ALL DAY
YOU GOTTA BE ALERT
JUST OPEN THE BAG
© 1999 PAWS, INC./Distributed by Universal Press Syndicate
www.garfield.com
JIM DAVIS 8-19

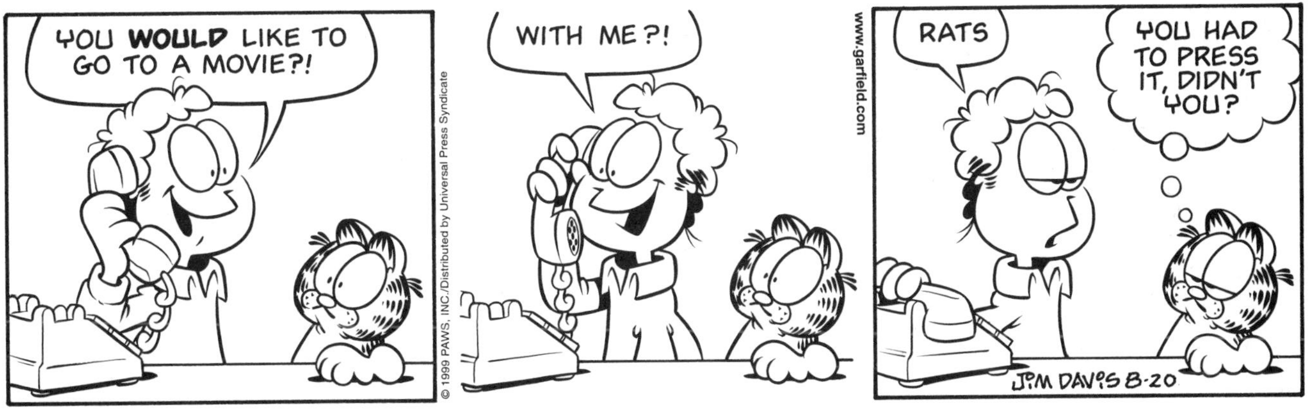
YOU WOULD LIKE TO GO TO A MOVIE?!
© 1999 PAWS, INC./Distributed by Universal Press Syndicate
WITH ME?!
www.garfield.com
RATS
YOU HAD TO PRESS IT, DIDN'T YOU?
JIM DAVIS 8-20

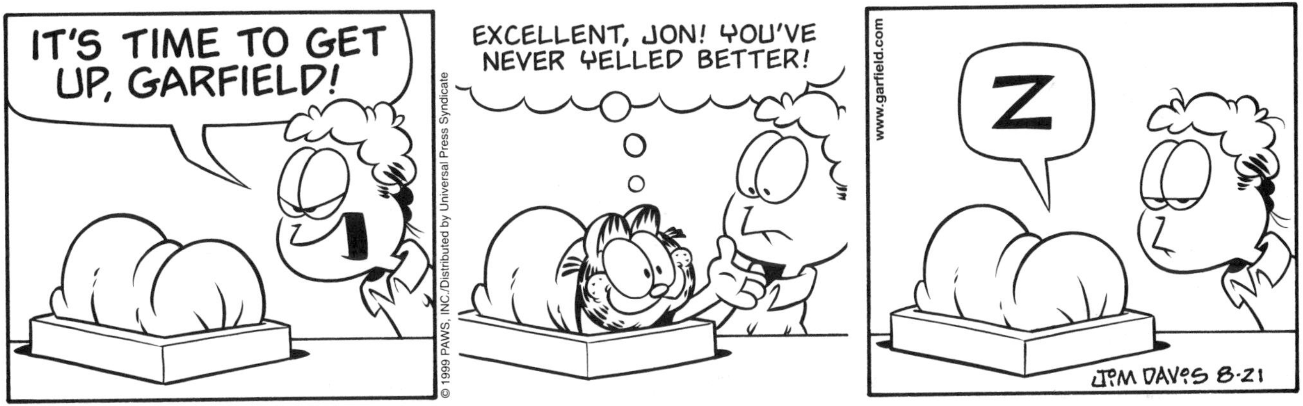
IT'S TIME TO GET UP, GARFIELD!
© 1999 PAWS, INC./Distributed by Universal Press Syndicate
EXCELLENT, JON! YOU'VE NEVER YELLED BETTER!
www.garfield.com
Z
JIM DAVIS 8-21

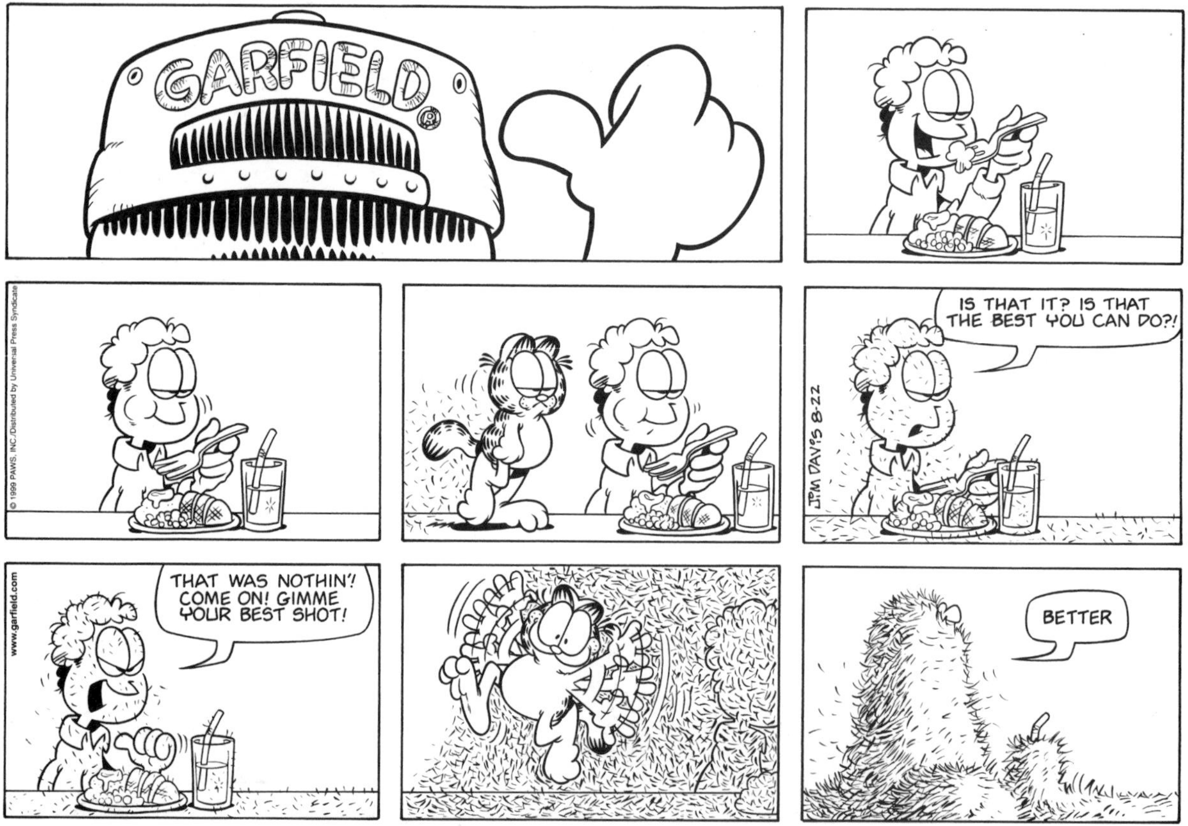
GARFIELD®
© 1999 PAWS, INC./Distributed by Universal Press Syndicate
JPM DAVIS 8-22
IS THAT IT? IS THAT THE BEST YOU CAN DO?!
www.garfield.com
THAT WAS NOTHIN'! COME ON! GIMME YOUR BEST SHOT!
BETTER

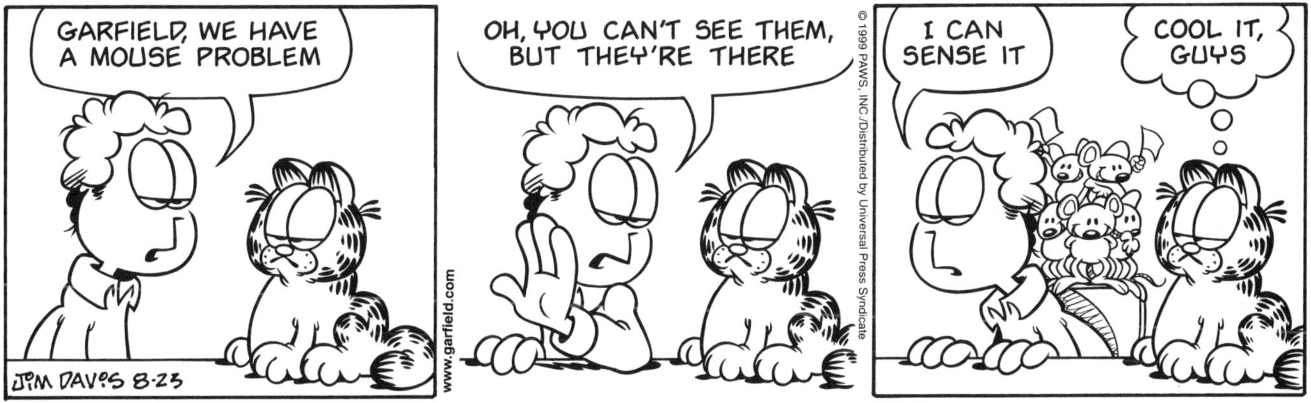
GARFIELD, WE HAVE A MOUSE PROBLEM
OH, YOU CAN'T SEE THEM, BUT THEY'RE THERE
I CAN SENSE IT
COOL IT, GUYS
JIM DAVIS 8-23
www.garfield.com
© 1999 PAWS, INC./Distributed by Universal Press Syndicate

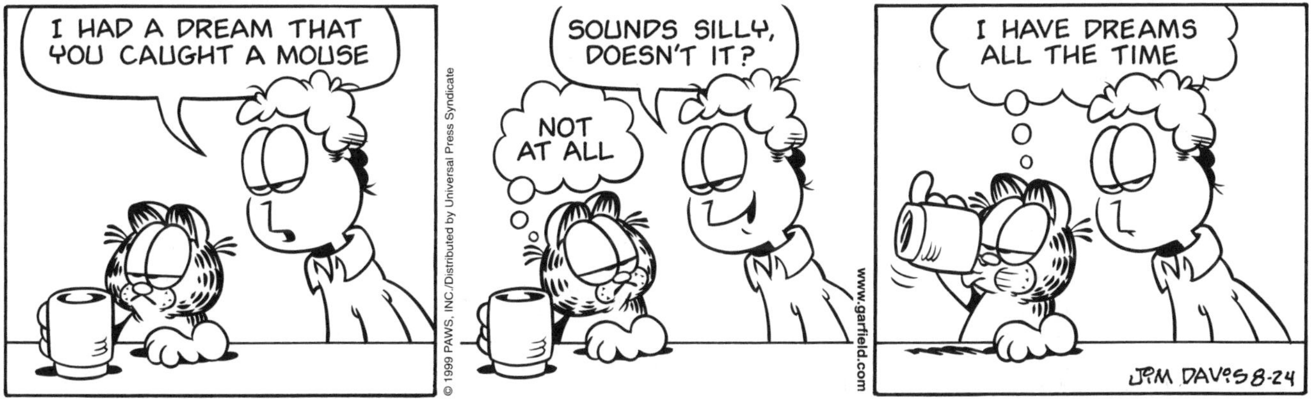
I HAD A DREAM THAT YOU CAUGHT A MOUSE
SOUNDS SILLY, DOESN'T IT?
NOT AT ALL
I HAVE DREAMS ALL THE TIME
JIM DAVIS 8-24
© 1999 PAWS, INC./Distributed by Universal Press Syndicate
www.garfield.com

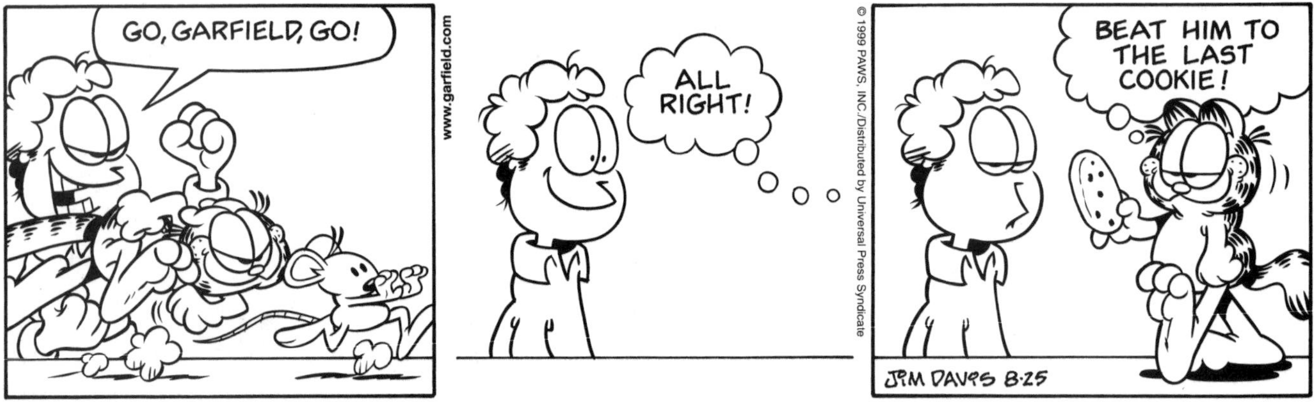
GO, GARFIELD, GO!
ALL RIGHT!
BEAT HIM TO THE LAST COOKIE!
JIM DAVIS 8-25
www.garfield.com
© 1999 PAWS, INC./Distributed by Universal Press Syndicate

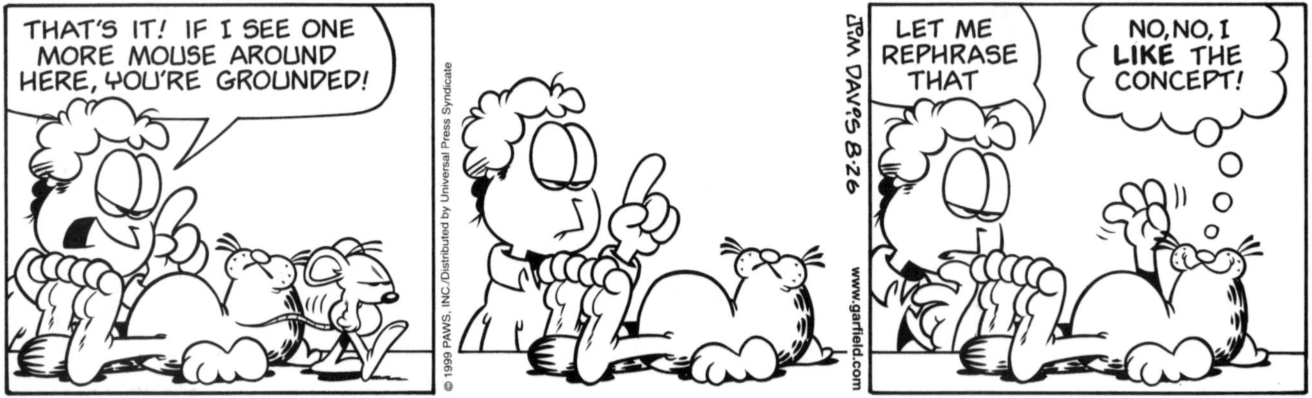
THAT'S IT! IF I SEE ONE MORE MOUSE AROUND HERE, YOU'RE GROUNDED!
LET ME REPHRASE THAT
NO, NO, I **LIKE** THE CONCEPT!
JIM DAVIS 8-26
© 1999 PAWS, INC./Distributed by Universal Press Syndicate
www.garfield.com

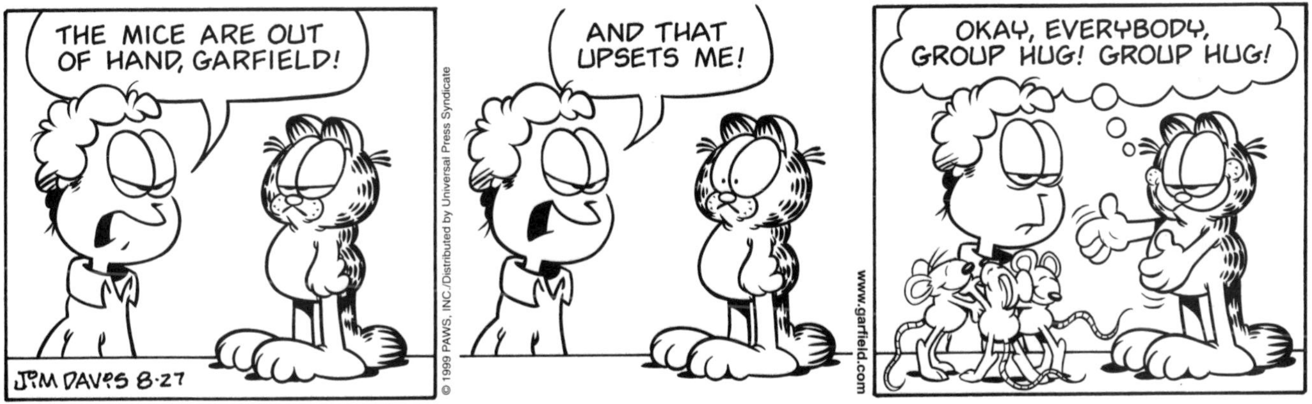
THE MICE ARE OUT OF HAND, GARFIELD!
JIM DAVIS 8-27
© 1999 PAWS, INC./Distributed by Universal Press Syndicate
AND THAT UPSETS ME!
www.garfield.com
OKAY, EVERYBODY, GROUP HUG! GROUP HUG!

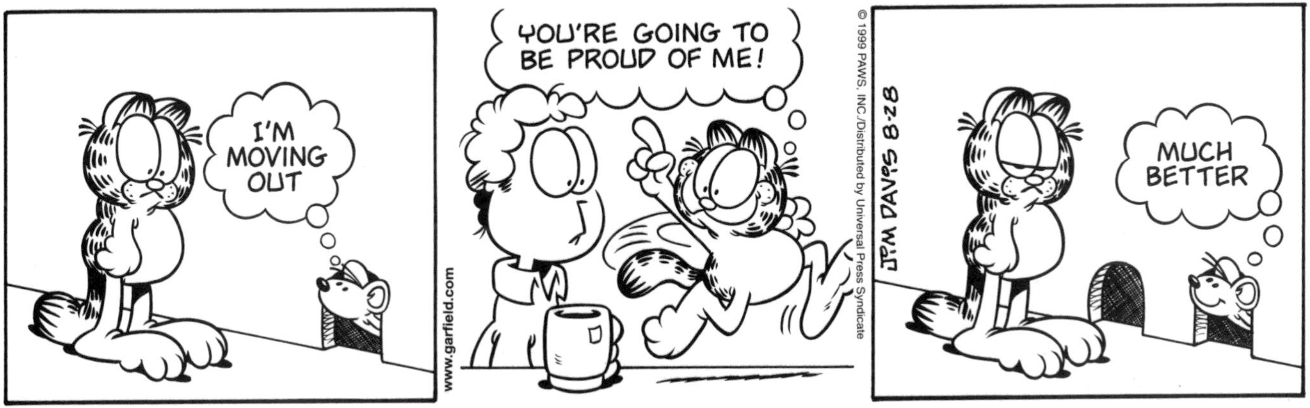
I'M MOVING OUT
www.garfield.com
YOU'RE GOING TO BE PROUD OF ME!
© 1999 PAWS, INC./Distributed by Universal Press Syndicate
JIM DAVIS 8-28
MUCH BETTER

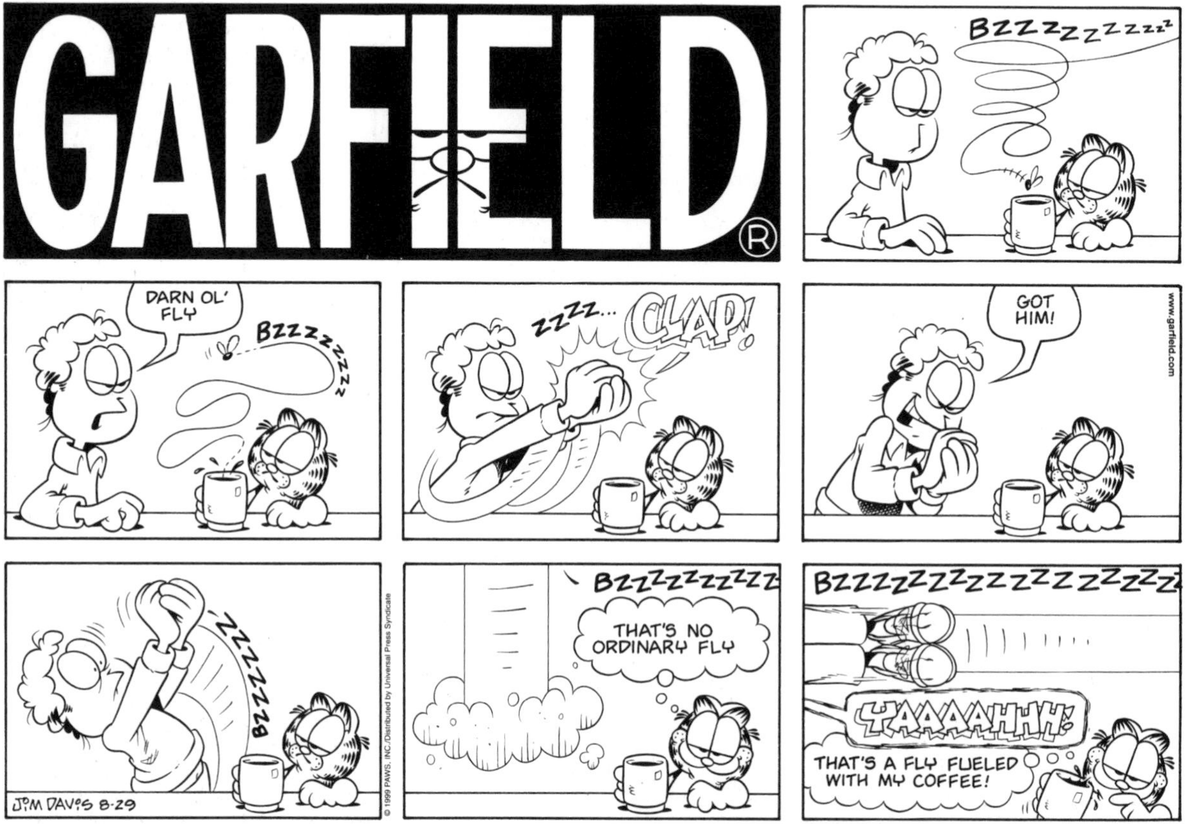
GARFIELD
BZZZZZZZZZZ
DARN OL' FLY
BZZZZZZZZZ
ZZZZ...
CLAP!
GOT HIM!
www.garfield.com
ZZZZZZZZ
JIM DAVIS 8-29
© 1999 PAWS, INC./Distributed by Universal Press Syndicate
BZZZZZZZZZZZ
THAT'S NO ORDINARY FLY
BZZZZZZZZZZZZZZZZZZ
YAAAAHHH!
THAT'S A FLY FUELED WITH MY COFFEE!

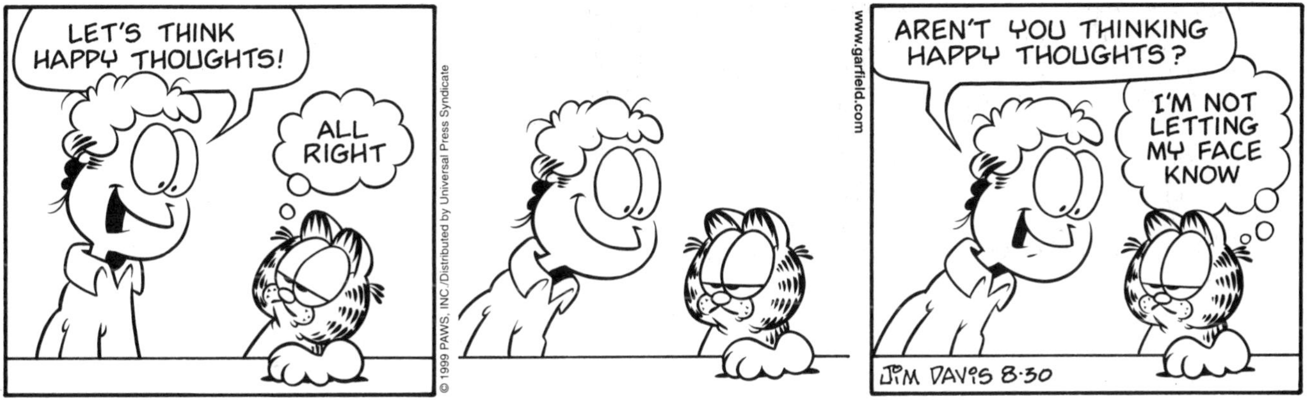
LET'S THINK HAPPY THOUGHTS!
ALL RIGHT
AREN'T YOU THINKING HAPPY THOUGHTS?
I'M NOT LETTING MY FACE KNOW
JIM DAVIS 8·30
© 1999 PAWS, INC./Distributed by Universal Press Syndicate
www.garfield.com

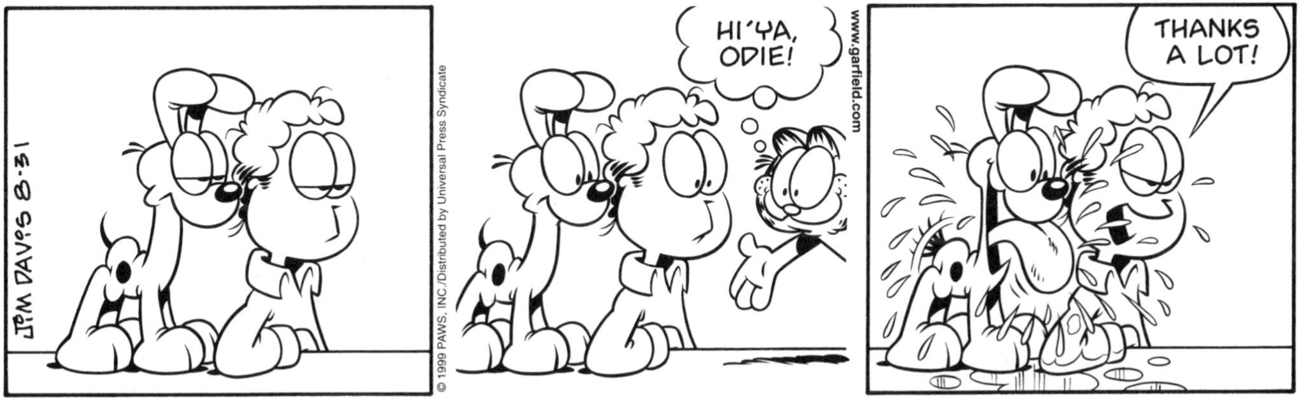
JIM DAVIS 8·31
HI'YA, ODIE!
THANKS A LOT!
© 1999 PAWS, INC./Distributed by Universal Press Syndicate
www.garfield.com

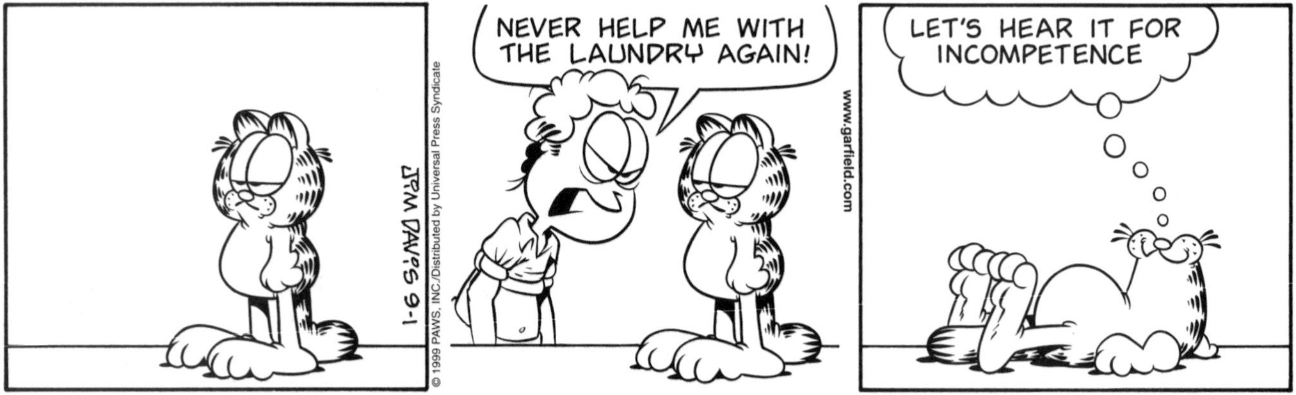
NEVER HELP ME WITH THE LAUNDRY AGAIN!
LET'S HEAR IT FOR INCOMPETENCE
© 1999 PAWS, INC./Distributed by Universal Press Syndicate
www.garfield.com

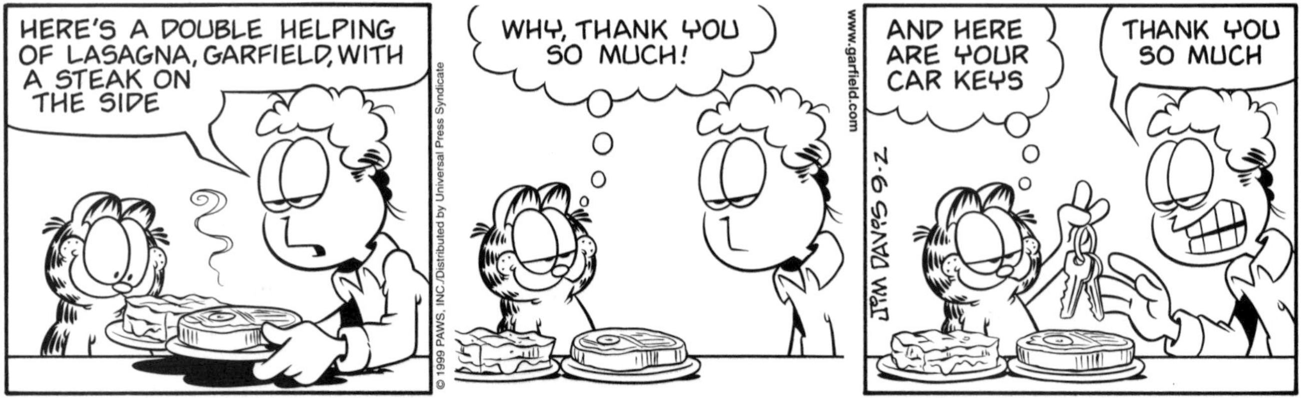
HERE'S A DOUBLE HELPING OF LASAGNA, GARFIELD, WITH A STEAK ON THE SIDE
WHY, THANK YOU SO MUCH!
AND HERE ARE YOUR CAR KEYS
THANK YOU SO MUCH
© 1999 PAWS, INC./Distributed by Universal Press Syndicate
www.garfield.com

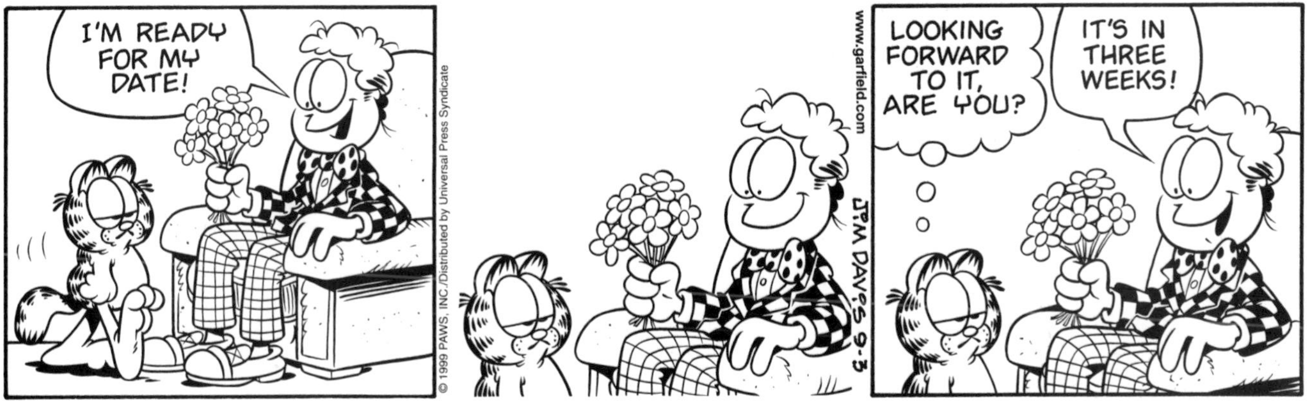
I'M READY FOR MY DATE!
LOOKING FORWARD TO IT, ARE YOU?
IT'S IN THREE WEEKS!
JIM DAVIS 9-3
© 1999 PAWS, INC./Distributed by Universal Press Syndicate
www.garfield.com

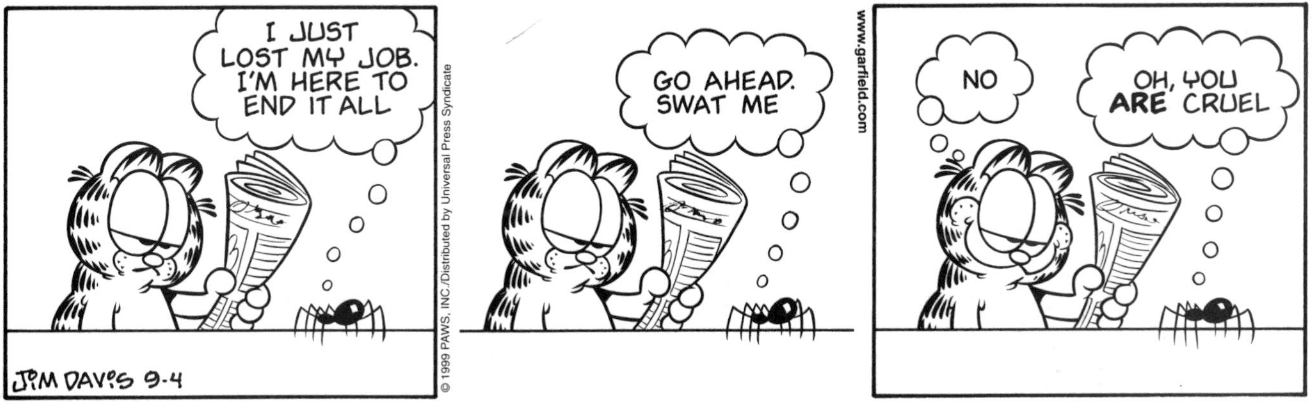
I JUST LOST MY JOB. I'M HERE TO END IT ALL
GO AHEAD. SWAT ME
NO
OH, YOU **ARE** CRUEL
JIM DAVIS 9-4
© 1999 PAWS, INC./Distributed by Universal Press Syndicate
www.garfield.com

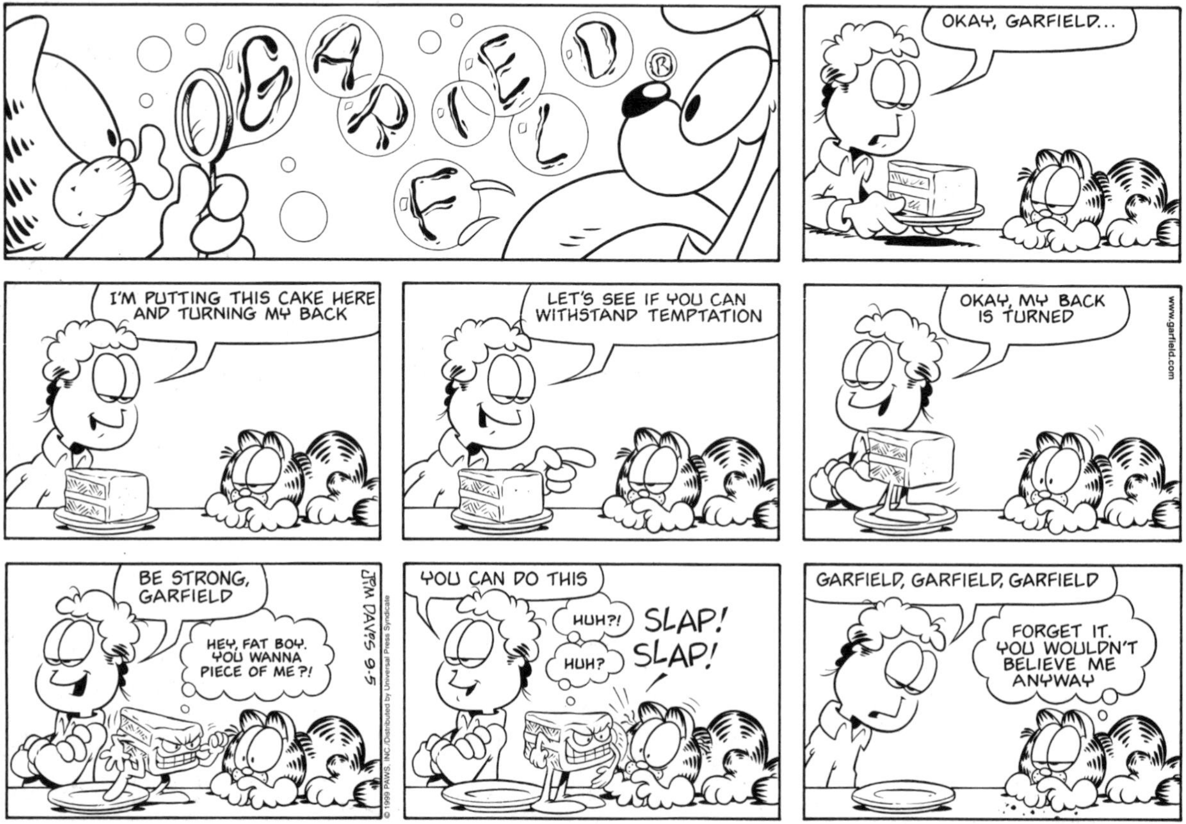

GARFIELD®
OKAY, GARFIELD...
I'M PUTTING THIS CAKE HERE AND TURNING MY BACK
LET'S SEE IF YOU CAN WITHSTAND TEMPTATION
OKAY, MY BACK IS TURNED
www.garfield.com
BE STRONG, GARFIELD
HEY, FAT BOY. YOU WANNA PIECE OF ME?!
JIM DAVIS 9-5
© 1999 PAWS, INC./Distributed by Universal Press Syndicate
YOU CAN DO THIS
HUH?!
HUH?
SLAP! SLAP!
GARFIELD, GARFIELD, GARFIELD
FORGET IT. YOU WOULDN'T BELIEVE ME ANYWAY

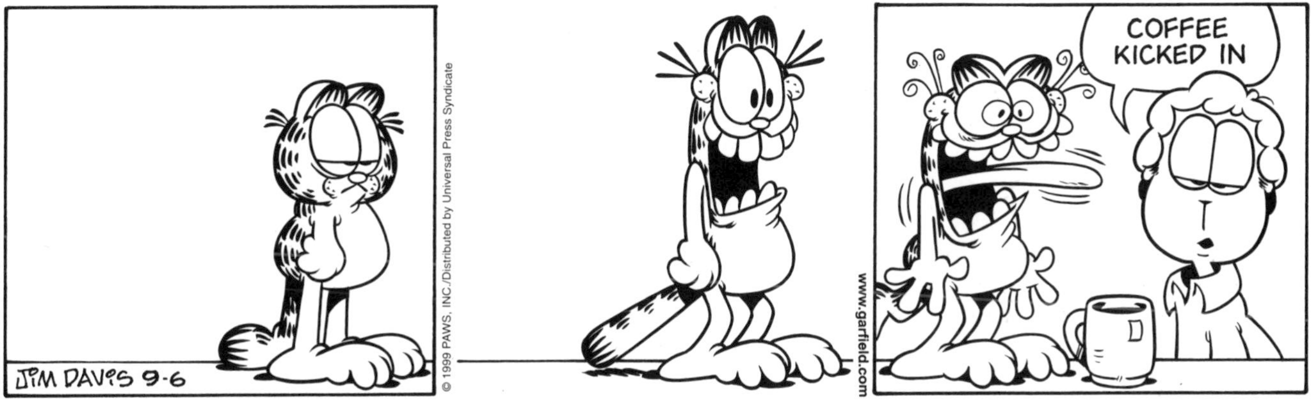
JIM DAVIS 9-6
© 1999 PAWS, INC./Distributed by Universal Press Syndicate
www.garfield.com
COFFEE KICKED IN

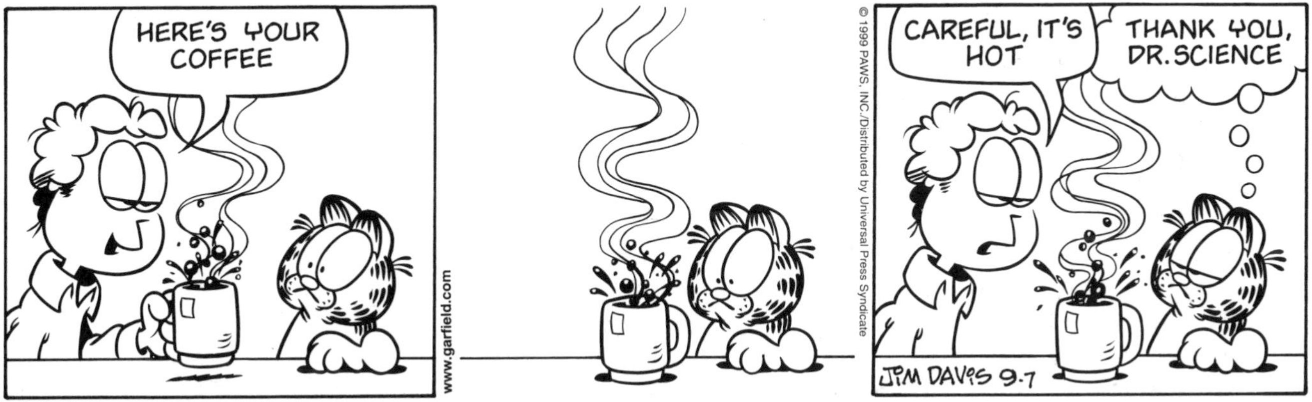
HERE'S YOUR COFFEE
www.garfield.com
© 1999 PAWS, INC./Distributed by Universal Press Syndicate
CAREFUL, IT'S HOT
THANK YOU, DR. SCIENCE
JIM DAVIS 9-7

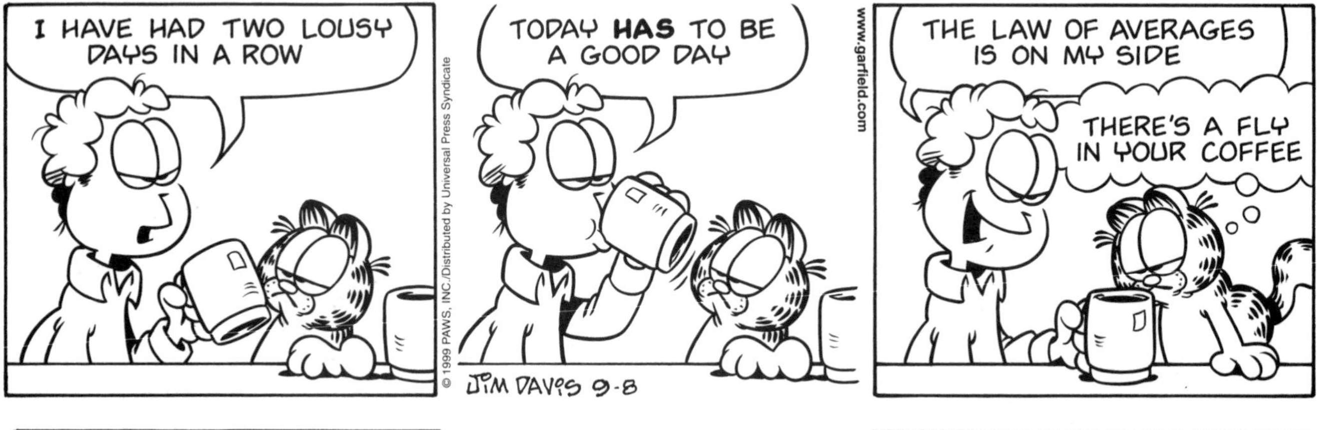
I HAVE HAD TWO LOUSY DAYS IN A ROW
TODAY **HAS** TO BE A GOOD DAY
THE LAW OF AVERAGES IS ON MY SIDE
THERE'S A FLY IN YOUR COFFEE
© 1999 PAWS, INC./Distributed by Universal Press Syndicate
www.garfield.com
JIM DAVIS 9-8

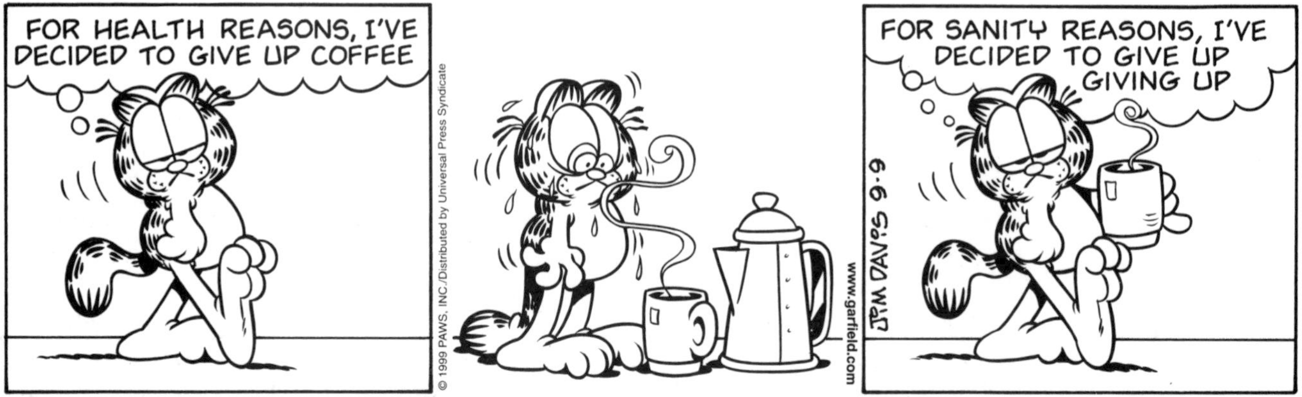
FOR HEALTH REASONS, I'VE DECIDED TO GIVE UP COFFEE
FOR SANITY REASONS, I'VE DECIDED TO GIVE UP GIVING UP
© 1999 PAWS, INC./Distributed by Universal Press Syndicate
www.garfield.com
JIM DAVIS 9-9

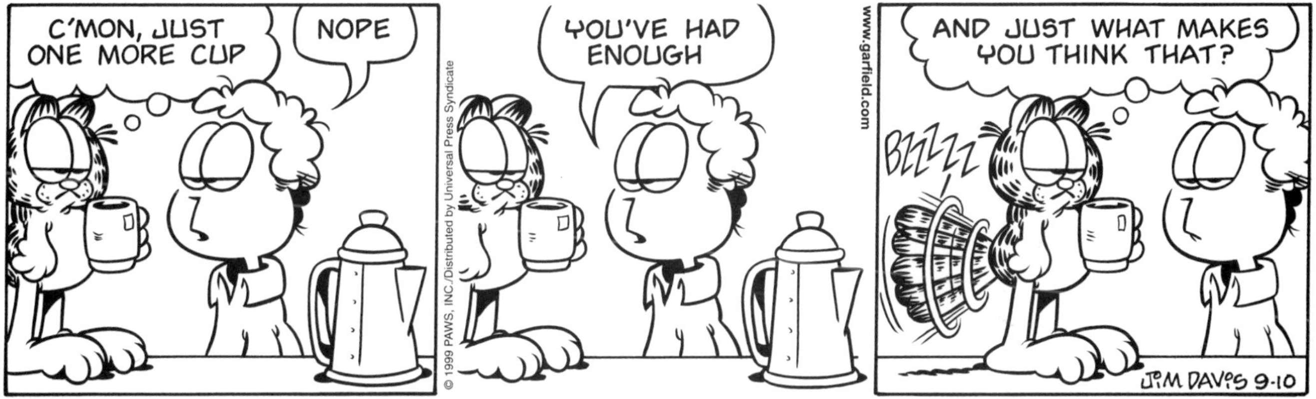
C'MON, JUST ONE MORE CUP
NOPE
YOU'VE HAD ENOUGH
AND JUST WHAT MAKES YOU THINK THAT?
BZZZZZ
JIM DAVIS 9-10
© 1999 PAWS, INC./Distributed by Universal Press Syndicate
www.garfield.com

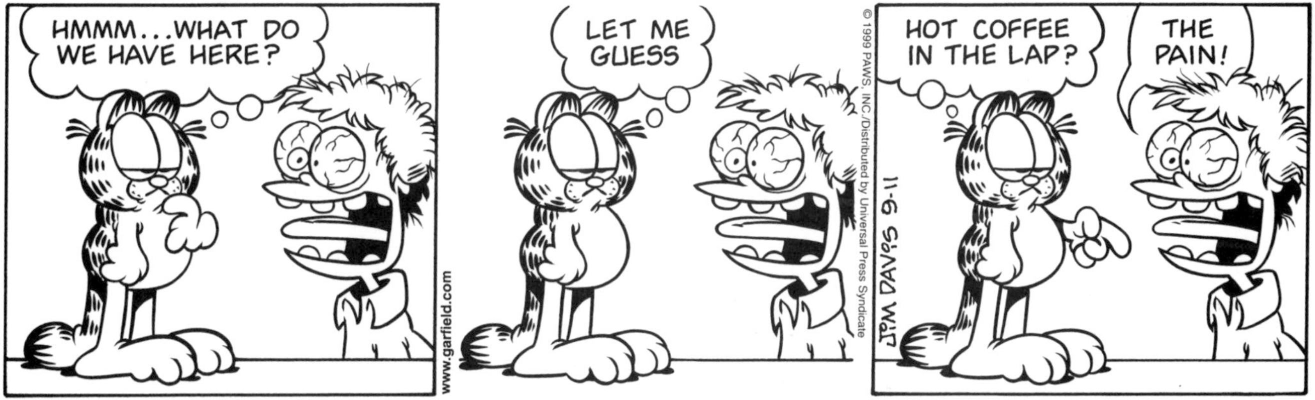
HMMM...WHAT DO WE HAVE HERE?
LET ME GUESS
HOT COFFEE IN THE LAP?
THE PAIN!
JIM DAVIS 9-11
© 1999 PAWS, INC./Distributed by Universal Press Syndicate
www.garfield.com

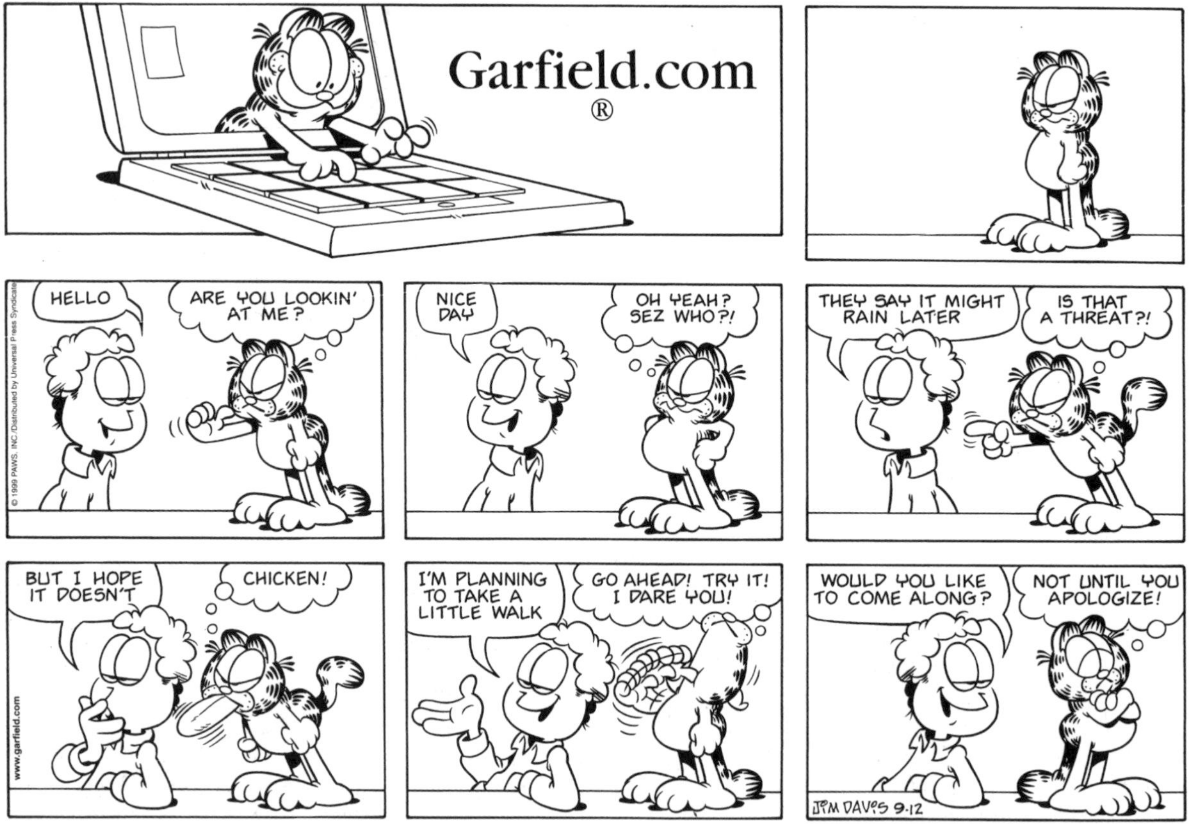
Garfield.com ®
© 1999 PAWS, INC./Distributed by Universal Press Syndicate
HELLO
ARE YOU LOOKIN' AT ME?
NICE DAY
OH YEAH? SEZ WHO?!
THEY SAY IT MIGHT RAIN LATER
IS THAT A THREAT?!
www.garfield.com
BUT I HOPE IT DOESN'T
CHICKEN!
I'M PLANNING TO TAKE A LITTLE WALK
GO AHEAD! TRY IT! I DARE YOU!
WOULD YOU LIKE TO COME ALONG?
NOT UNTIL YOU APOLOGIZE!
JIM DAVIS 9-12

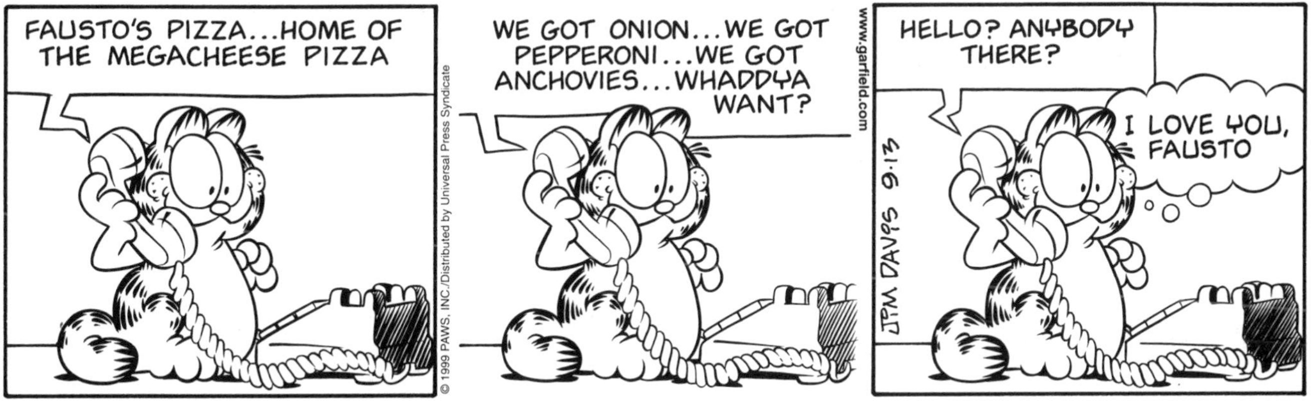
FAUSTO'S PIZZA...HOME OF THE MEGACHEESE PIZZA
WE GOT ONION...WE GOT PEPPERONI...WE GOT ANCHOVIES...WHADDYA WANT?
HELLO? ANYBODY THERE?
I LOVE YOU, FAUSTO
© 1999 PAWS, INC./Distributed by Universal Press Syndicate
www.garfield.com
JIM DAVIS 9·13

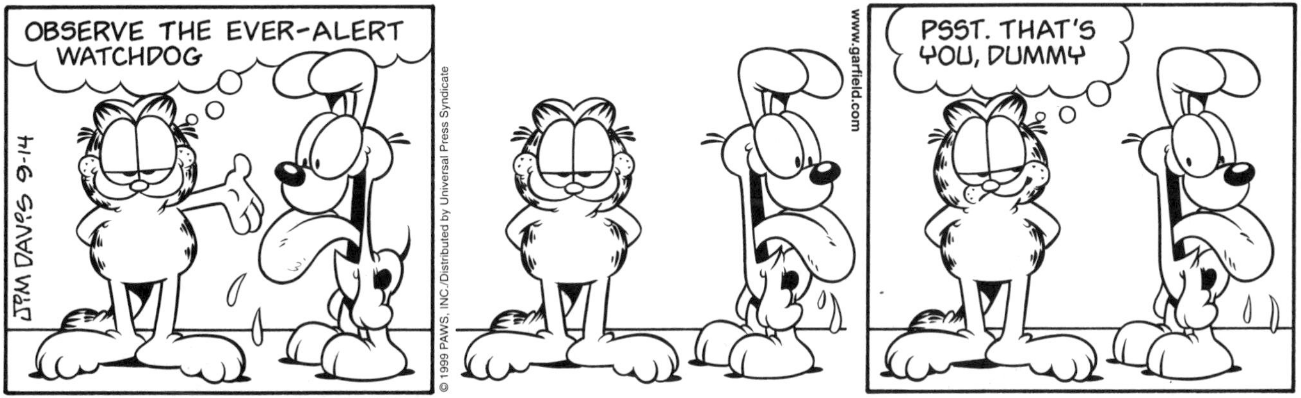
OBSERVE THE EVER-ALERT WATCHDOG
PSST. THAT'S YOU, DUMMY
JIM DAVIS 9·14
© 1999 PAWS, INC./Distributed by Universal Press Syndicate
www.garfield.com

Fat Cat Classics Vol. 2

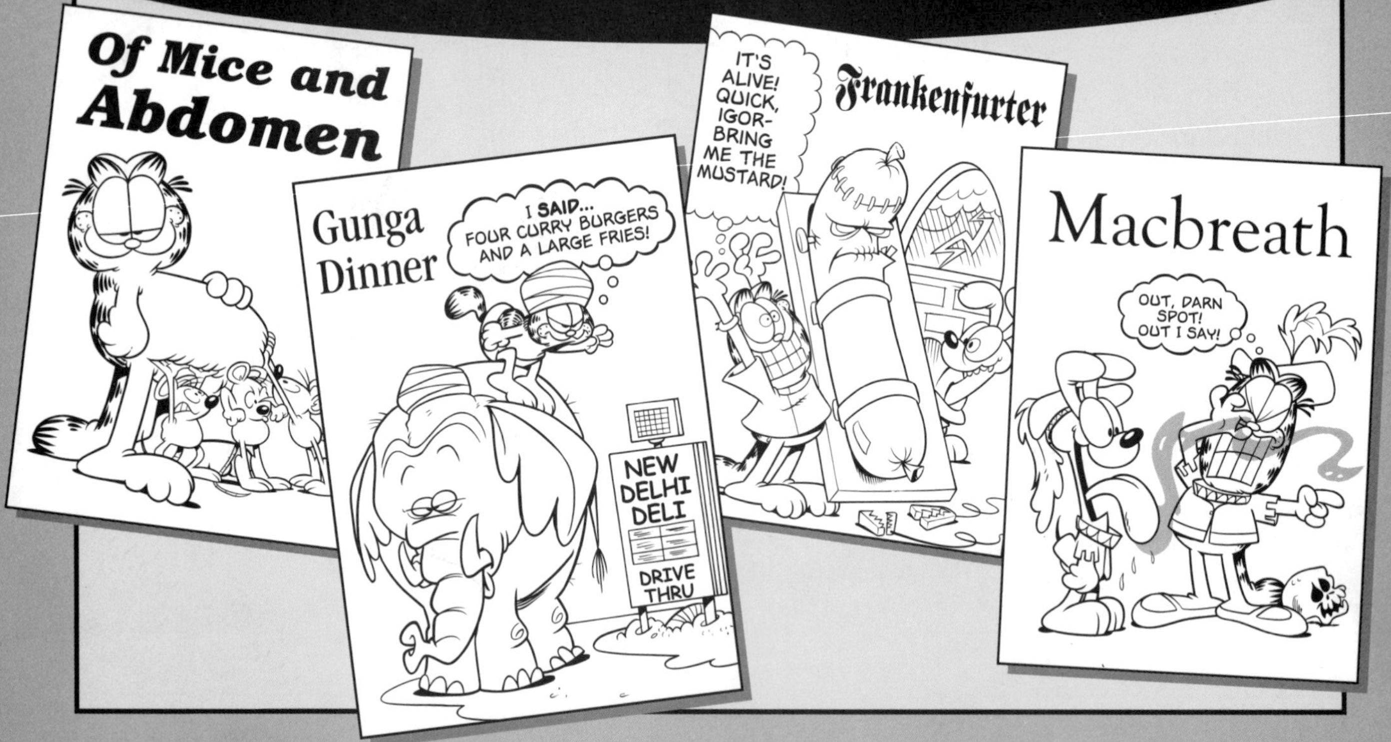
Of Mice and Abdomen
Gunga Dinner
I SAID... FOUR CURRY BURGERS AND A LARGE FRIES!
NEW DELHI DELI
DRIVE THRU
IT'S ALIVE! QUICK, IGOR- BRING ME THE MUSTARD!
Frankenfurter
Macbreath
OUT, DARN SPOT! OUT I SAY!

Like to get a **COOL CATalog** stuffed with great **GARFIELD** products? Then just write down the information below, stuff it in an envelope and mail it back to us...or you can fill in the card on our website - HTTP://www.GARFIELD.com. We'll get one out to you in two shakes of a cat's tail!

Name:
Address:
City:
State:
Zip:
Phone:
Date of Birth:
Sex:

Please mail your information to:

**Garfield Stuff Catalog
Dept.2BB38A
5804 Churchman By-Pass
Indianapolis, IN 46203-6109**

© PAWS